STAR WARS®

JEDI

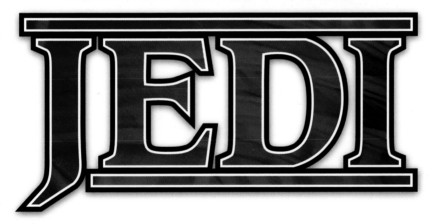

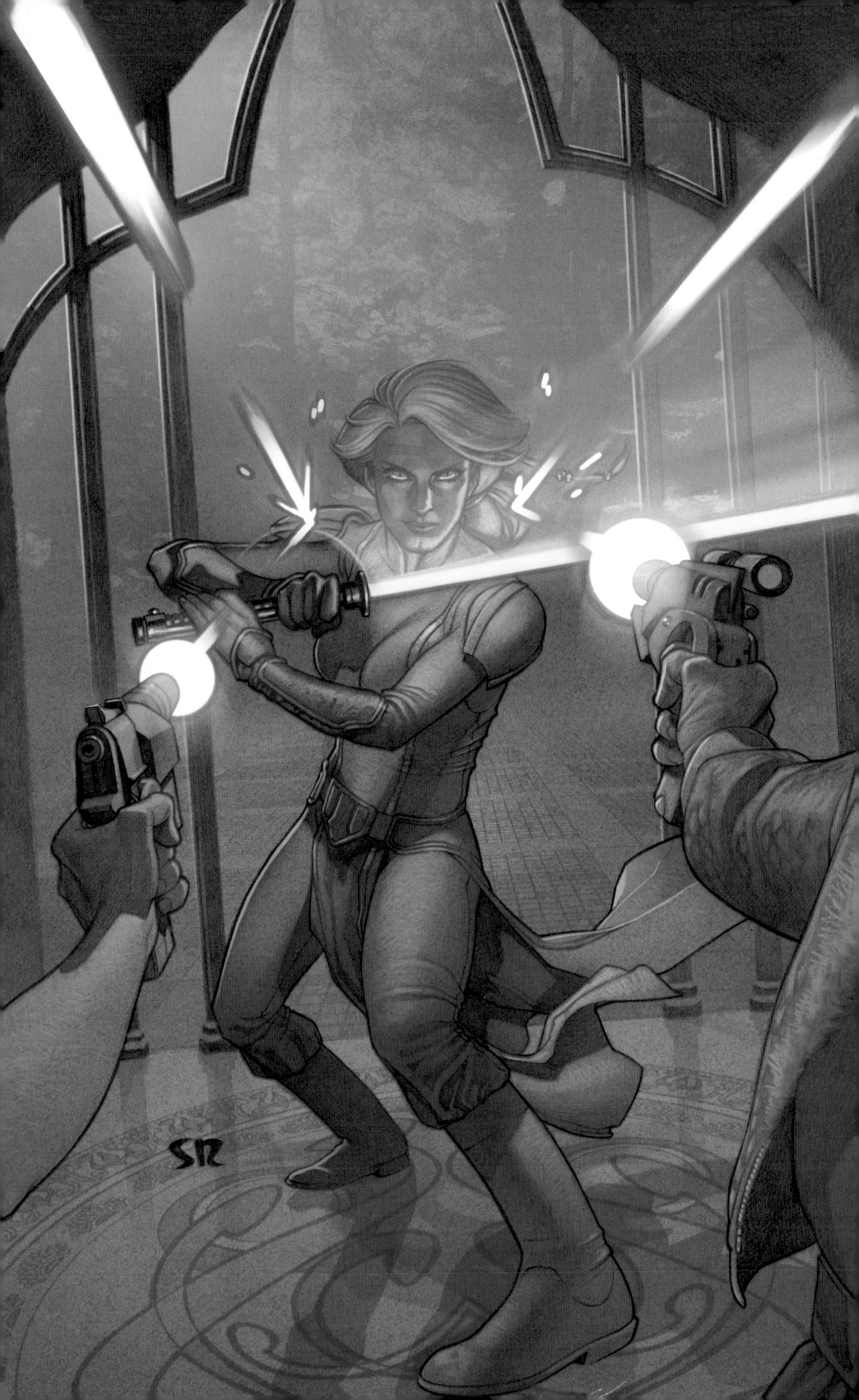
SR

STAR WARS® JEDI

VOLUME I
= THE DARK SIDE =

SCRIPT
SCOTT ALLIE

ART
MAHMUD ASRAR

COLORS
PAUL MOUNTS

LETTERS
MICHAEL HEISLER

COVER ART
STÉPHANE ROUX

DARK HORSE BOOKS

PRESIDENT AND PUBLISHER
MIKE RICHARDSON

COLLECTION DESIGNER
STEPHEN REICHERT

EDITOR
RANDY STRADLEY

ASSISTANT EDITOR
FREDDYE LINS

NEIL HANKERSON Executive Vice President • TOM WEDDLE Chief Financial Officer • RANDY STRADLEY Vice President of Publishing • MICHAEL MARTENS Vice President of Book Trade Sales • ANITA NELSON Vice President of Business Affairs • MICHA HERSHMAN Vice President of Marketing • DAVID SCROGGY Vice President of Product Development • DALE LAFOUNTAIN Vice President of Information Technology • DARLENE VOGEL Senior Director of Print, Design, and Production • KEN LIZZI General Counsel • DAVEY ESTRADA Editorial Director • SCOTT ALLIE Senior Managing Editor • CHRIS WARNER Senior Books Editor • DIANA SCHUTZ Executive Editor • CARY GRAZZINI Director of Print and Development • LIA RIBACCHI Art Director • CARA NIECE Director of Scheduling

Special thanks to J. W. Rinzler, Leland Chee, Troy Alders,
Carol Roeder, Jann Moorhead, and David Anderman at Lucas Licensing.

STAR WARS: JEDI—THE DARK SIDE

This volume collects issues #1–#5 of the Dark Horse comic-book series *Star Wars: Jedi—The Dark Side*.

Published by
Dark Horse Books
A division of Dark Horse Comics, Inc.
10956 SE Main Street
Milwaukie, OR 97222

DarkHorse.com | StarWars.com

To find a comics shop in your area, call the Comic Shop Locator Service toll-free at 1-888-266-4226

Library of Congress Cataloging-in-Publication Data

Allie, Scott.
Star wars, Jedi. Vol. 1, The dark side / script, Scott Allie ; art, Mahmud Asrar ; colors, Paul Mounts ;
letters, Michael Heisler ; cover art, Stéphane Roux.
p. cm.
Summary: "A political assassination sends Jedi Master Qui-Gon Jinn to prevent a
civil war on the homeworld of his headstrong Padawan, Xanatos"–Provided by publisher.
ISBN 978-1-59582-840-8
1. Graphic novels. I. Asrar, Mahmud A., ill. II. Roux, Stéphane, ill. III. Title. IV. Title: Dark side.
PZ7.7.A37Stj 2012
741.5'973–dc22
2011038197

First edition: March 2012
ISBN 978-1-59582-840-8

1 3 5 7 9 10 8 6 4 2
Printed at Midas Printing International, Ltd., Huizhou, China

THE RISE OF THE EMPIRE (1,000–0 YEARS BEFORE THE BATTLE OF YAVIN)

After the seeming final defeat of the Sith, the Republic enters a state of complacency. In the waning years of the Republic, the Senate is rife with corruption, and the ambitious Senator Palpatine has himself elected Supreme Chancellor. This is the era of the prequel trilogy.

The events in this story take place approximately fifty-three years before the Battle of Yavin.

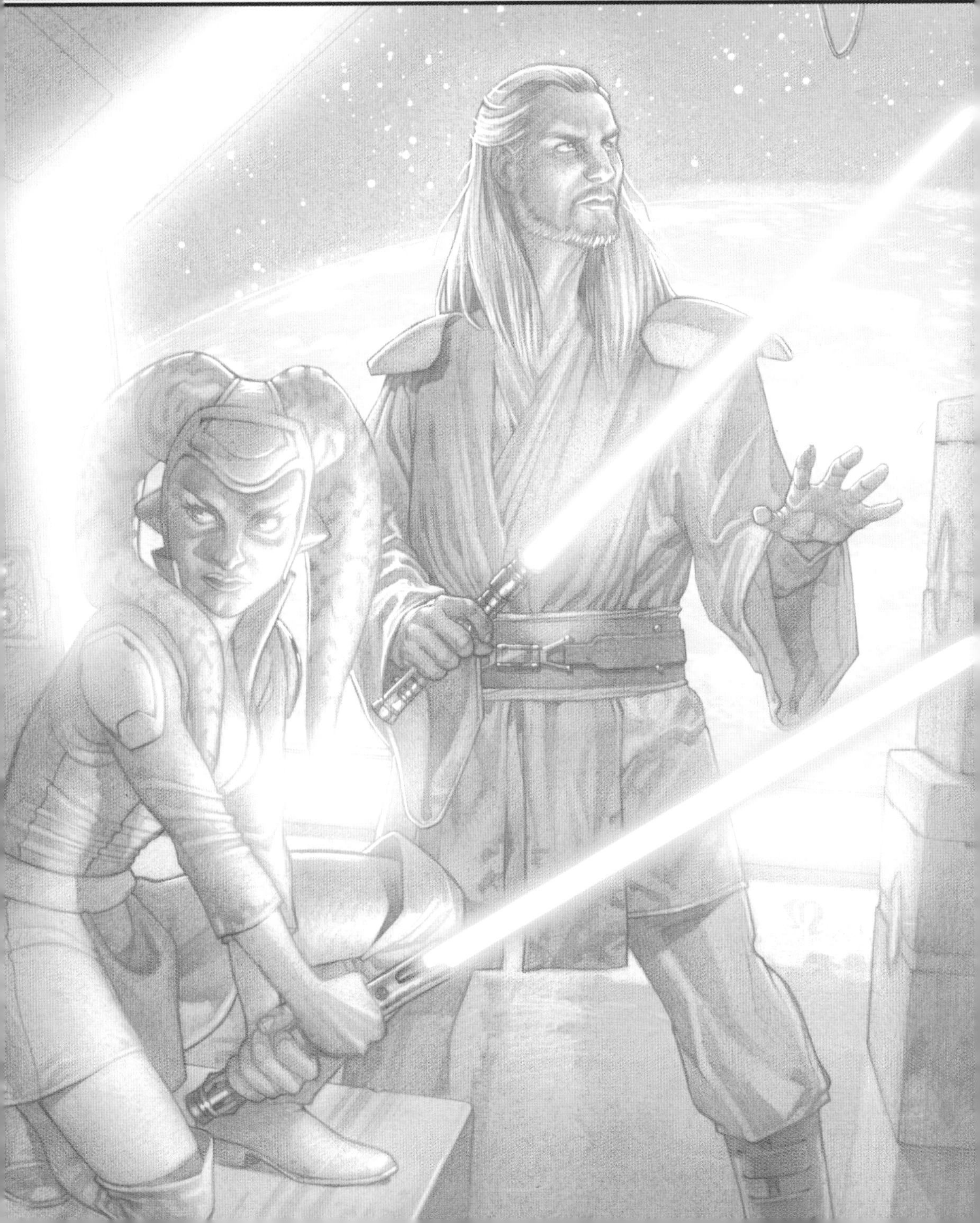

It is a time of relative peace in the galaxy. Nearly a thousand years have passed since the Jedi defeated the Sith on the broken plains of Ruusan.

Now, at the Jedi Temple on Coruscant, the Jedi train their Padawans in the ways of the Force, preparing them to become the Jedi Knights of the always-uncertain future.

For despite the current galactic peace, the Jedi are still called upon to mediate—or quell—smaller, localized conflicts . . .

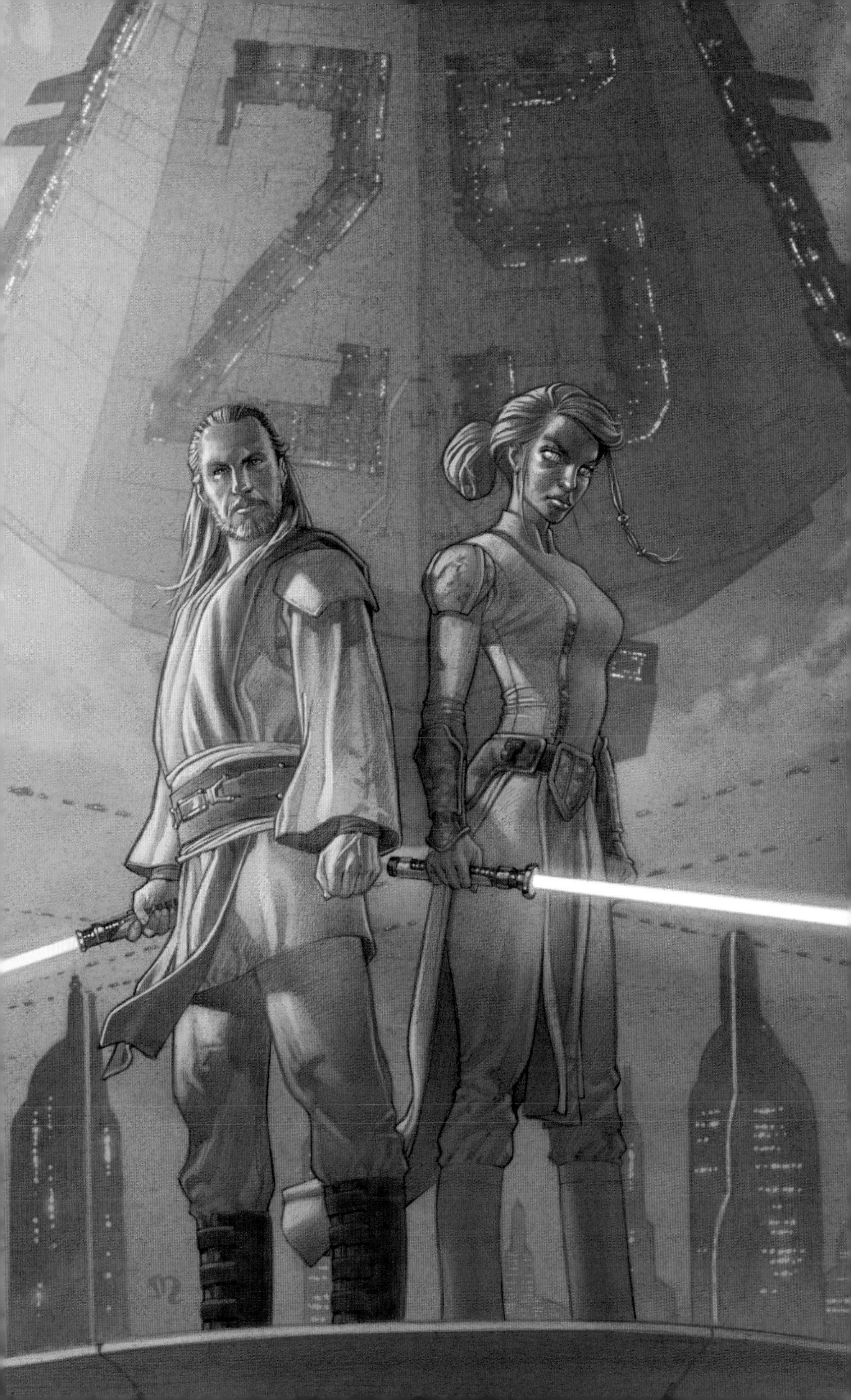

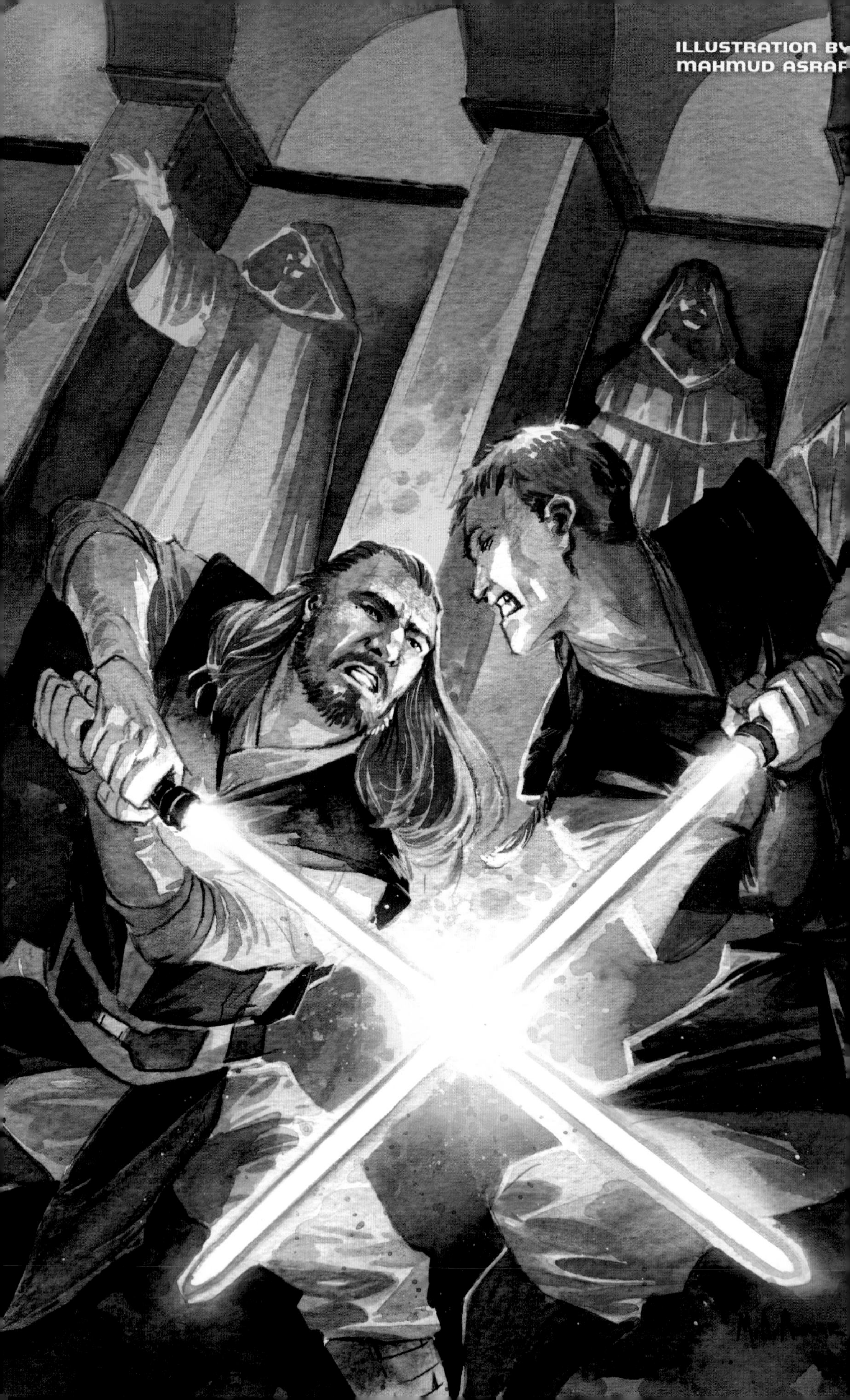

ILLUSTRATION BY
MAHMUD ASRAR

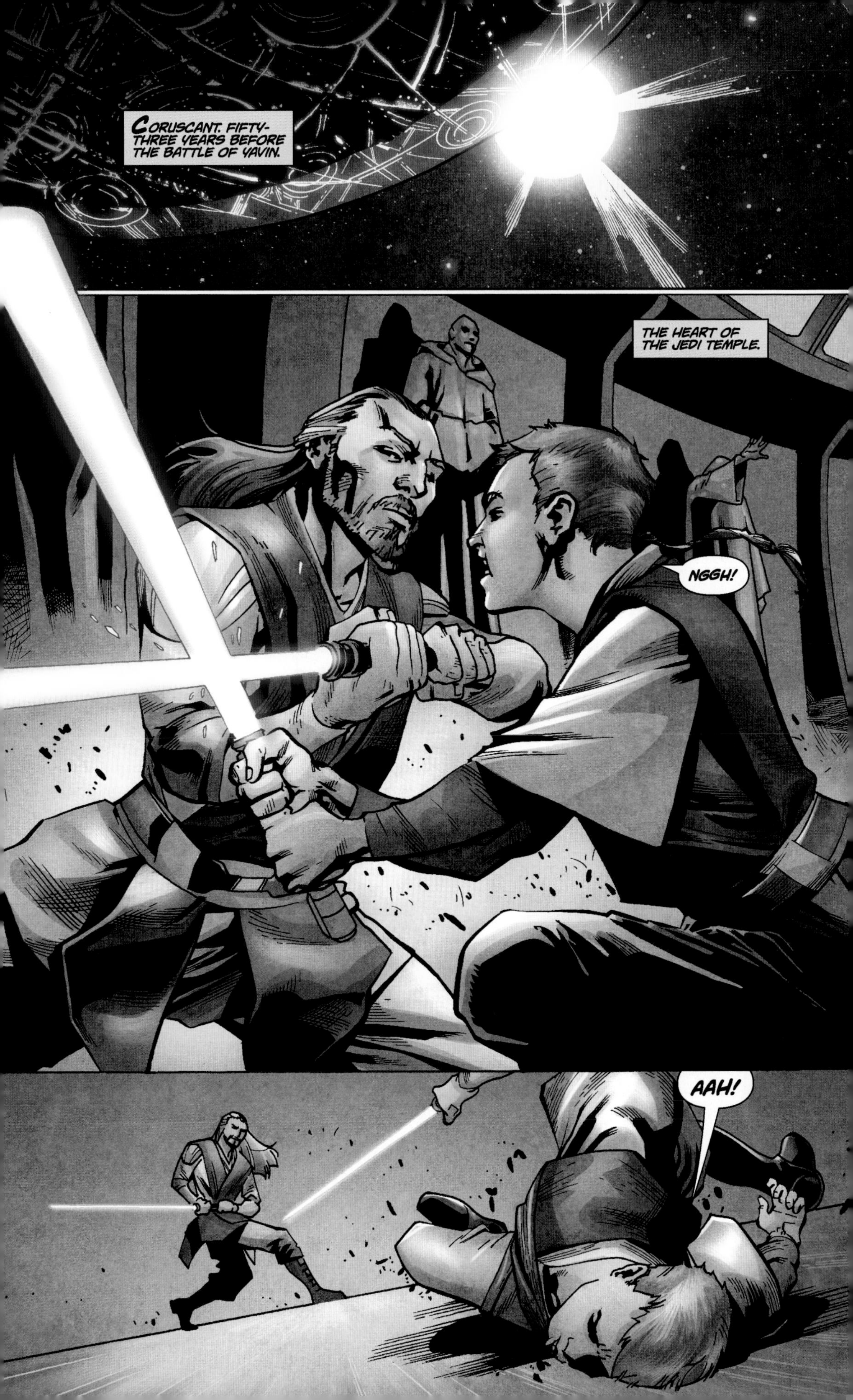
CORUSCANT. FIFTY-THREE YEARS BEFORE THE BATTLE OF YAVIN.
THE HEART OF THE JEDI TEMPLE.
NGGH!
AAH!

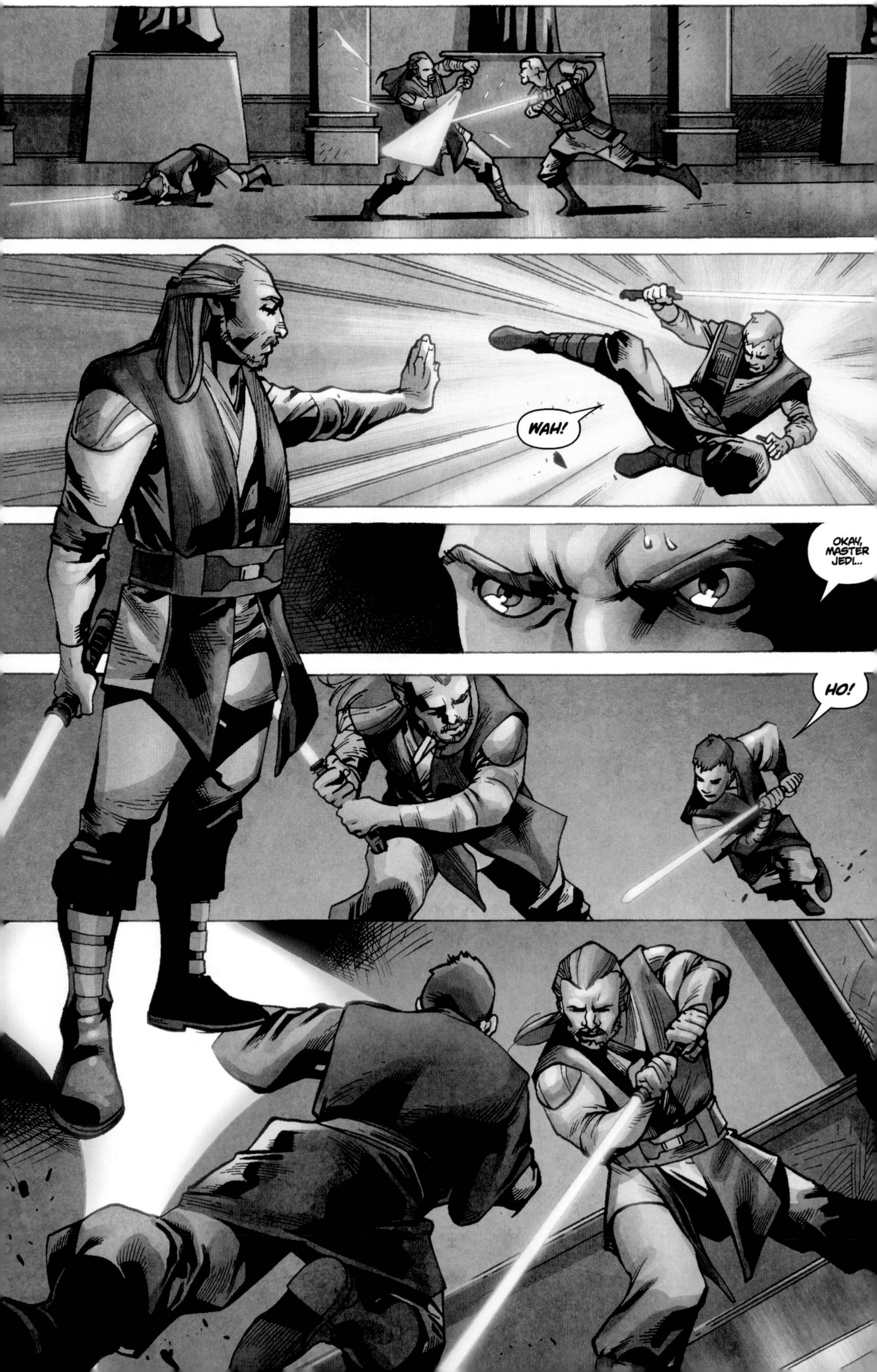
WAH!
OKAY, MASTER JEDI...
HO!

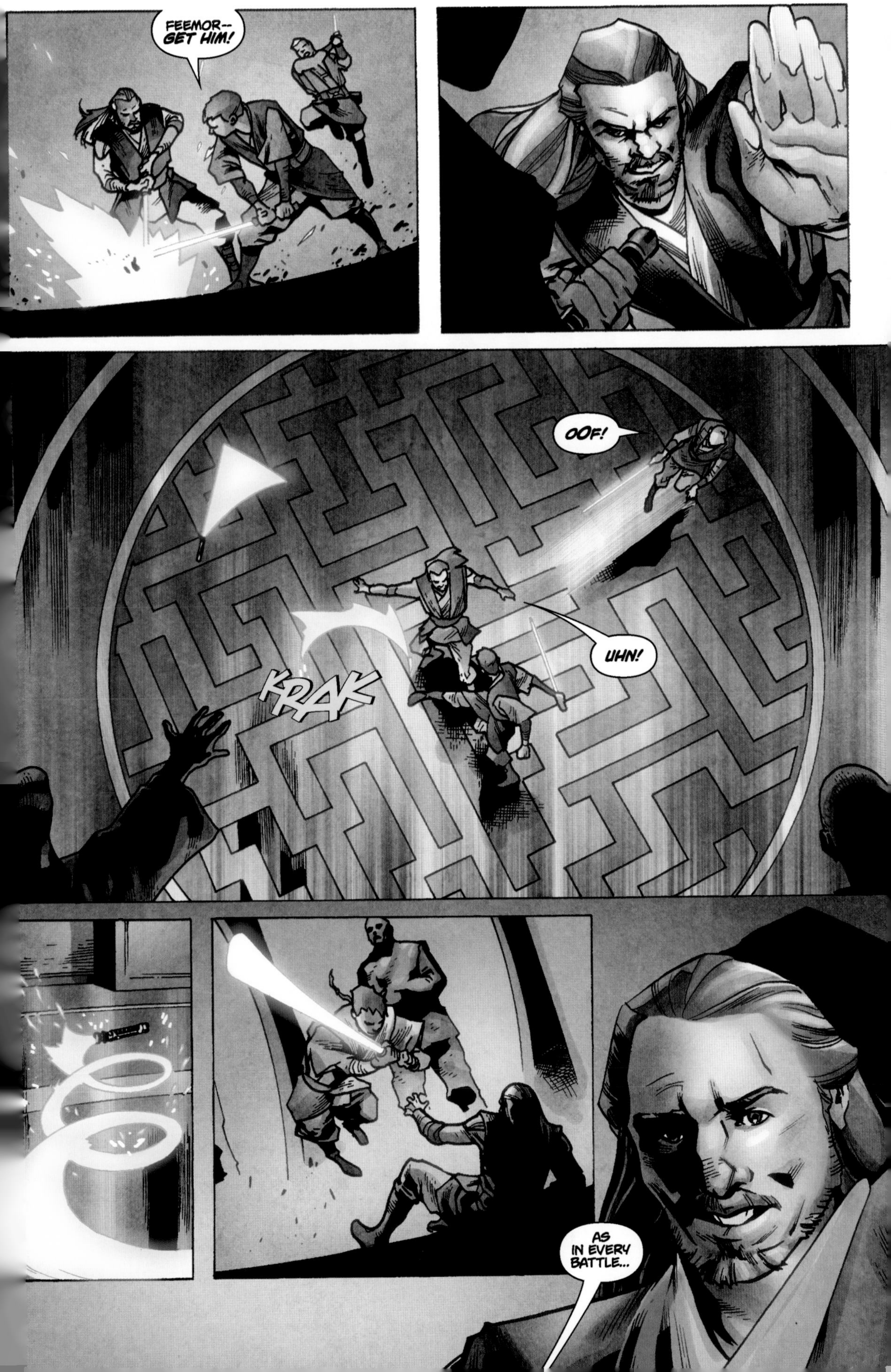
FEEMOR-- GET HIM!
OOF!
UHN!
KRAK
AS IN EVERY BATTLE...

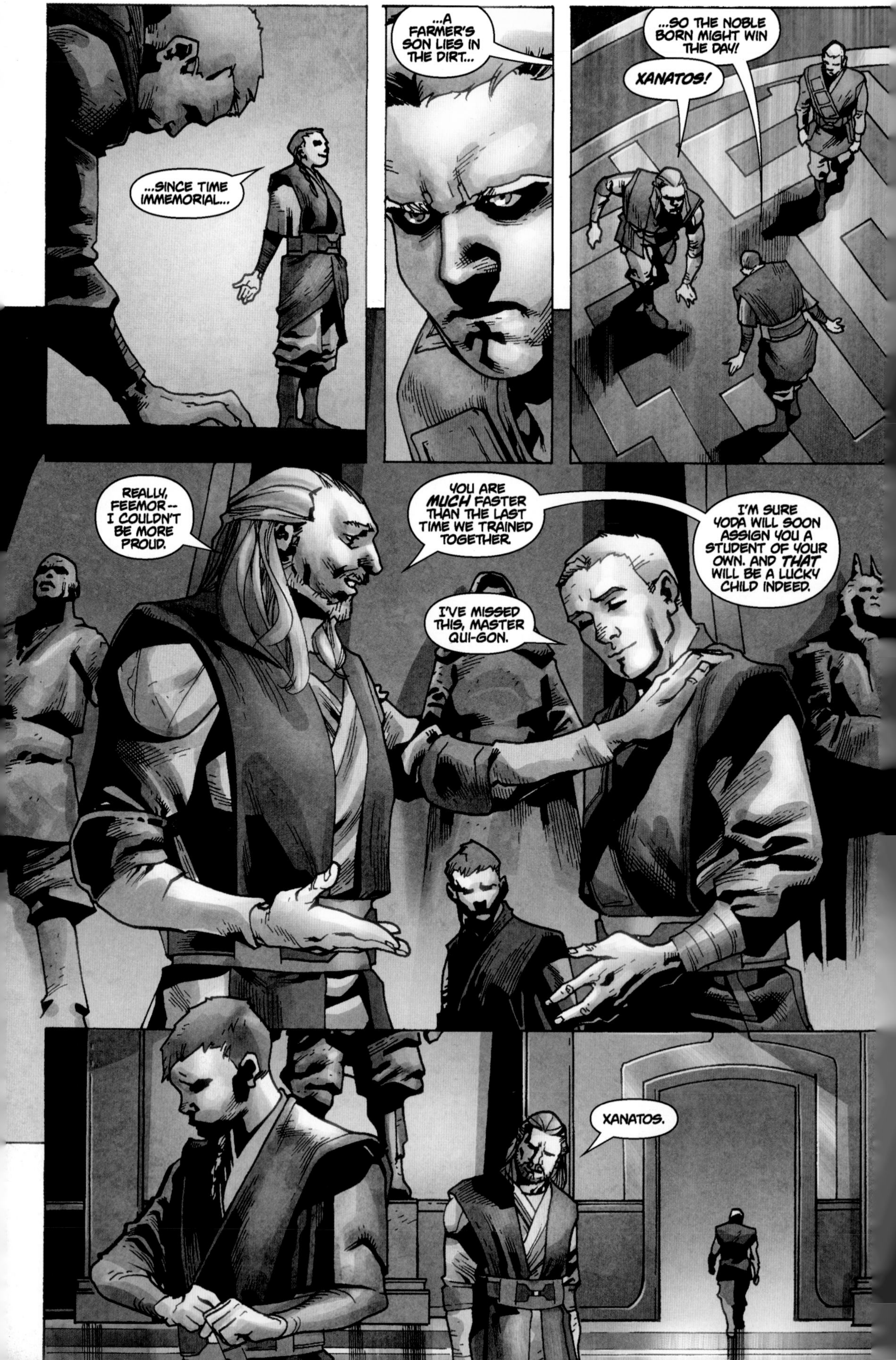
...SINCE TIME IMMEMORIAL...
...A FARMER'S SON LIES IN THE DIRT...
...SO THE NOBLE BORN MIGHT WIN THE DAY!
XANATOS!
REALLY, FEEMOR-- I COULDN'T BE MORE PROUD.
YOU ARE MUCH FASTER THAN THE LAST TIME WE TRAINED TOGETHER.
I'M SURE YODA WILL SOON ASSIGN YOU A STUDENT OF YOUR OWN. AND THAT WILL BE A LUCKY CHILD INDEED.
I'VE MISSED THIS, MASTER QUI-GON.
XANATOS.

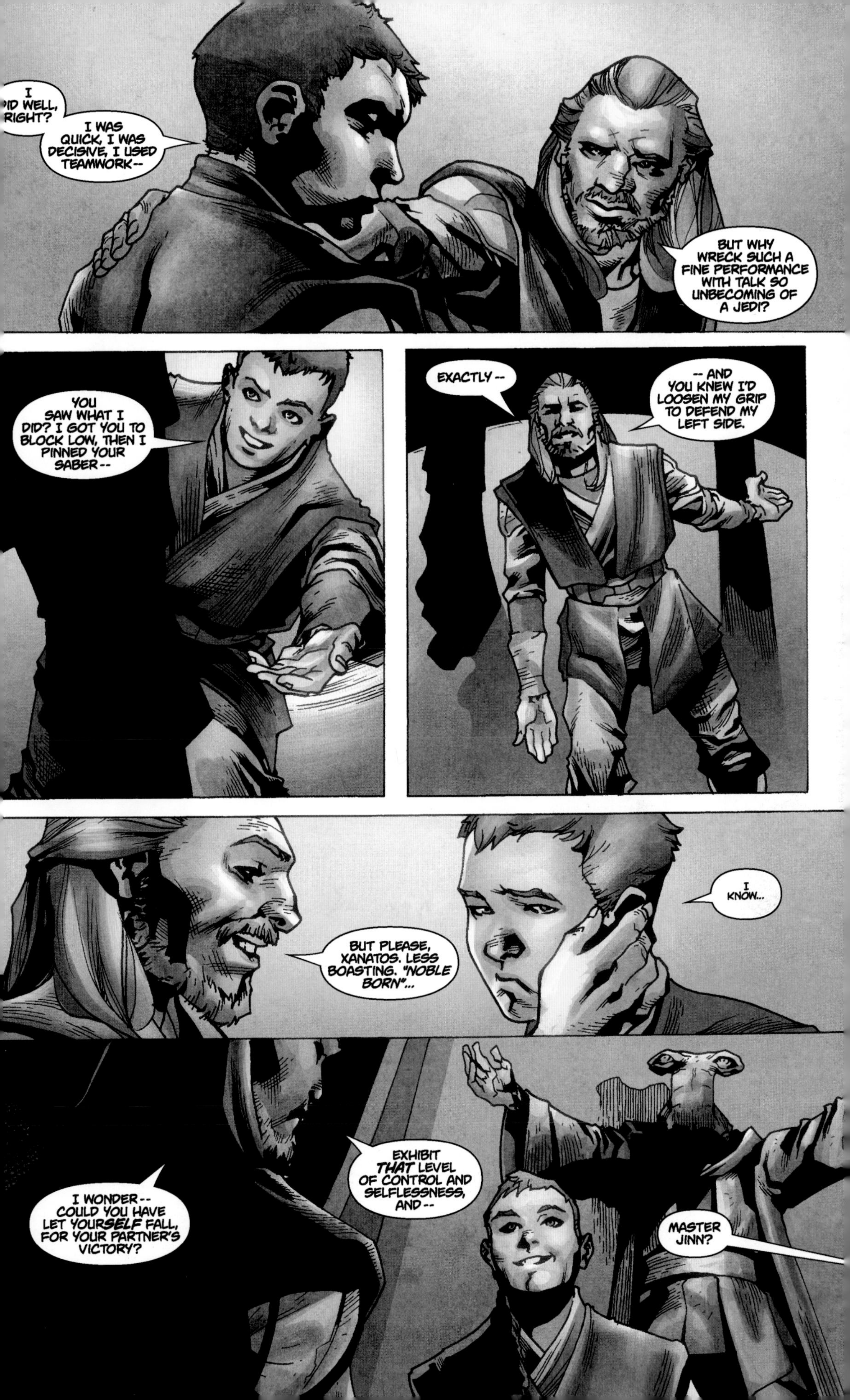
I DID WELL, RIGHT?
I WAS QUICK, I WAS DECISIVE, I USED TEAMWORK--
BUT WHY WRECK SUCH A FINE PERFORMANCE WITH TALK SO UNBECOMING OF A JEDI?
YOU SAW WHAT I DID? I GOT YOU TO BLOCK LOW, THEN I PINNED YOUR SABER--
EXACTLY--
--AND YOU KNEW I'D LOOSEN MY GRIP TO DEFEND MY LEFT SIDE.
I KNOW...
BUT PLEASE, XANATOS. LESS BOASTING. "NOBLE BORN"...
I WONDER-- COULD YOU HAVE LET YOURSELF FALL, FOR YOUR PARTNER'S VICTORY?
EXHIBIT THAT LEVEL OF CONTROL AND SELFLESSNESS, AND--
MASTER JINN?

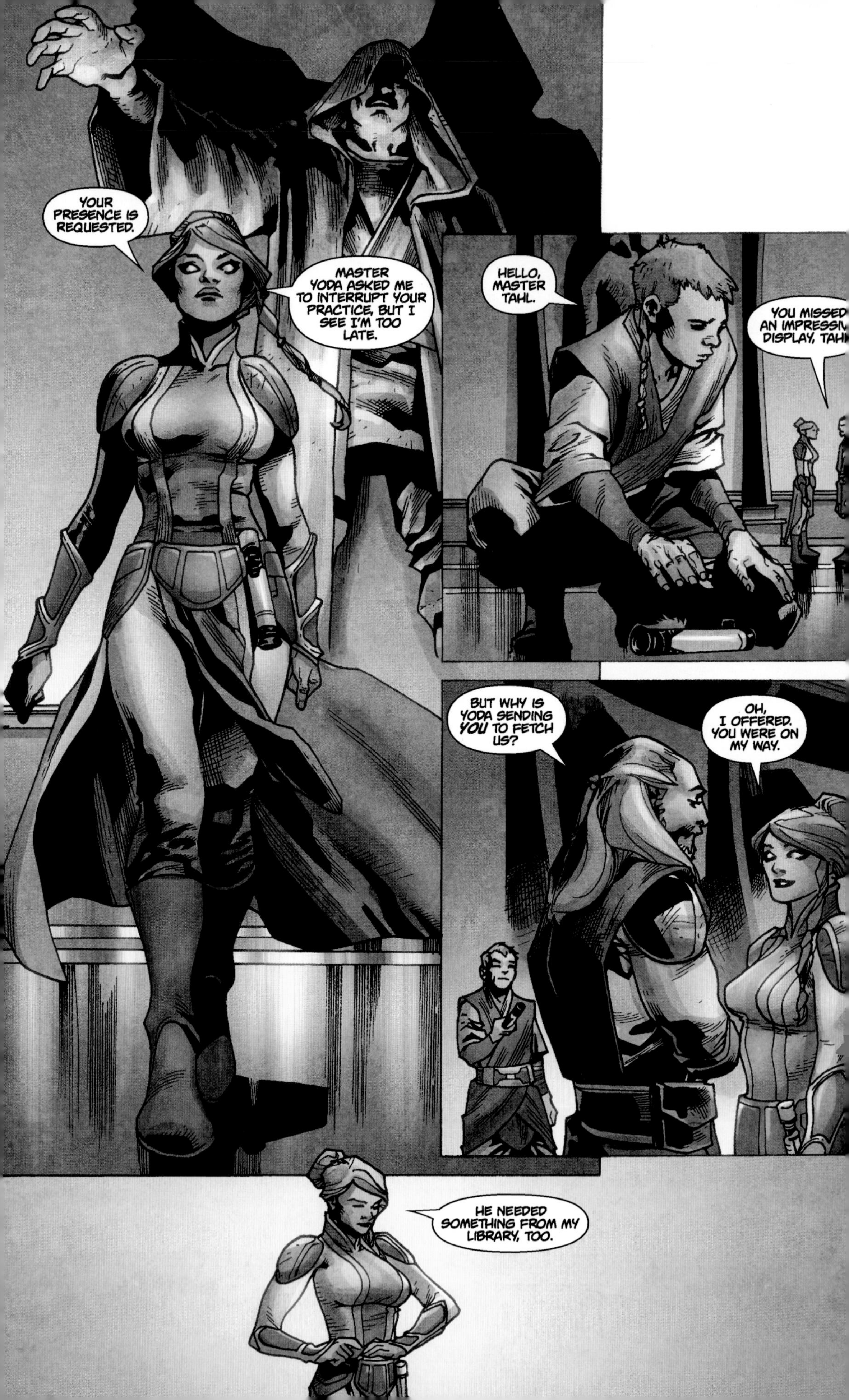
YOUR PRESENCE IS REQUESTED.
MASTER YODA ASKED ME TO INTERRUPT YOUR PRACTICE, BUT I SEE I'M TOO LATE.
HELLO, MASTER TAHL.
YOU MISSED AN IMPRESSIV DISPLAY, TAH
BUT WHY IS YODA SENDING *YOU* TO FETCH US?
OH, I OFFERED. YOU WERE ON MY WAY.
HE NEEDED SOMETHING FROM MY LIBRARY, TOO.

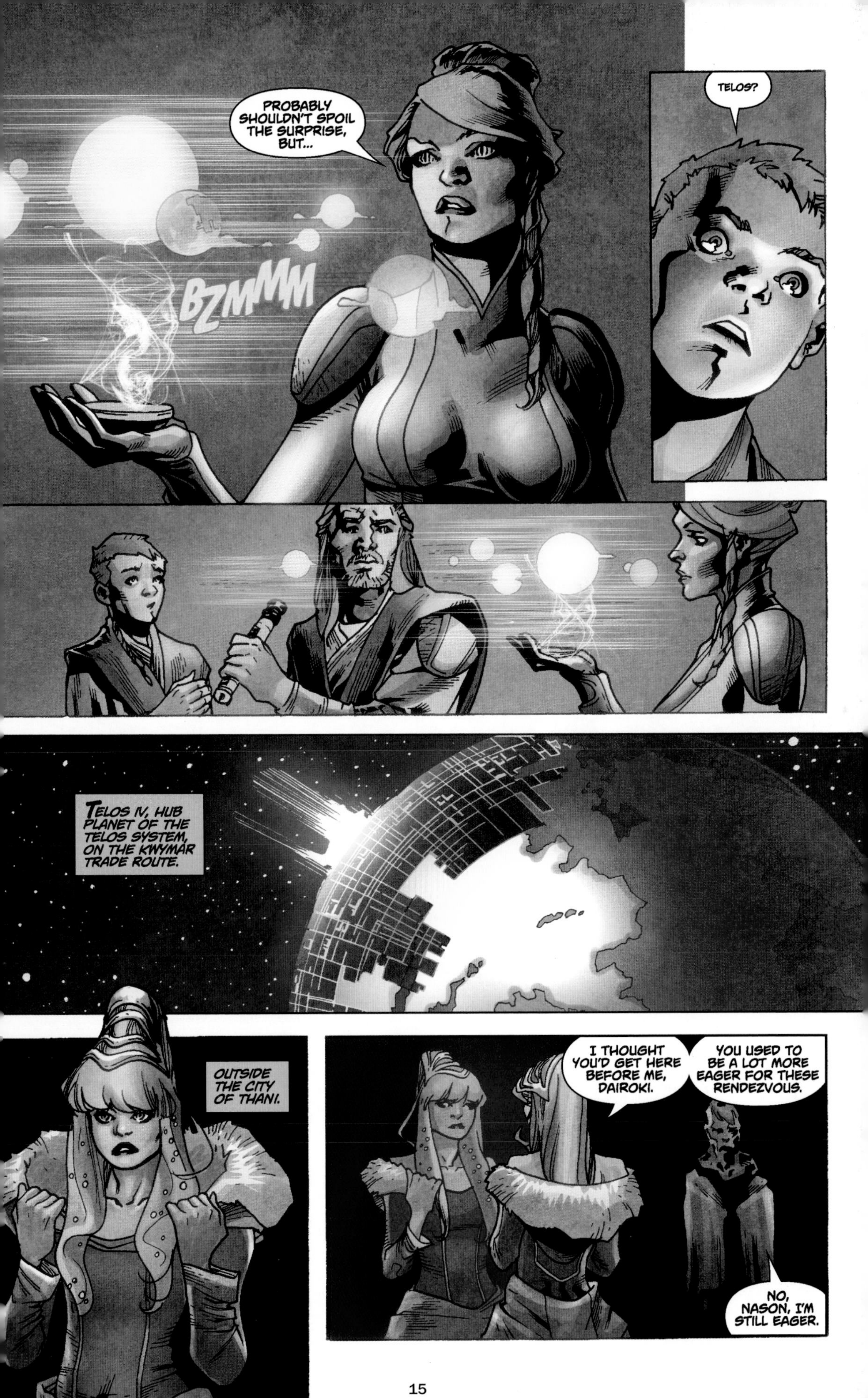
PROBABLY SHOULDN'T SPOIL THE SURPRISE, BUT...
BZMMM
TELOS?
TELOS IV, HUB PLANET OF THE TELOS SYSTEM, ON THE KWYMAR TRADE ROUTE.
OUTSIDE THE CITY OF THANI.
I THOUGHT YOU'D GET HERE BEFORE ME, DAIROKI.
YOU USED TO BE A LOT MORE EAGER FOR THESE RENDEZVOUS.
NO, NASON, I'M STILL EAGER.

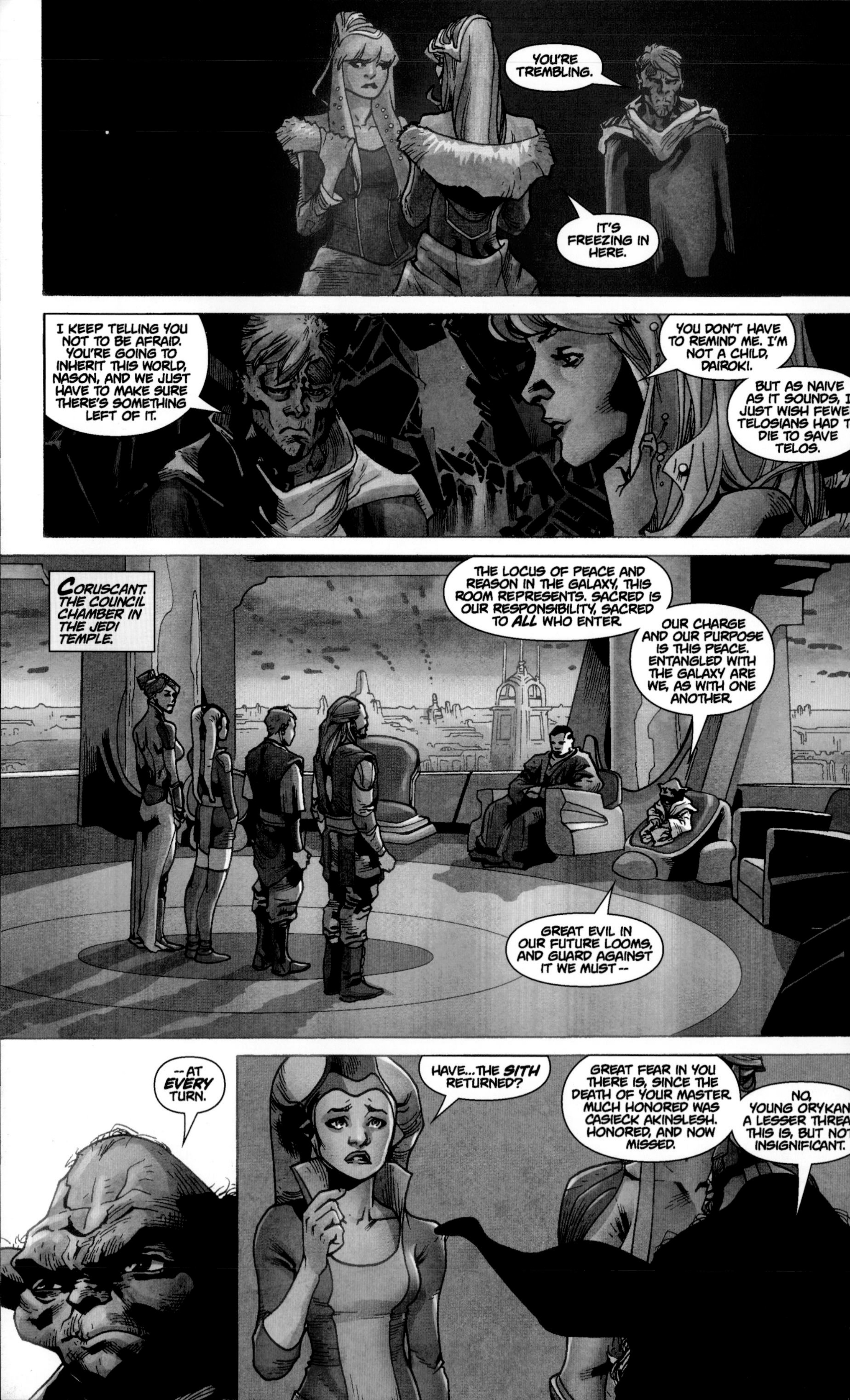
YOU'RE TREMBLING.
IT'S FREEZING IN HERE.
I KEEP TELLING YOU NOT TO BE AFRAID. YOU'RE GOING TO INHERIT THIS WORLD, NASON, AND WE JUST HAVE TO MAKE SURE THERE'S SOMETHING LEFT OF IT.
YOU DON'T HAVE TO REMIND ME. I'M NOT A CHILD, DAIROKI.
BUT AS NAIVE AS IT SOUNDS, I JUST WISH FEWER TELOSIANS HAD TO DIE TO SAVE TELOS.
CORUSCANT. THE COUNCIL CHAMBER IN THE JEDI TEMPLE.
THE LOCUS OF PEACE AND REASON IN THE GALAXY, THIS ROOM REPRESENTS. SACRED IS OUR RESPONSIBILITY, SACRED TO ALL WHO ENTER.
OUR CHARGE AND OUR PURPOSE IS THIS PEACE. ENTANGLED WITH THE GALAXY ARE WE, AS WITH ONE ANOTHER.
GREAT EVIL IN OUR FUTURE LOOMS, AND GUARD AGAINST IT WE MUST --
--AT EVERY TURN.
HAVE...THE SITH RETURNED?
GREAT FEAR IN YOU THERE IS, SINCE THE DEATH OF YOUR MASTER. MUCH HONORED WAS CASIECK AKINSLESH. HONORED, AND NOW MISSED.
NO, YOUNG ORYKAN. A LESSER THREAT THIS IS, BUT NOT INSIGNIFICANT.

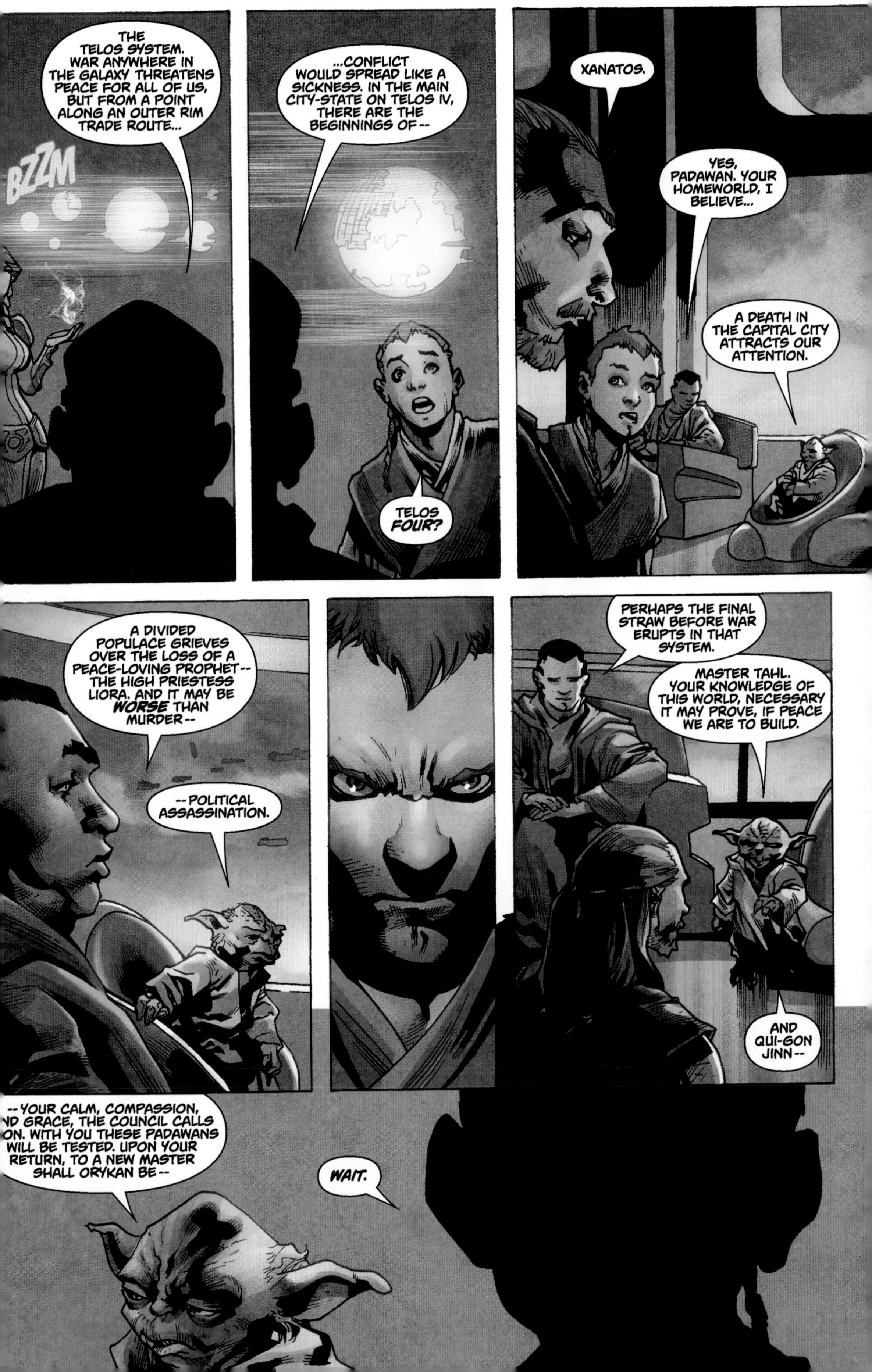
THE TELOS SYSTEM. WAR ANYWHERE IN THE GALAXY THREATENS PEACE FOR ALL OF US, BUT FROM A POINT ALONG AN OUTER RIM TRADE ROUTE...
BZZM
...CONFLICT WOULD SPREAD LIKE A SICKNESS. IN THE MAIN CITY-STATE ON TELOS IV, THERE ARE THE BEGINNINGS OF--
TELOS *FOUR?*
XANATOS.
YES, PADAWAN. YOUR HOMEWORLD, I BELIEVE...
A DEATH IN THE CAPITAL CITY ATTRACTS OUR ATTENTION.
A DIVIDED POPULACE GRIEVES OVER THE LOSS OF A PEACE-LOVING PROPHET--THE HIGH PRIESTESS LIORA. AND IT MAY BE *WORSE* THAN MURDER--
--POLITICAL ASSASSINATION.
PERHAPS THE FINAL STRAW BEFORE WAR ERUPTS IN THAT SYSTEM.
MASTER TAHL. YOUR KNOWLEDGE OF THIS WORLD, NECESSARY IT MAY PROVE, IF PEACE WE ARE TO BUILD.
AND QUI-GON JINN--
--YOUR CALM, COMPASSION, ND GRACE, THE COUNCIL CALLS ON. WITH YOU THESE PADAWANS WILL BE TESTED. UPON YOUR RETURN, TO A NEW MASTER SHALL ORYKAN BE--
WAIT.

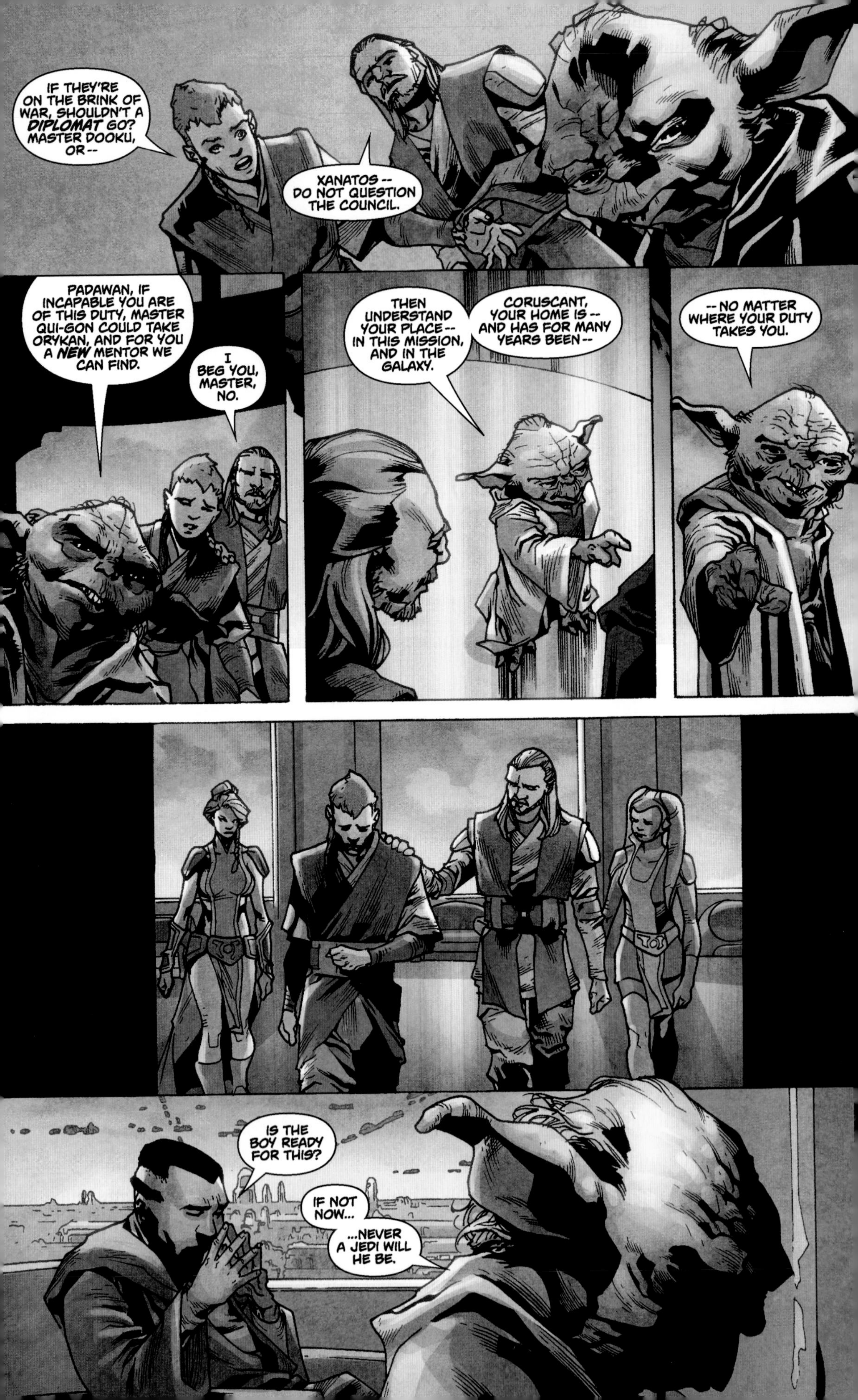

IF THEY'RE ON THE BRINK OF WAR, SHOULDN'T A *DIPLOMAT* GO? MASTER DOOKU, OR--
XANATOS -- DO NOT QUESTION THE COUNCIL.
PADAWAN, IF INCAPABLE YOU ARE OF THIS DUTY, MASTER QUI-GON COULD TAKE ORYKAN, AND FOR YOU A *NEW* MENTOR WE CAN FIND.
I BEG YOU, MASTER, NO.
THEN UNDERSTAND YOUR PLACE-- IN THIS MISSION, AND IN THE GALAXY.
CORUSCANT, YOUR HOME IS -- AND HAS FOR MANY YEARS BEEN --
-- NO MATTER WHERE YOUR DUTY TAKES YOU.
IS THE BOY READY FOR THIS?
IF NOT NOW...
...NEVER A JEDI WILL HE BE.

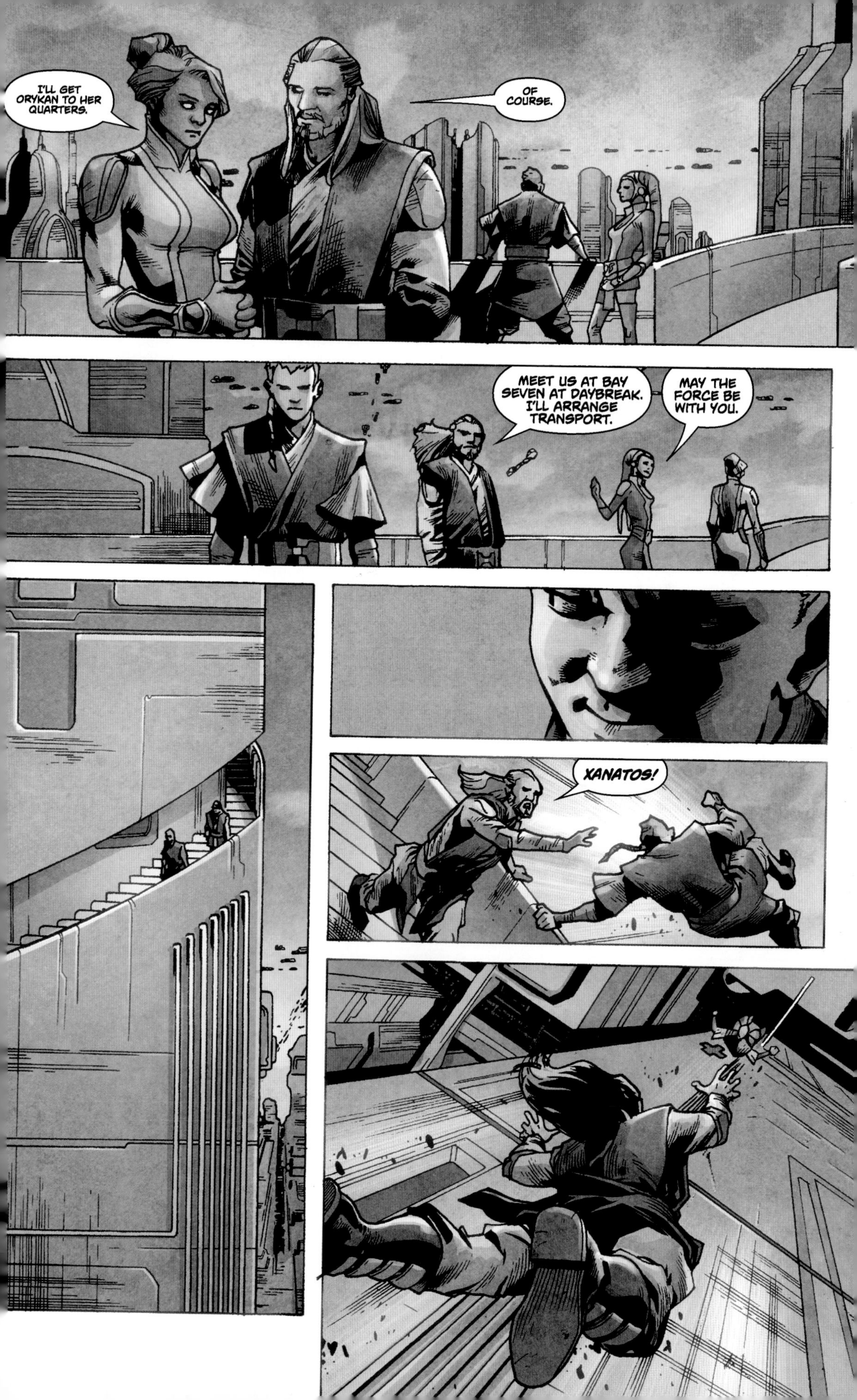
I'LL GET ORYKAN TO HER QUARTERS.
OF COURSE.
MEET US AT BAY SEVEN AT DAYBREAK. I'LL ARRANGE TRANSPORT.
MAY THE FORCE BE WITH YOU.
XANATOS!

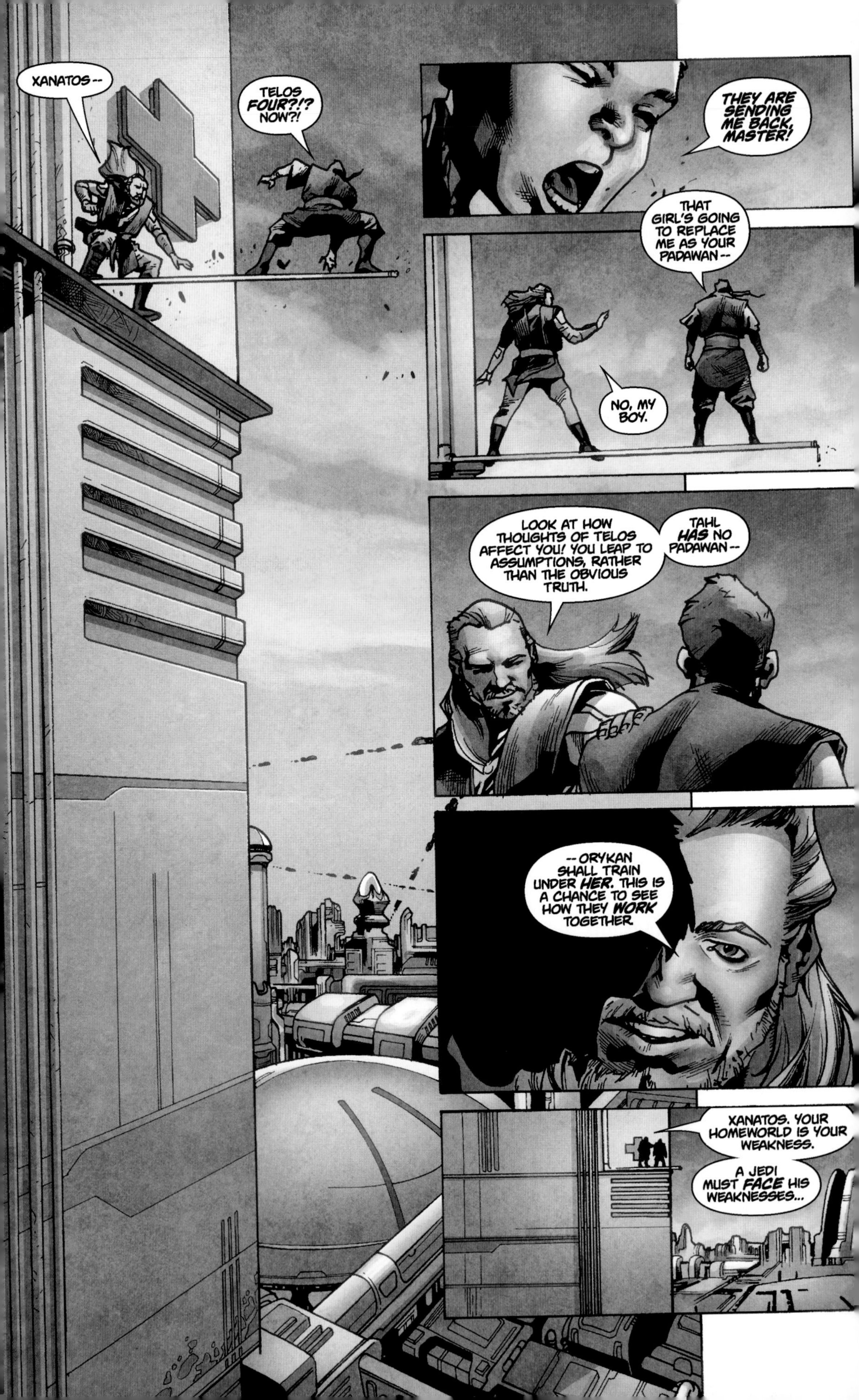
XANATOS --
TELOS FOUR?!? NOW?!
THEY ARE SENDING ME BACK, MASTER!
THAT GIRL'S GOING TO REPLACE ME AS YOUR PADAWAN --
NO, MY BOY.
LOOK AT HOW THOUGHTS OF TELOS AFFECT YOU! YOU LEAP TO ASSUMPTIONS, RATHER THAN THE OBVIOUS TRUTH.
TAHL HAS NO PADAWAN --
-- ORYKAN SHALL TRAIN UNDER HER. THIS IS A CHANCE TO SEE HOW THEY WORK TOGETHER.
XANATOS. YOUR HOMEWORLD IS YOUR WEAKNESS.
A JEDI MUST FACE HIS WEAKNESSES...

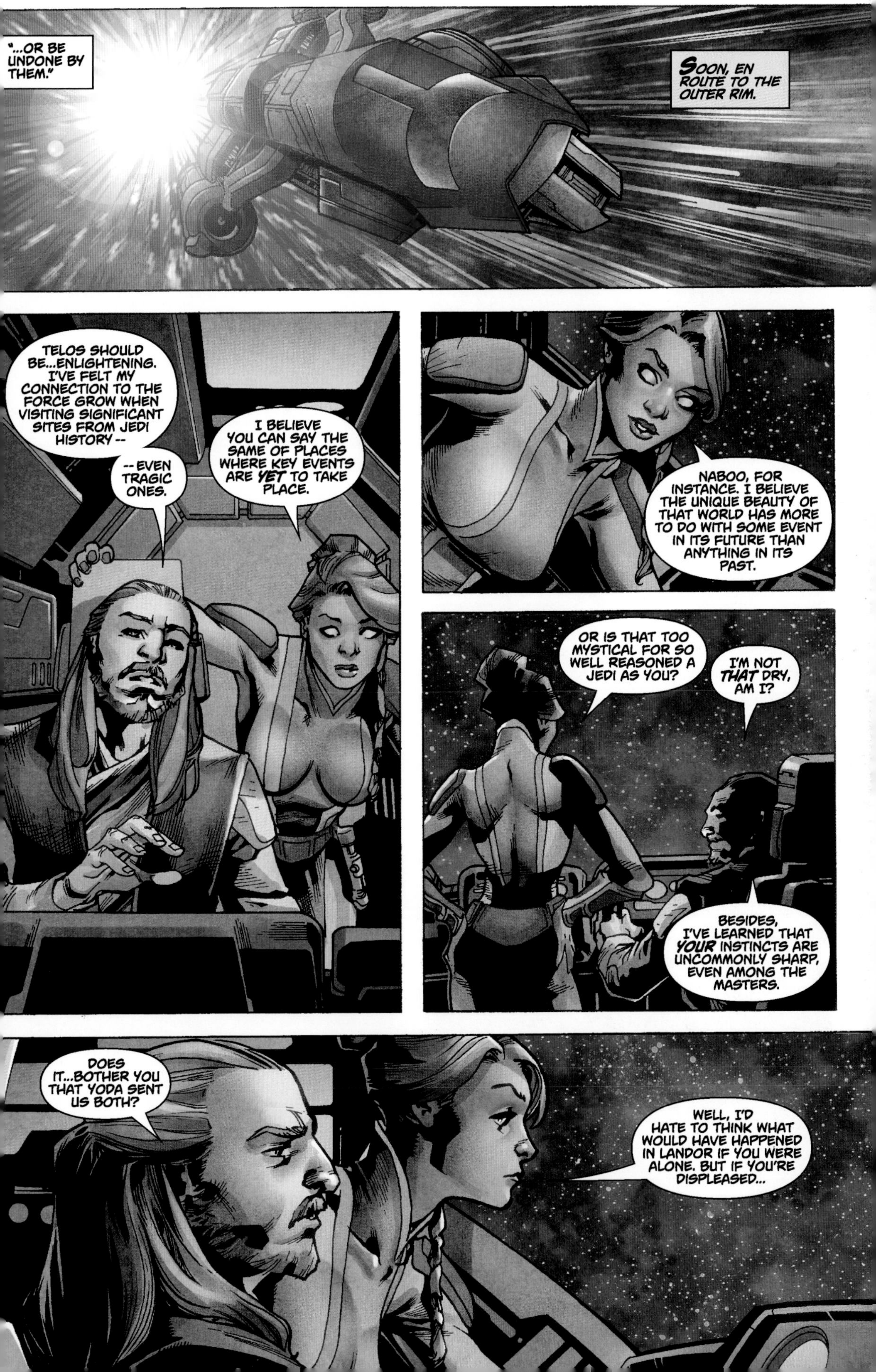
"...OR BE UNDONE BY THEM."
SOON, EN ROUTE TO THE OUTER RIM.
TELOS SHOULD BE...ENLIGHTENING. I'VE FELT MY CONNECTION TO THE FORCE GROW WHEN VISITING SIGNIFICANT SITES FROM JEDI HISTORY --
-- EVEN TRAGIC ONES.
I BELIEVE YOU CAN SAY THE SAME OF PLACES WHERE KEY EVENTS ARE *YET* TO TAKE PLACE.
NABOO, FOR INSTANCE. I BELIEVE THE UNIQUE BEAUTY OF THAT WORLD HAS MORE TO DO WITH SOME EVENT IN ITS FUTURE THAN ANYTHING IN ITS PAST.
OR IS THAT TOO MYSTICAL FOR SO WELL REASONED A JEDI AS YOU?
I'M NOT *THAT* DRY, AM I?
BESIDES, I'VE LEARNED THAT *YOUR* INSTINCTS ARE UNCOMMONLY SHARP, EVEN AMONG THE MASTERS.
DOES IT...BOTHER YOU THAT YODA SENT US BOTH?
WELL, I'D HATE TO THINK WHAT WOULD HAVE HAPPENED IN LANDOR IF YOU WERE ALONE. BUT IF YOU'RE DISPLEASED...

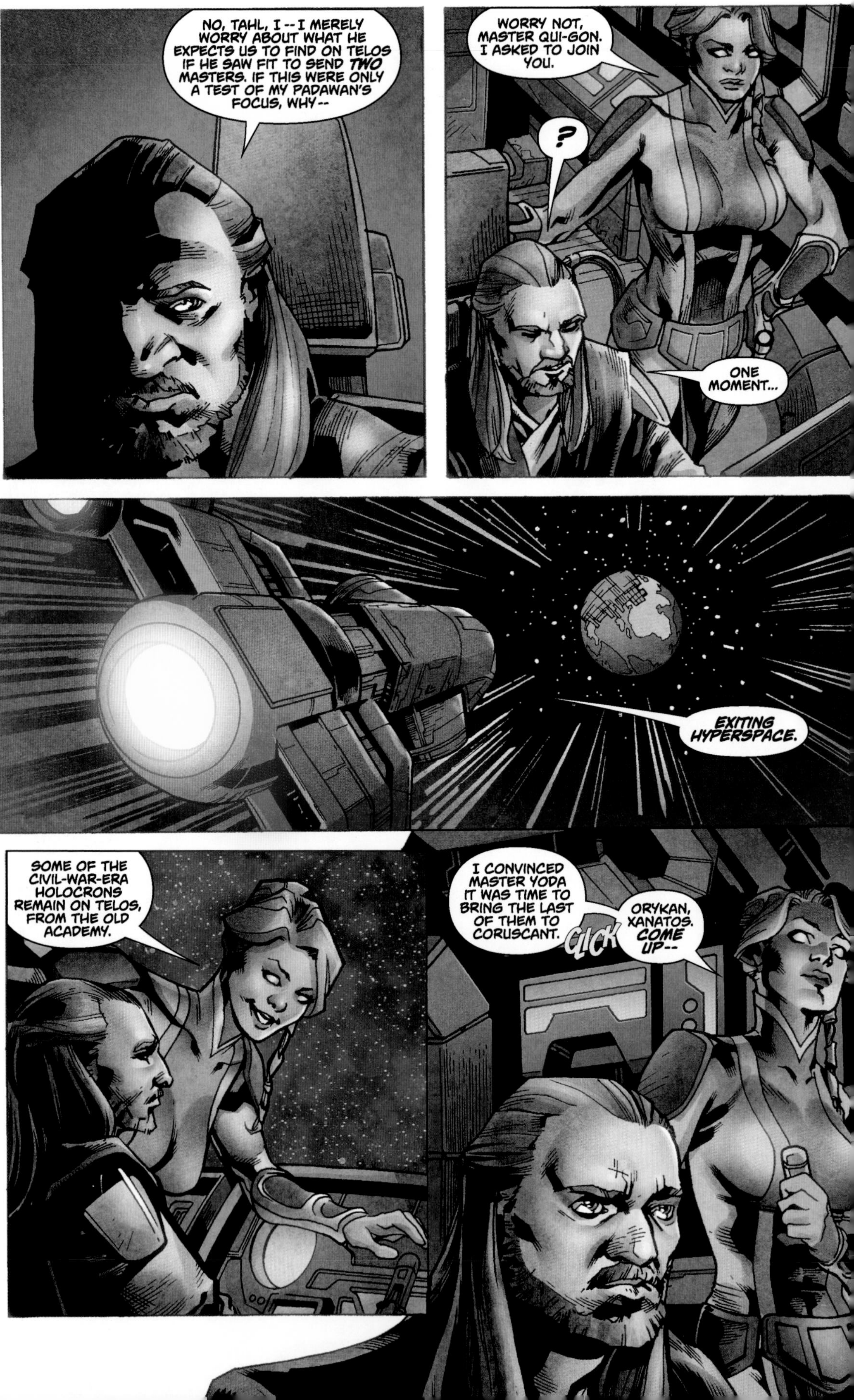
NO, TAHL, I -- I MERELY WORRY ABOUT WHAT HE EXPECTS US TO FIND ON TELOS IF HE SAW FIT TO SEND TWO MASTERS. IF THIS WERE ONLY A TEST OF MY PADAWAN'S FOCUS, WHY--
WORRY NOT, MASTER QUI-GON. I ASKED TO JOIN YOU.
?
ONE MOMENT...
EXITING HYPERSPACE.
SOME OF THE CIVIL-WAR-ERA HOLOCRONS REMAIN ON TELOS, FROM THE OLD ACADEMY.
I CONVINCED MASTER YODA IT WAS TIME TO BRING THE LAST OF THEM TO CORUSCANT.
CLICK
ORYKAN, XANATOS. COME UP--

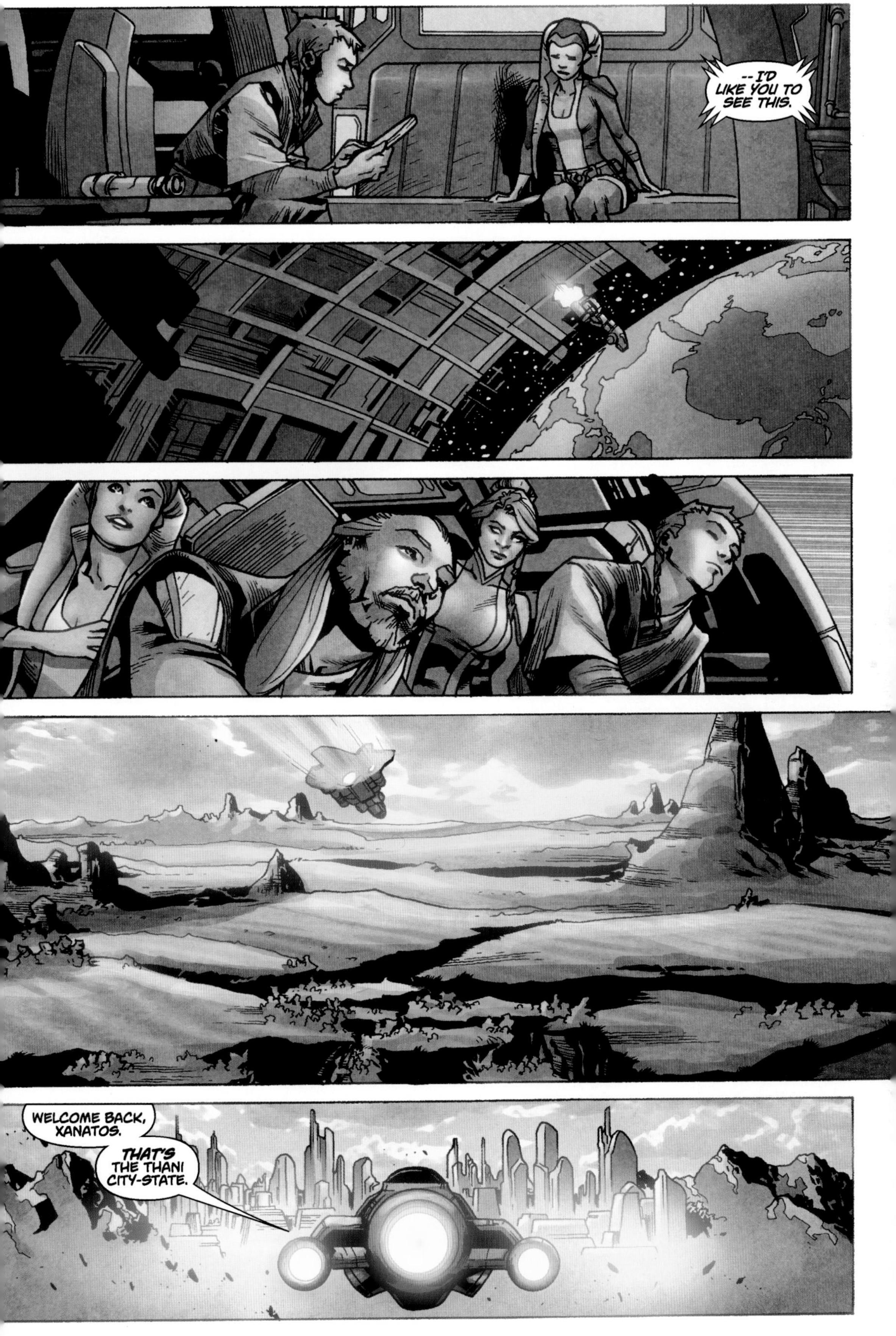
--I'D LIKE YOU TO SEE THIS.
WELCOME BACK, XANATOS.
THAT'S THE THANI CITY-STATE.

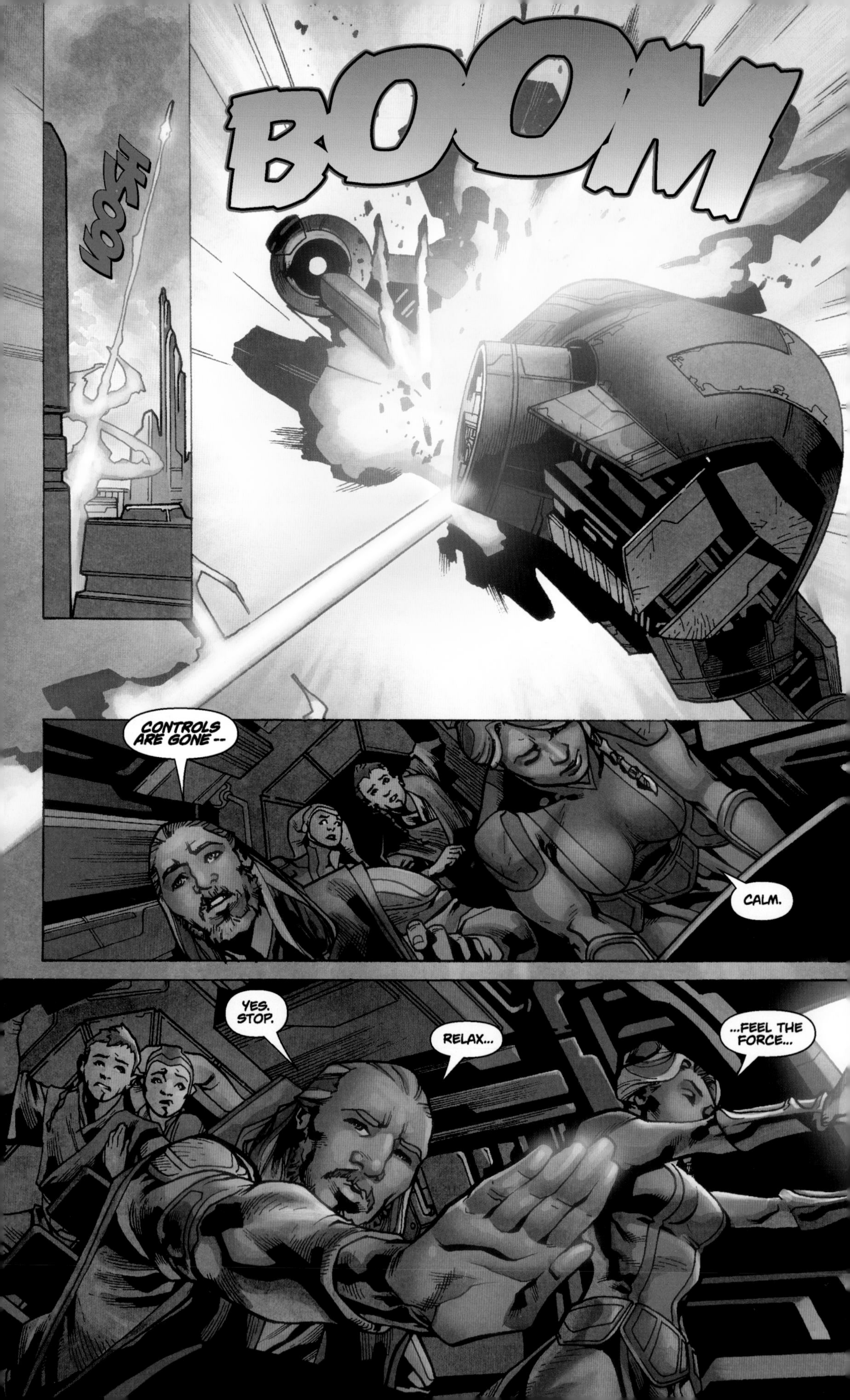
VOOSH
BOOM
CONTROLS ARE GONE --
CALM.
YES. STOP.
RELAX...
...FEEL THE FORCE...

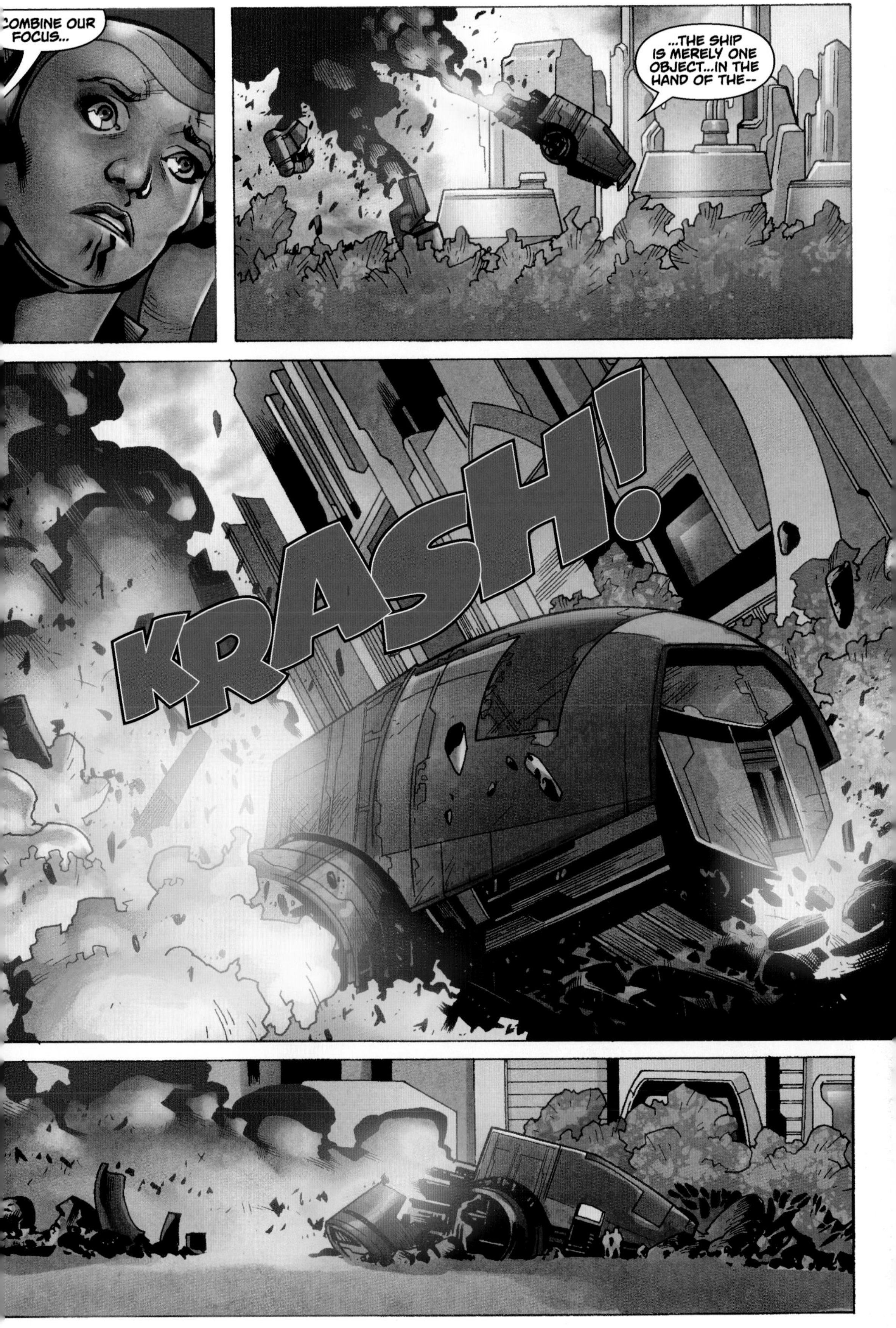
COMBINE OUR FOCUS...
...THE SHIP IS MERELY ONE OBJECT...IN THE HAND OF THE--
KRASH!

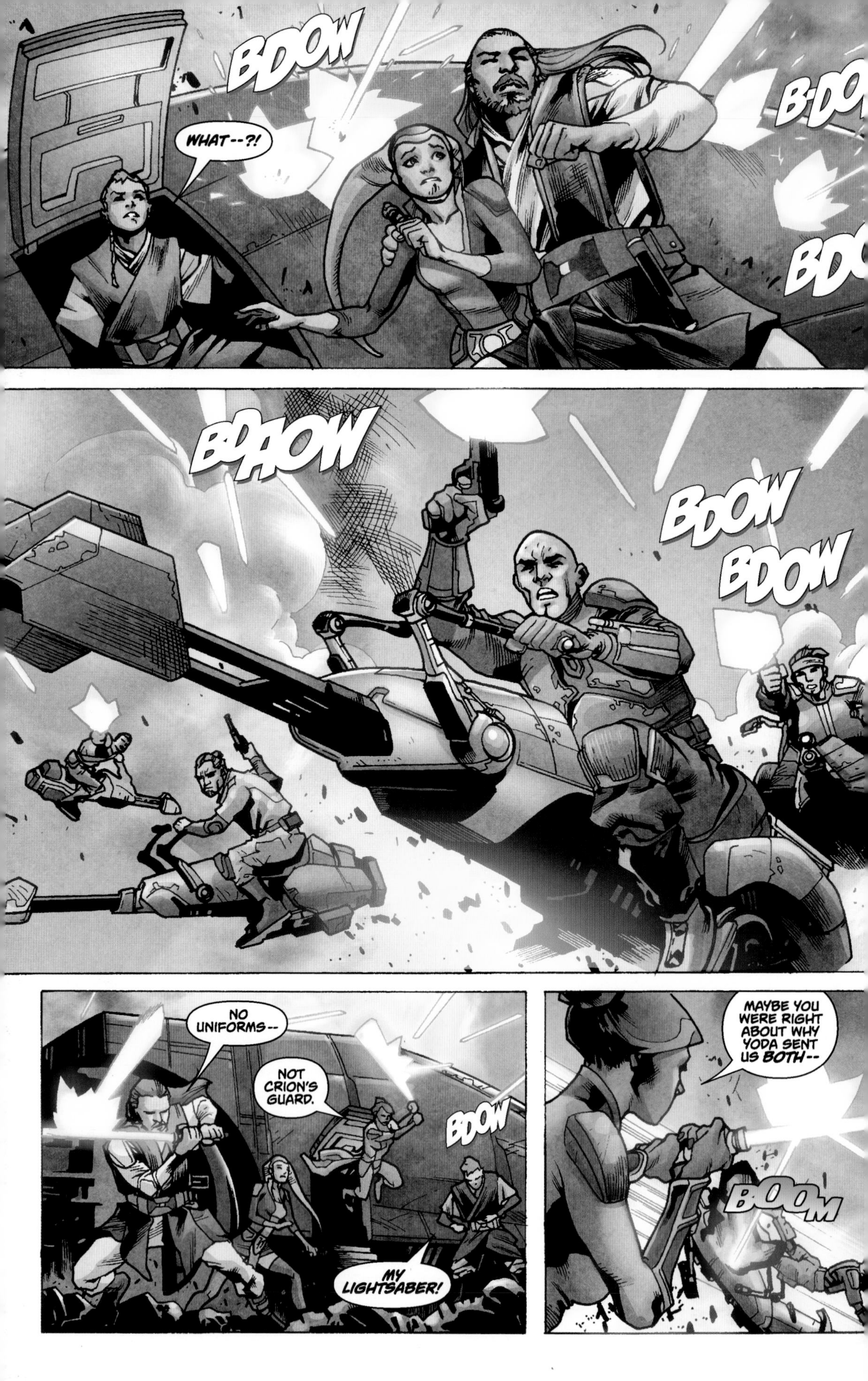
BDOW
WHAT--?!
B-DO
BDO
BDAOW
BDOW
BDOW
NO UNIFORMS--
NOT CRION'S GUARD.
BDOW
MY LIGHTSABER!
MAYBE YOU WERE RIGHT ABOUT WHY YODA SENT US *BOTH*--
BOOM

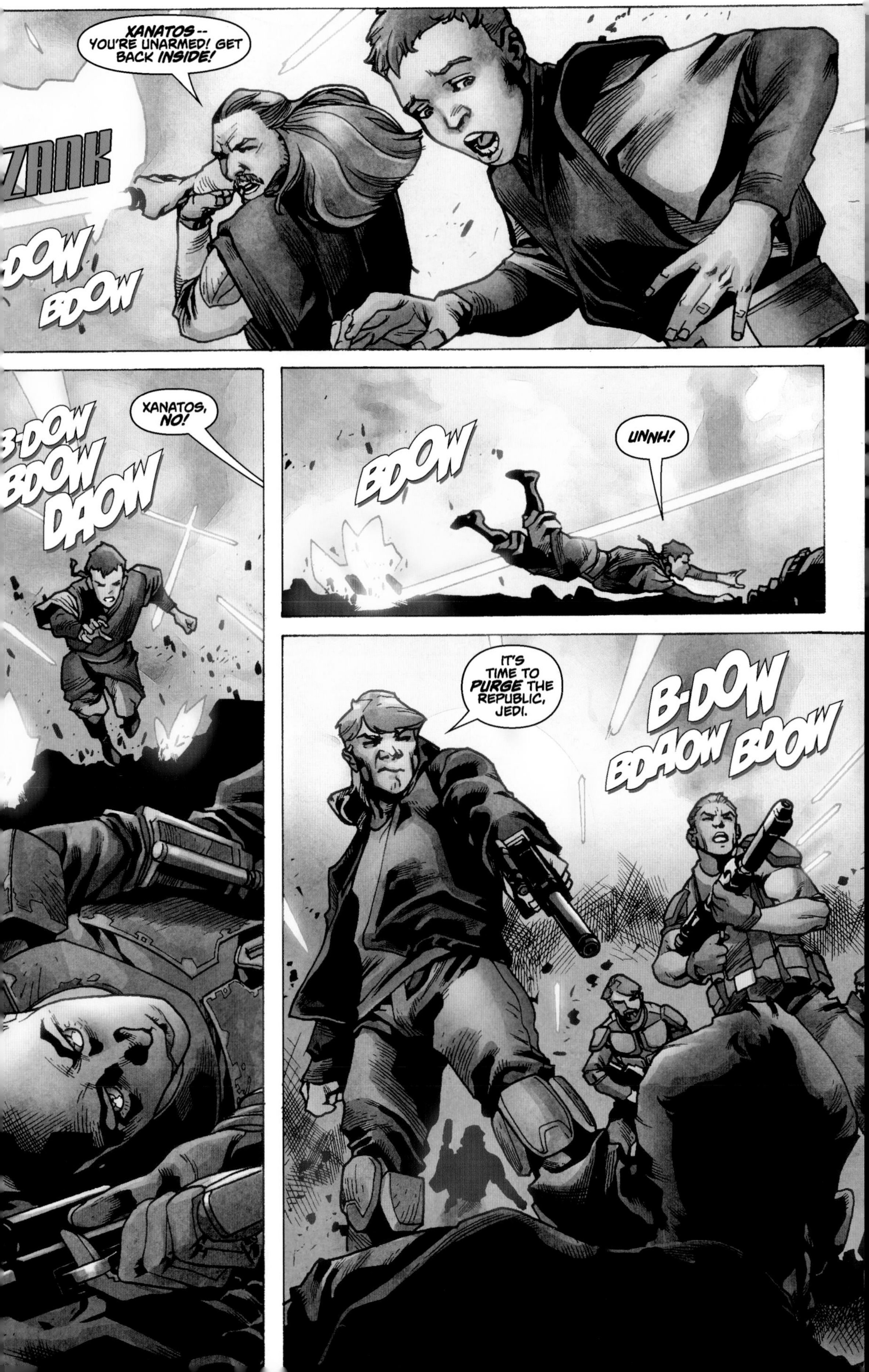
XANATOS -- YOU'RE UNARMED! GET BACK INSIDE!
ZANK
B-DOW
BDOW
XANATOS, NO!
B-DOW
BDOW
DAOW
BDOW
UNNH!
IT'S TIME TO PURGE THE REPUBLIC, JEDI.
B-DOW
BDAOW BDOW

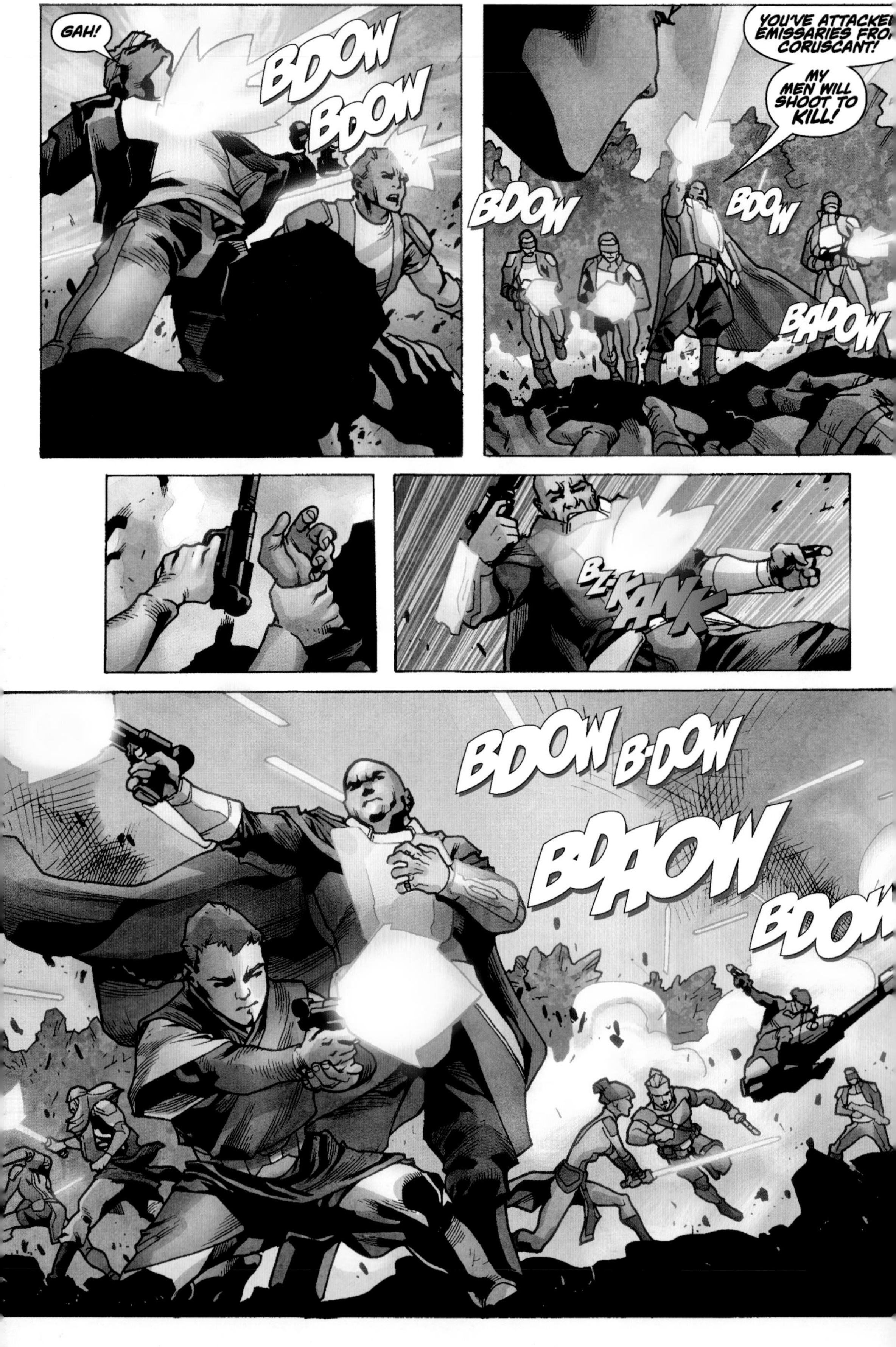
GAH!
BDOW
BDOW
YOU'VE ATTACKE
EMISSARIES FRO
CORUSCANT!
MY MEN WILL SHOOT TO KILL!
BDOW
BDOW
BADOW
BZ-KANK
BDOW B-DOW
BDAOW
BDO

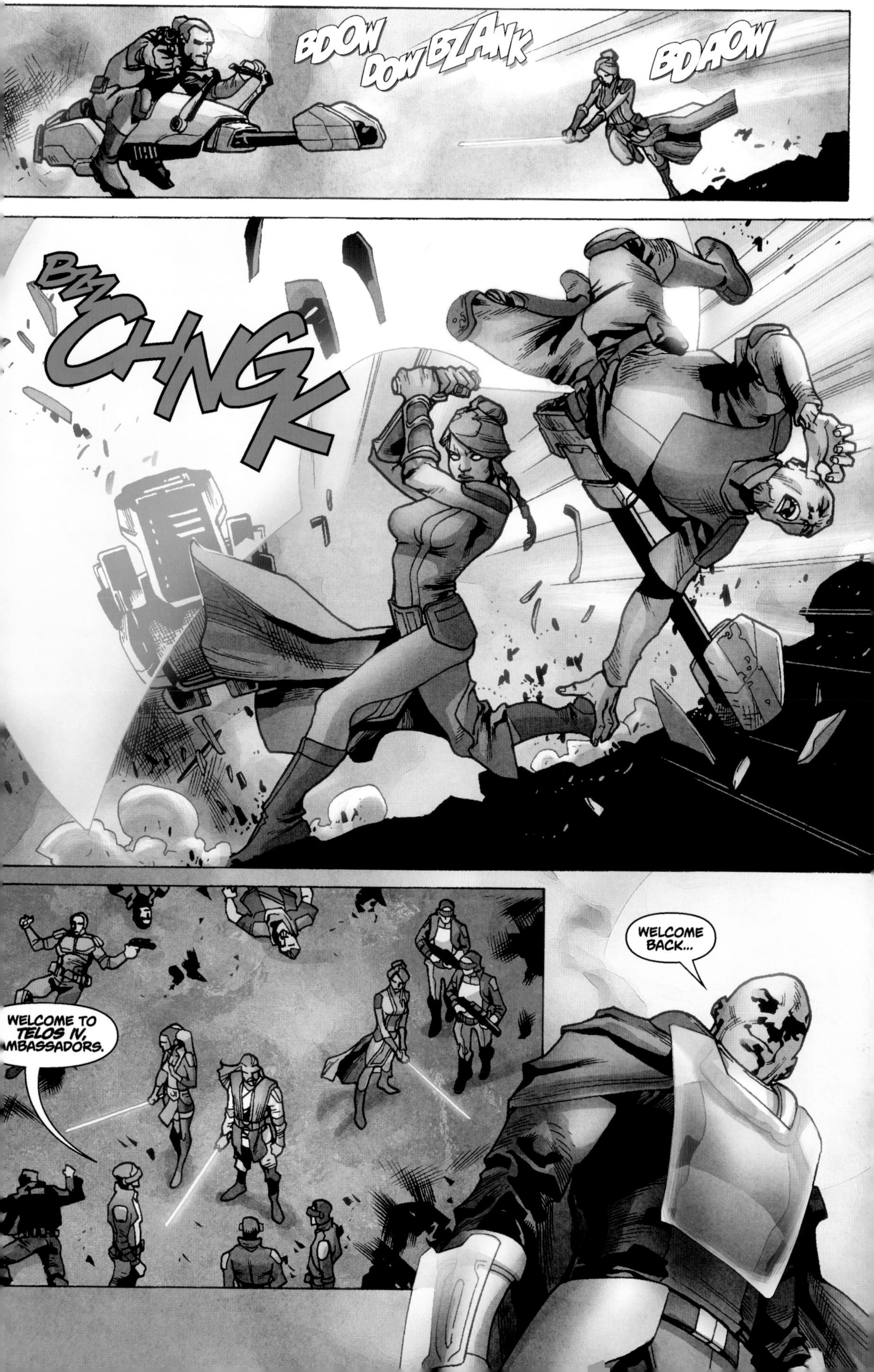
BDOW
DOW BZANK
BDAOW
BZZ CHNGK
WELCOME BACK...
WELCOME TO TELOS IV, AMBASSADORS.

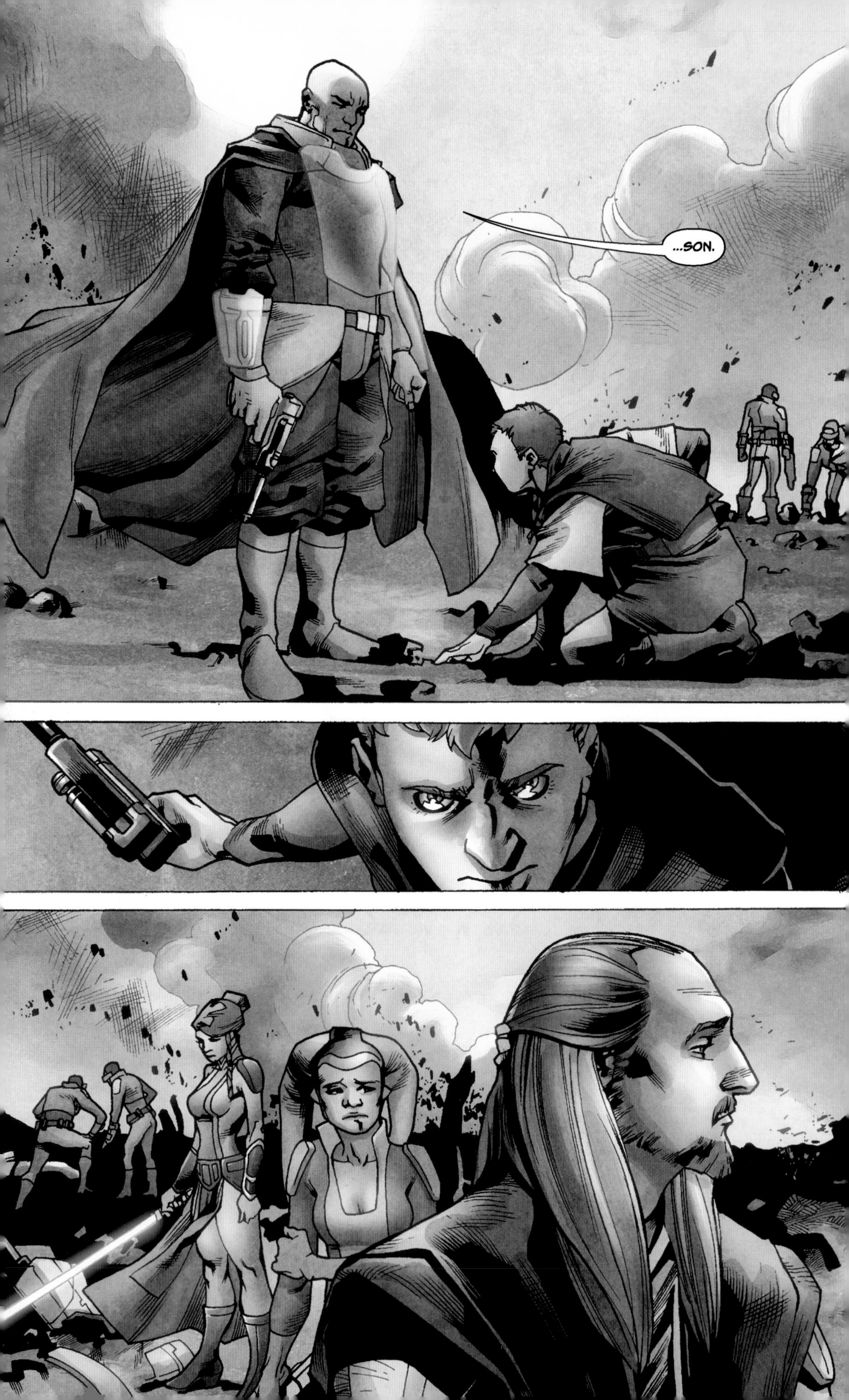
...SON.

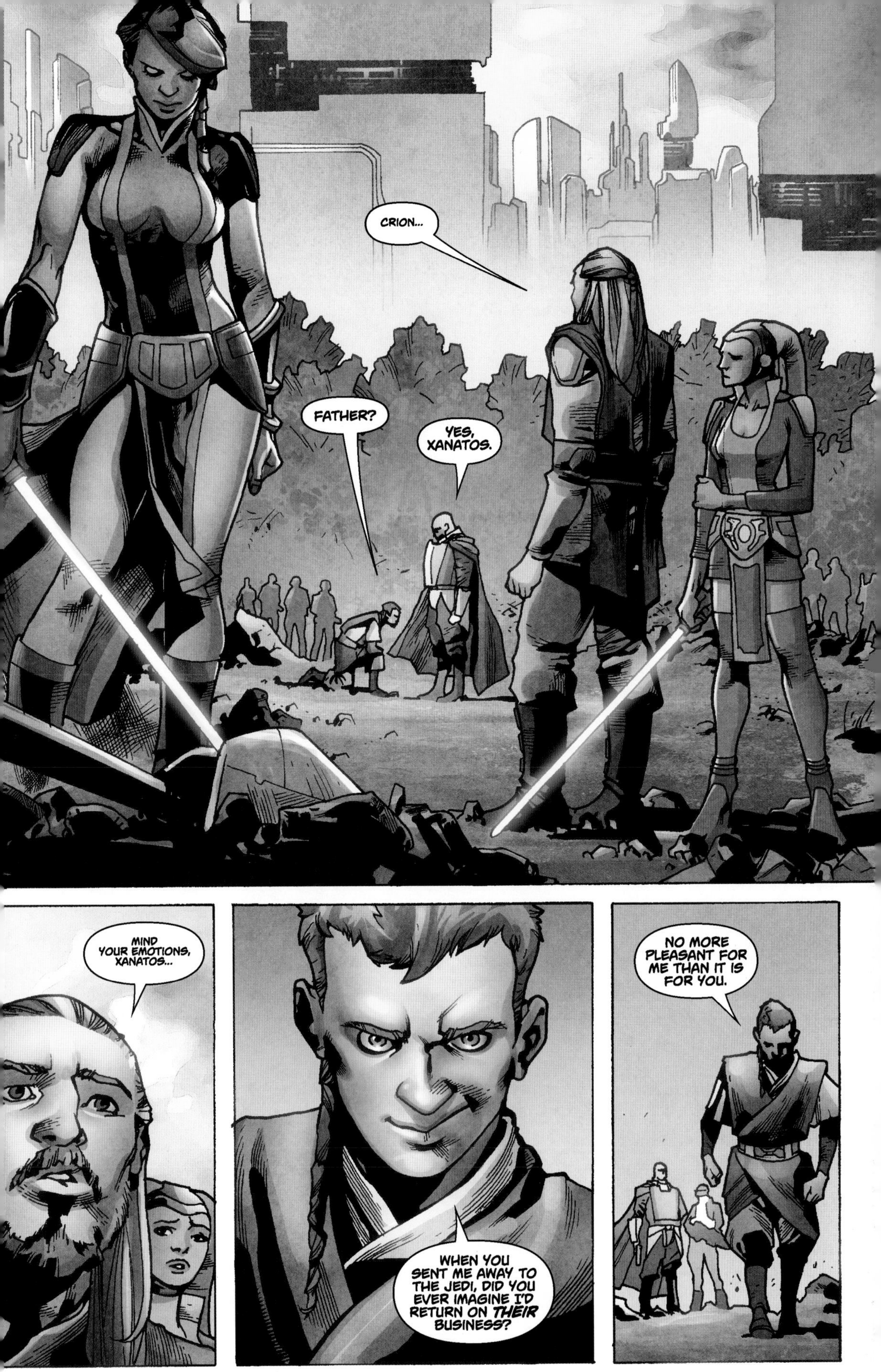
CRION...
FATHER?
YES, XANATOS.
MIND YOUR EMOTIONS, XANATOS...
WHEN YOU SENT ME AWAY TO THE JEDI, DID YOU EVER IMAGINE I'D RETURN ON *THEIR* BUSINESS?
NO MORE PLEASANT FOR ME THAN IT IS FOR YOU.

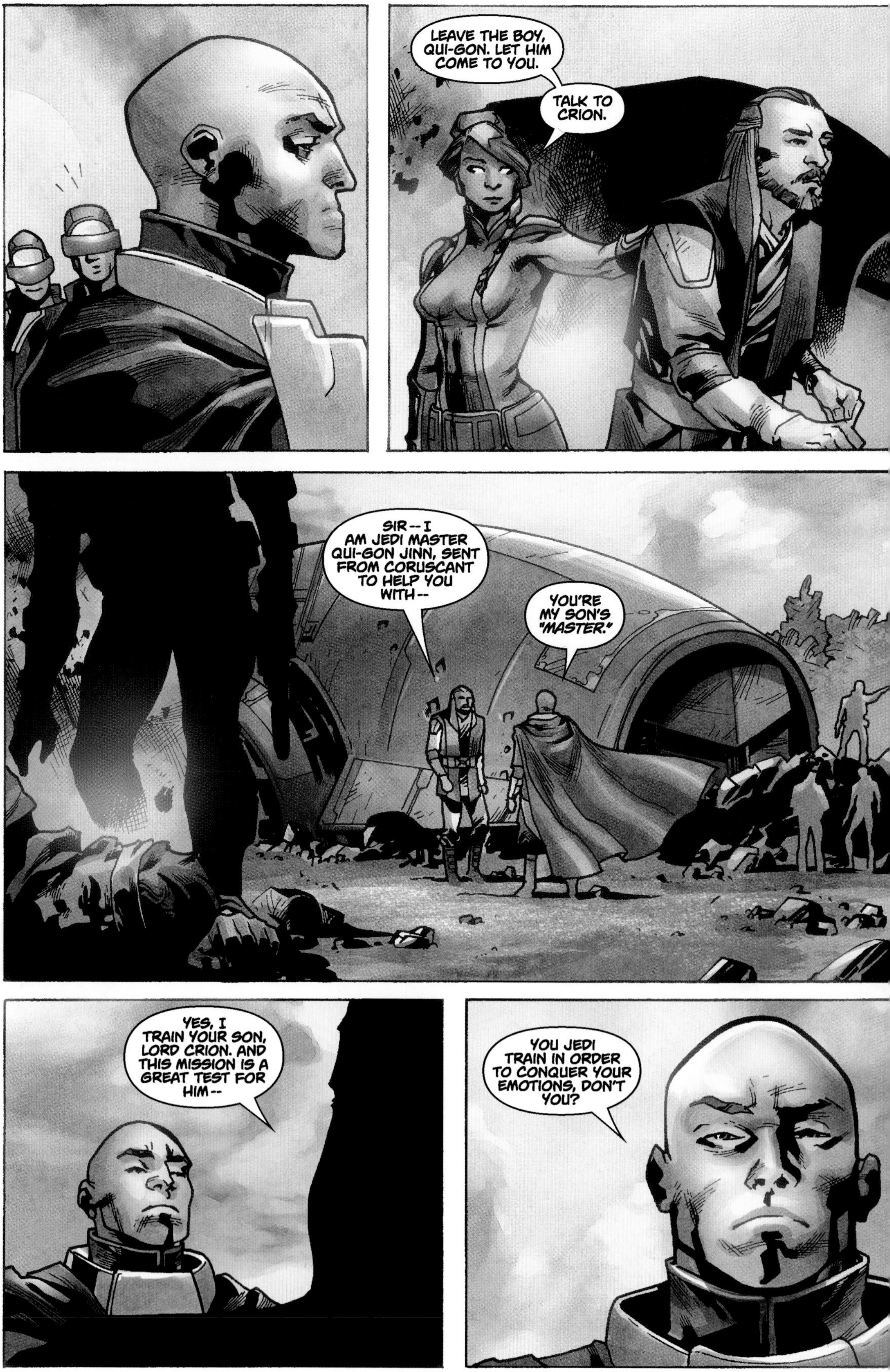
LEAVE THE BOY, QUI-GON. LET HIM COME TO YOU.
TALK TO CRION.
SIR -- I AM JEDI MASTER QUI-GON JINN, SENT FROM CORUSCANT TO HELP YOU WITH --
YOU'RE MY SON'S "MASTER."
YES, I TRAIN YOUR SON, LORD CRION. AND THIS MISSION IS A GREAT TEST FOR HIM --
YOU JEDI TRAIN IN ORDER TO CONQUER YOUR EMOTIONS, DON'T YOU?

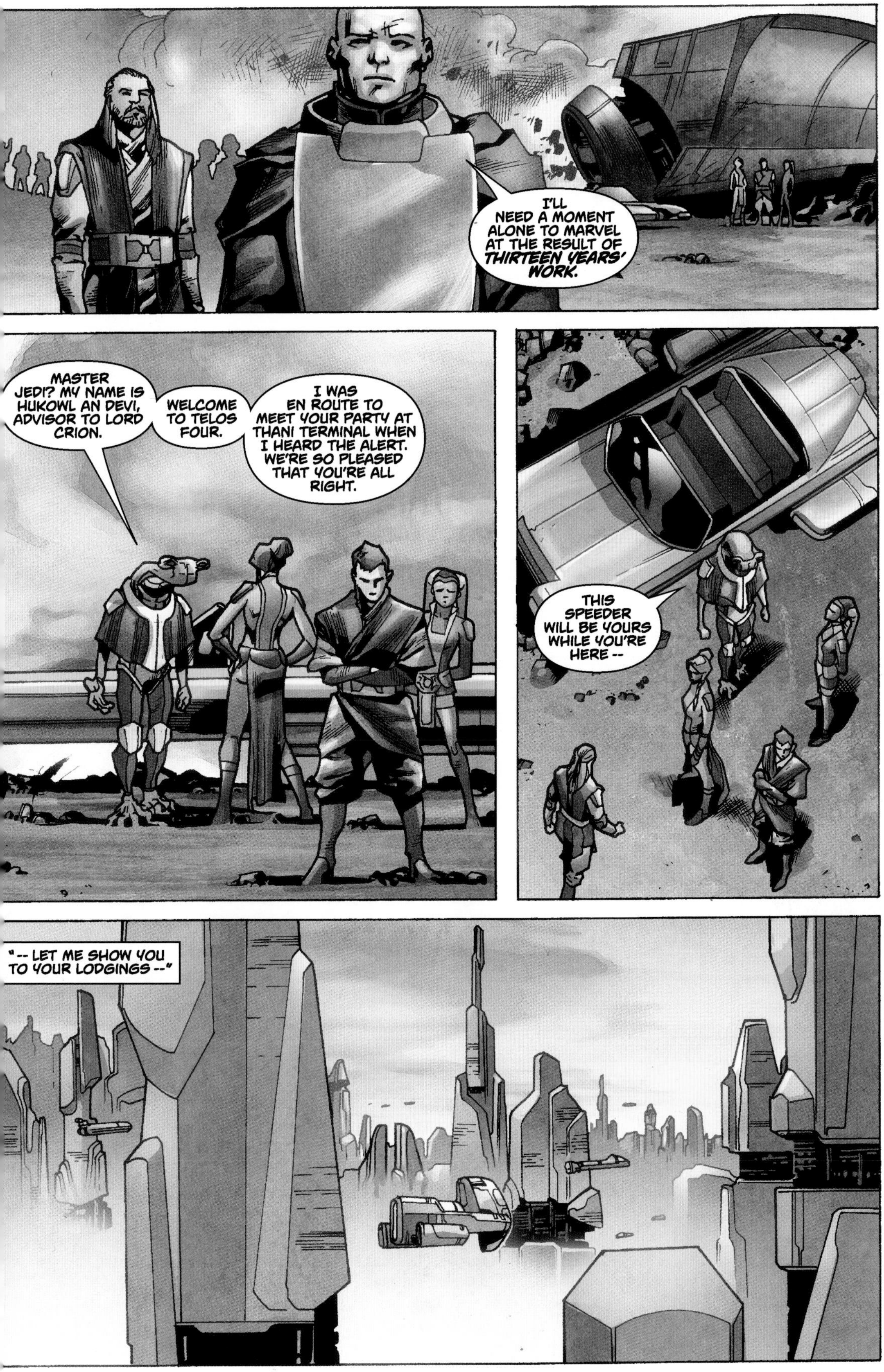
I'LL NEED A MOMENT ALONE TO MARVEL AT THE RESULT OF THIRTEEN YEARS' WORK.
MASTER JEDI? MY NAME IS HUKOWL AN DEVI, ADVISOR TO LORD CRION.
WELCOME TO TELOS FOUR.
I WAS EN ROUTE TO MEET YOUR PARTY AT THANI TERMINAL WHEN I HEARD THE ALERT. WE'RE SO PLEASED THAT YOU'RE ALL RIGHT.
THIS SPEEDER WILL BE YOURS WHILE YOU'RE HERE --
"-- LET ME SHOW YOU TO YOUR LODGINGS --"

" -- I'M CERTAIN YOU'LL FIND THEM TO YOUR LIKING."

LOOK AT THE SCREEN.

WHAT?

SOME OF THESE LIGHT FIXTURES HAVE CAMS IN THEM. WE'RE AMBASSADORS, BUT IT DOESN'T STOP THE TELOSIANS FROM SPYING ON US. THEY HATE OFF-WORLDERS. SO WATCH YOURSELF.

BUT IF I DO THIS...

I SAID LOOK AT THE SCREEN.

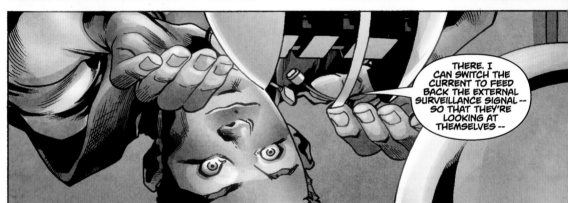

THERE. I CAN SWITCH THE CURRENT TO FEED BACK THE EXTERNAL SURVEILLANCE SIGNAL -- SO THAT THEY'RE LOOKING AT THEMSELVES --

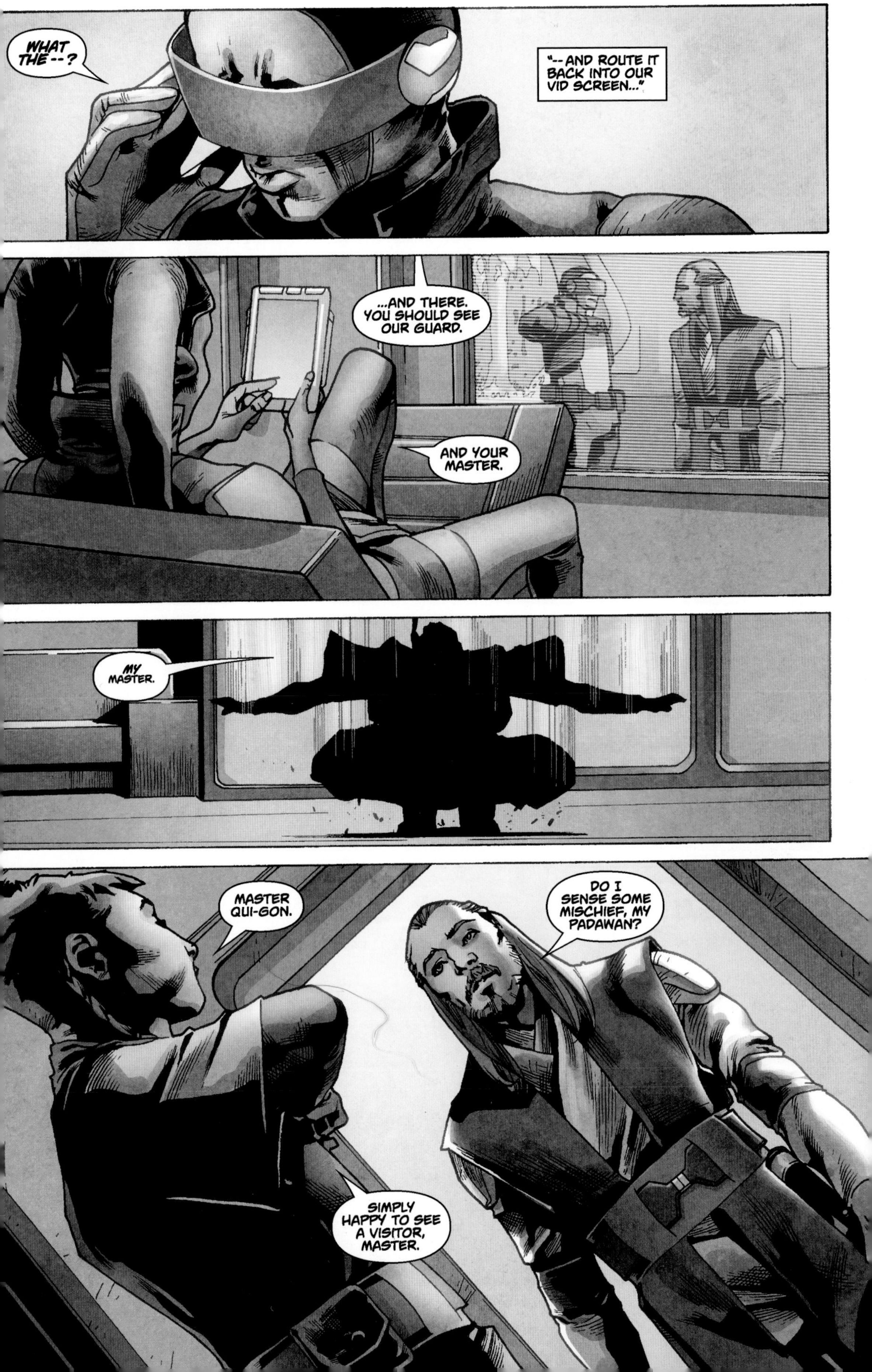
WHAT THE--?
"--AND ROUTE IT BACK INTO OUR VID SCREEN..."
...AND THERE. YOU SHOULD SEE OUR GUARD.
AND YOUR MASTER.
MY MASTER.
MASTER QUI-GON.
DO I SENSE SOME MISCHIEF, MY PADAWAN?
SIMPLY HAPPY TO SEE A VISITOR, MASTER.

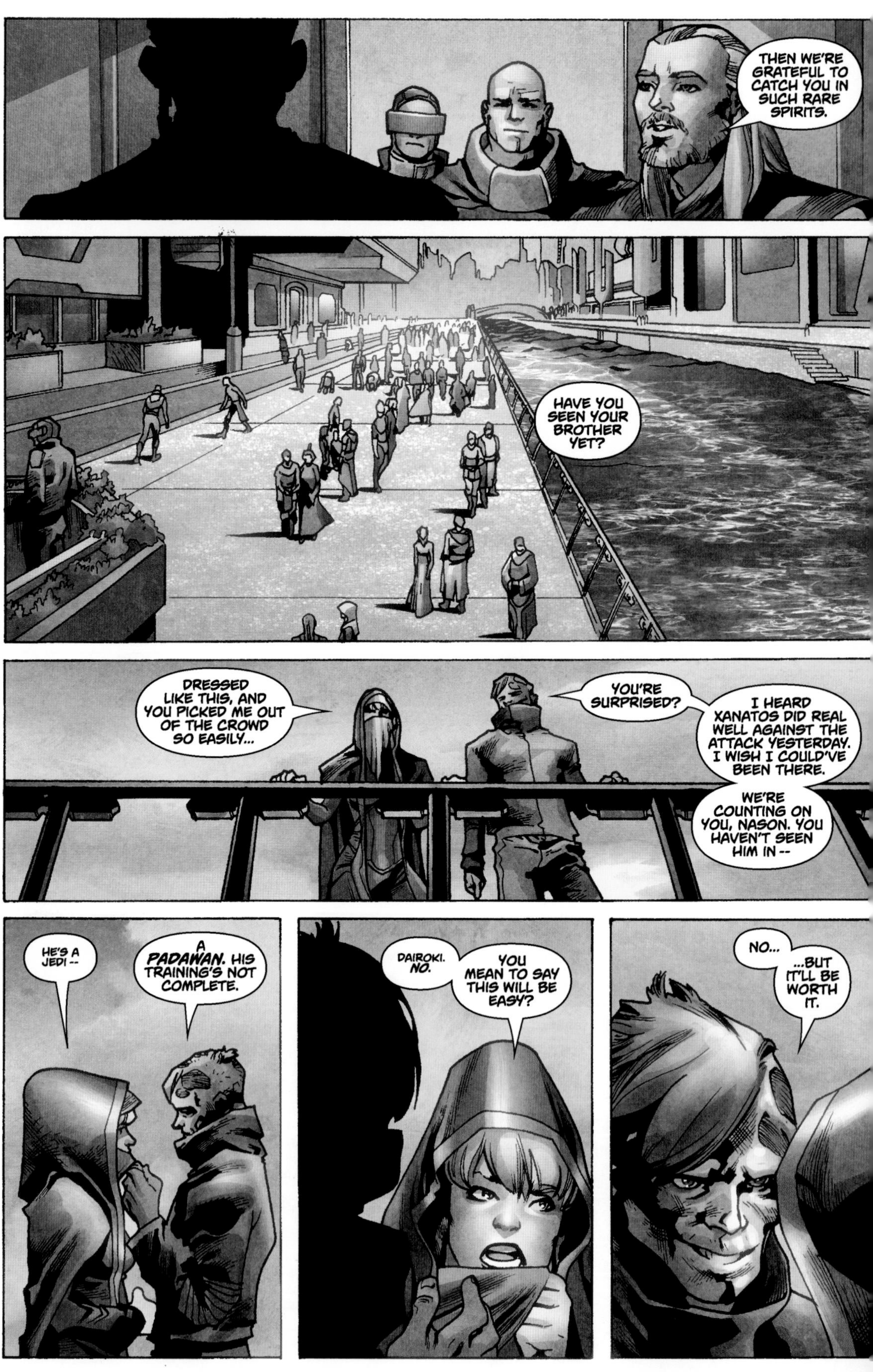
THEN WE'RE GRATEFUL TO CATCH YOU IN SUCH RARE SPIRITS.
HAVE YOU SEEN YOUR BROTHER YET?
DRESSED LIKE THIS, AND YOU PICKED ME OUT OF THE CROWD SO EASILY...
YOU'RE SURPRISED?
I HEARD XANATOS DID REAL WELL AGAINST THE ATTACK YESTERDAY. I WISH I COULD'VE BEEN THERE.
WE'RE COUNTING ON YOU, NASON. YOU HAVEN'T SEEN HIM IN --
HE'S A JEDI --
A PADAWAN. HIS TRAINING'S NOT COMPLETE.
DAIROKI. NO.
YOU MEAN TO SAY THIS WILL BE EASY?
NO...
...BUT IT'LL BE WORTH IT.

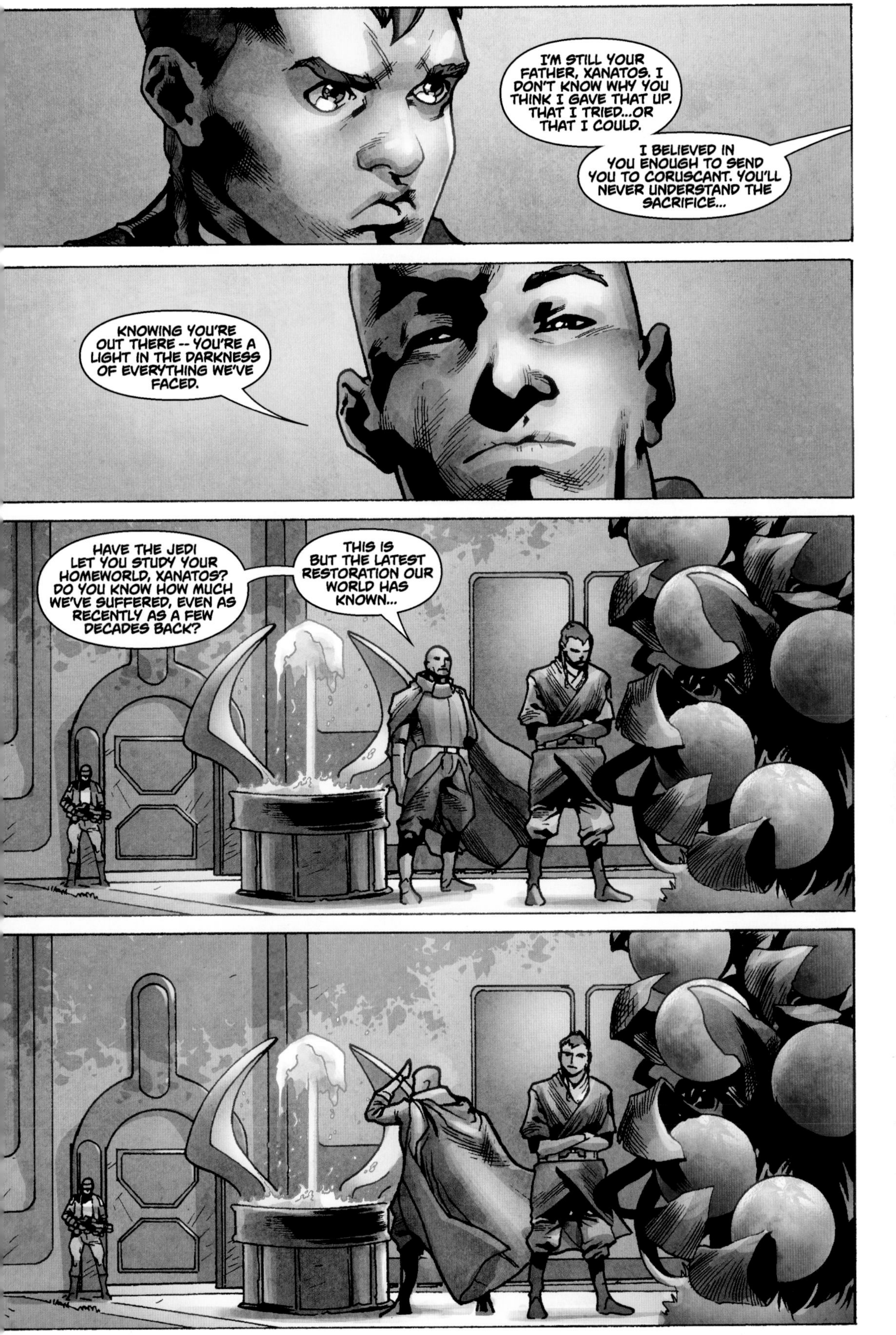
I'M STILL YOUR FATHER, XANATOS. I DON'T KNOW WHY YOU THINK I GAVE THAT UP. THAT I TRIED...OR THAT I COULD.
I BELIEVED IN YOU ENOUGH TO SEND YOU TO CORUSCANT. YOU'LL NEVER UNDERSTAND THE SACRIFICE...
KNOWING YOU'RE OUT THERE -- YOU'RE A LIGHT IN THE DARKNESS OF EVERYTHING WE'VE FACED.
HAVE THE JEDI LET YOU STUDY YOUR HOMEWORLD, XANATOS? DO YOU KNOW HOW MUCH WE'VE SUFFERED, EVEN AS RECENTLY AS A FEW DECADES BACK?
THIS IS BUT THE LATEST RESTORATION OUR WORLD HAS KNOWN...

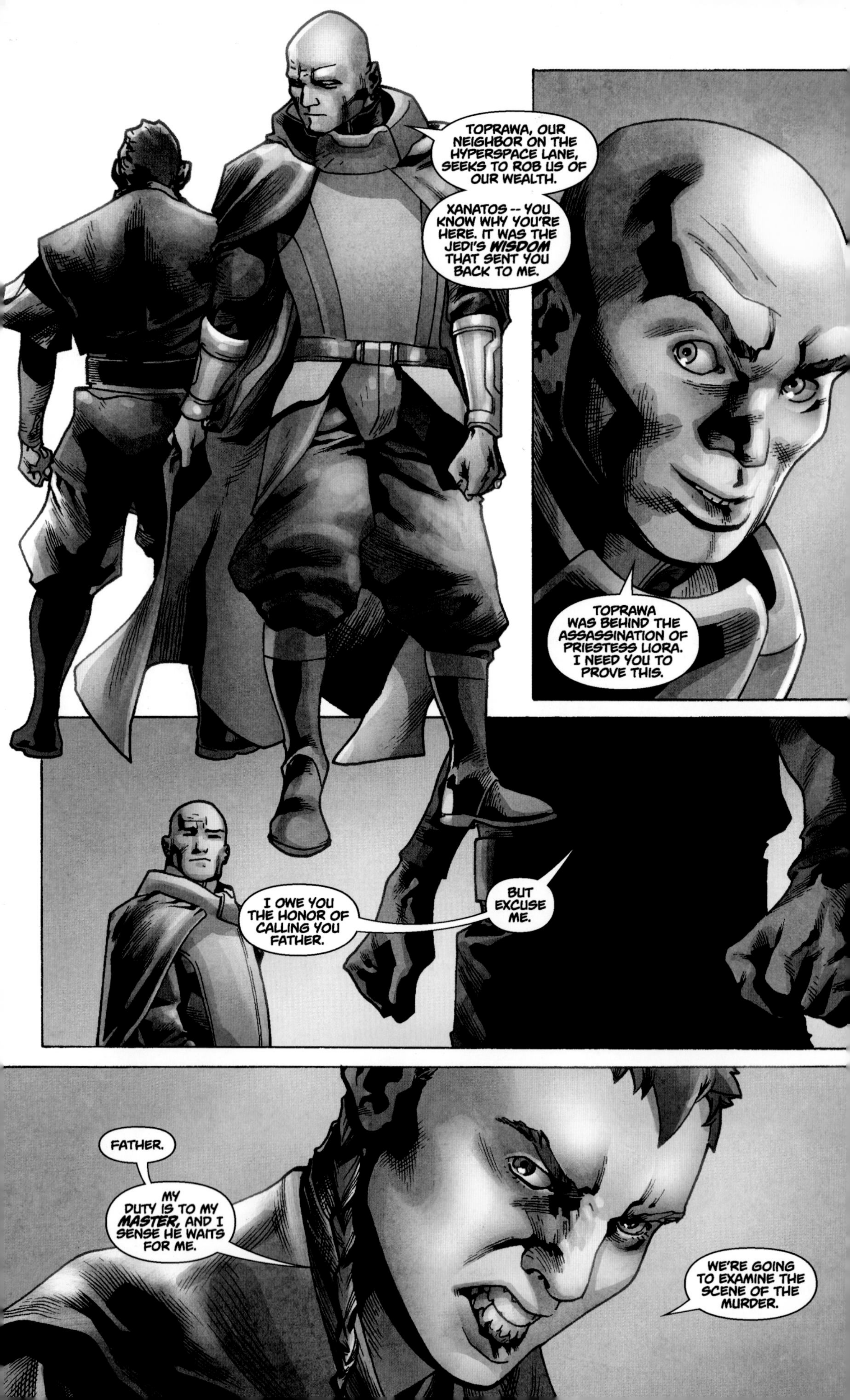

TOPRAWA, OUR NEIGHBOR ON THE HYPERSPACE LANE, SEEKS TO ROB US OF OUR WEALTH.
XANATOS -- YOU KNOW WHY YOU'RE HERE. IT WAS THE JEDI'S *WISDOM* THAT SENT YOU BACK TO ME.
TOPRAWA WAS BEHIND THE ASSASSINATION OF PRIESTESS LIORA. I NEED YOU TO PROVE THIS.
I OWE YOU THE HONOR OF CALLING YOU FATHER.
BUT EXCUSE ME.
FATHER.
MY DUTY IS TO MY *MASTER,* AND I SENSE HE WAITS FOR ME.
WE'RE GOING TO EXAMINE THE SCENE OF THE MURDER.

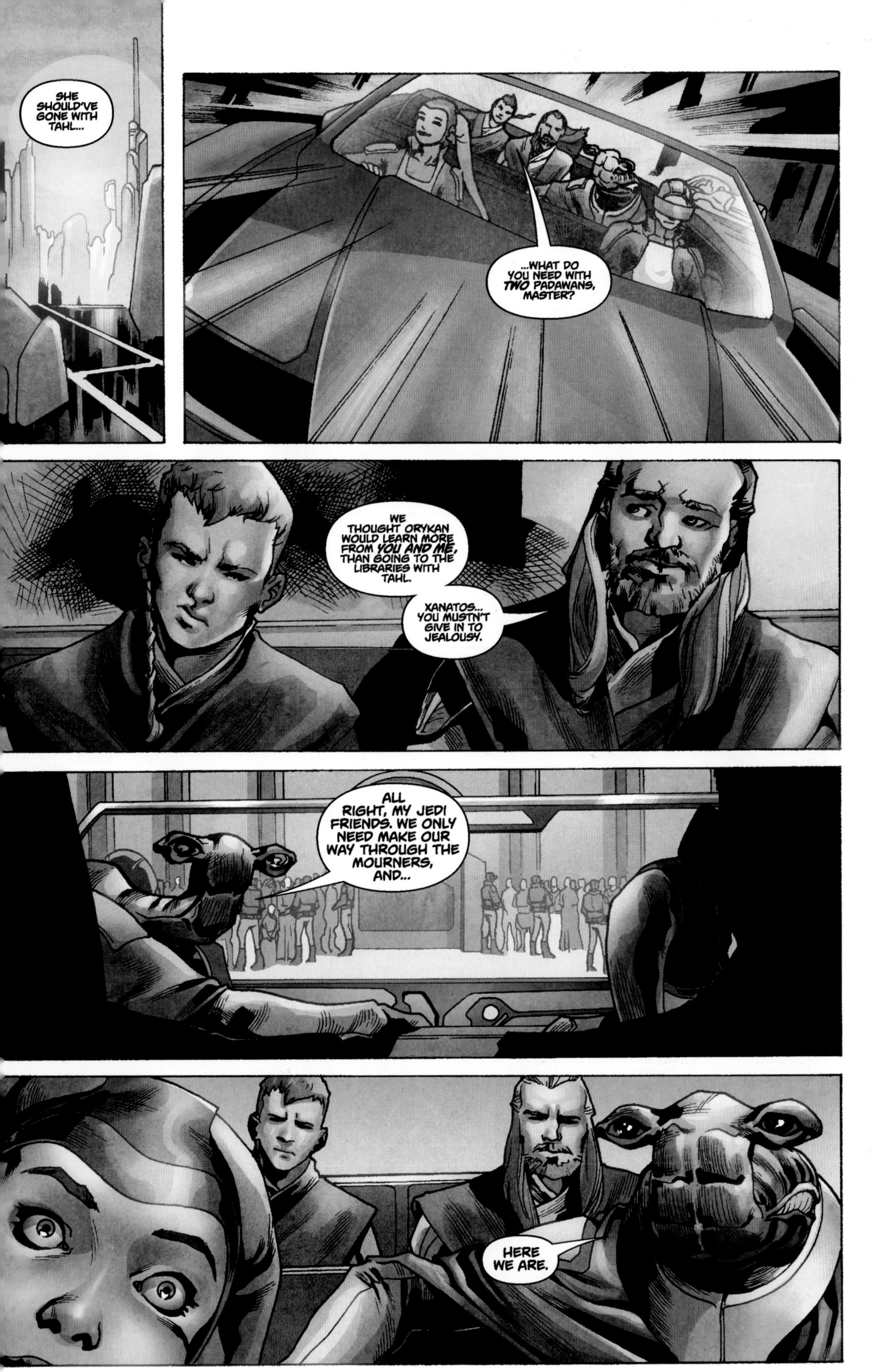
SHE SHOULD'VE GONE WITH TAHL...
...WHAT DO YOU NEED WITH *TWO* PADAWANS, MASTER?
WE THOUGHT ORYKAN WOULD LEARN MORE FROM *YOU AND ME*, THAN GOING TO THE LIBRARIES WITH TAHL.
XANATOS... YOU MUSTN'T GIVE IN TO JEALOUSY.
ALL RIGHT, MY JEDI FRIENDS. WE ONLY NEED MAKE OUR WAY THROUGH THE MOURNERS, AND...
HERE WE ARE.

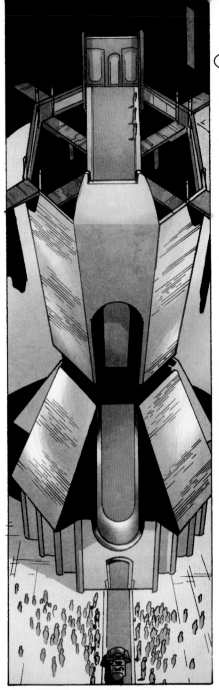

OFFWORLDERS! WE DON'T NEED *JEDI POLICE* TO TAKE CARE OF *OUR* BUSINESS!

TELOSIANS ARE A FIERCELY INDEPENDENT PEOPLE, MY FRIENDS.

PLEASE DON'T TAKE THOSE OUTCRIES SERIOUSLY.

THERE'S NO ANTI-JEDI SENTIMENT HERE.

MAYBE WE *DON'T* BELONG, MASTER.

XANATOS...

NO -- I MERELY MEAN, MAYBE THERE WAS NO MURDER.

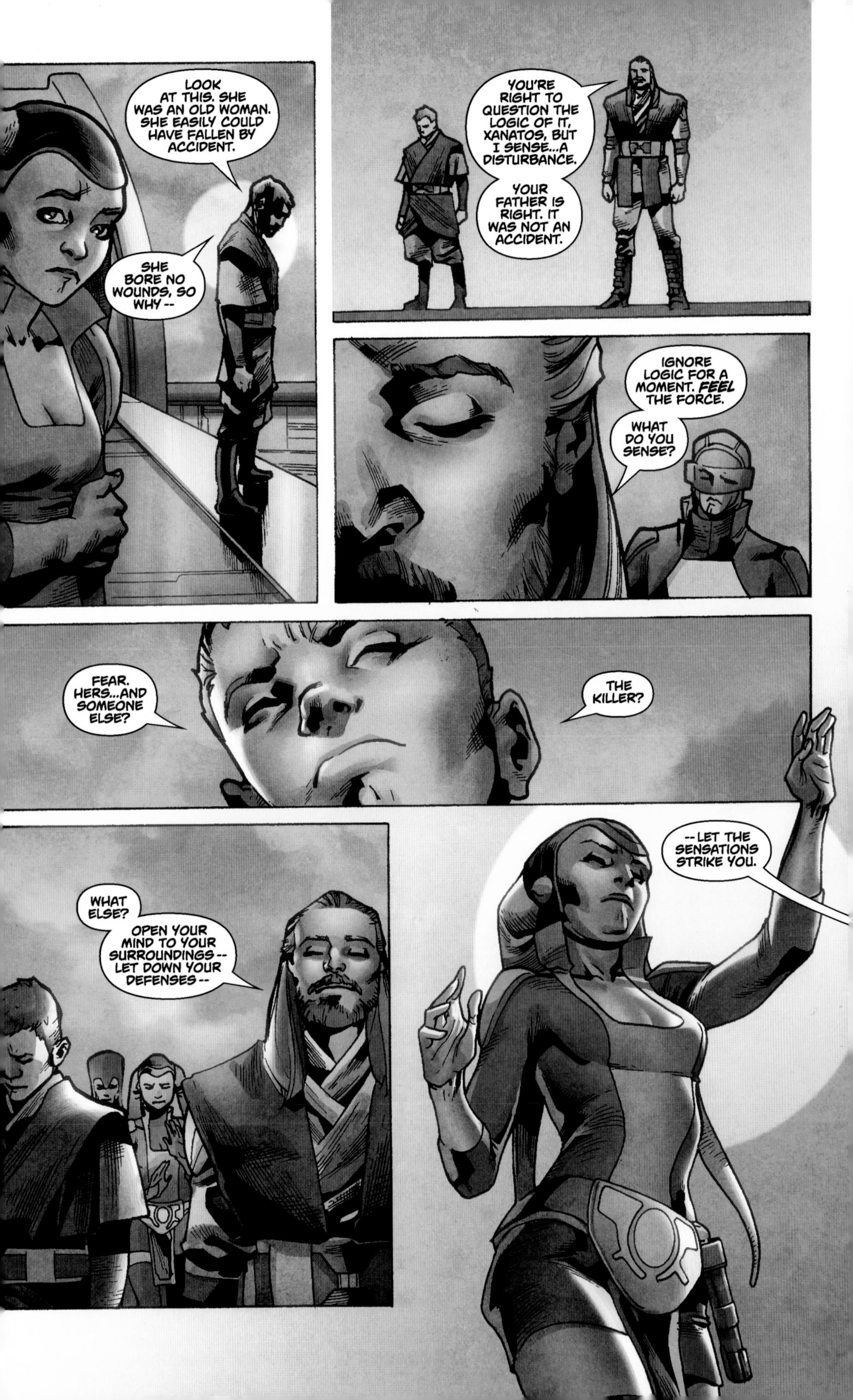
LOOK AT THIS. SHE WAS AN OLD WOMAN. SHE EASILY COULD HAVE FALLEN BY ACCIDENT.
SHE BORE NO WOUNDS, SO WHY --
YOU'RE RIGHT TO QUESTION THE LOGIC OF IT, XANATOS, BUT I SENSE...A DISTURBANCE.
YOUR FATHER IS RIGHT. IT WAS NOT AN ACCIDENT.
IGNORE LOGIC FOR A MOMENT. FEEL THE FORCE.
WHAT DO YOU SENSE?
FEAR. HERS...AND SOMEONE ELSE?
THE KILLER?
WHAT ELSE?
OPEN YOUR MIND TO YOUR SURROUNDINGS -- LET DOWN YOUR DEFENSES --
-- LET THE SENSATIONS STRIKE YOU.

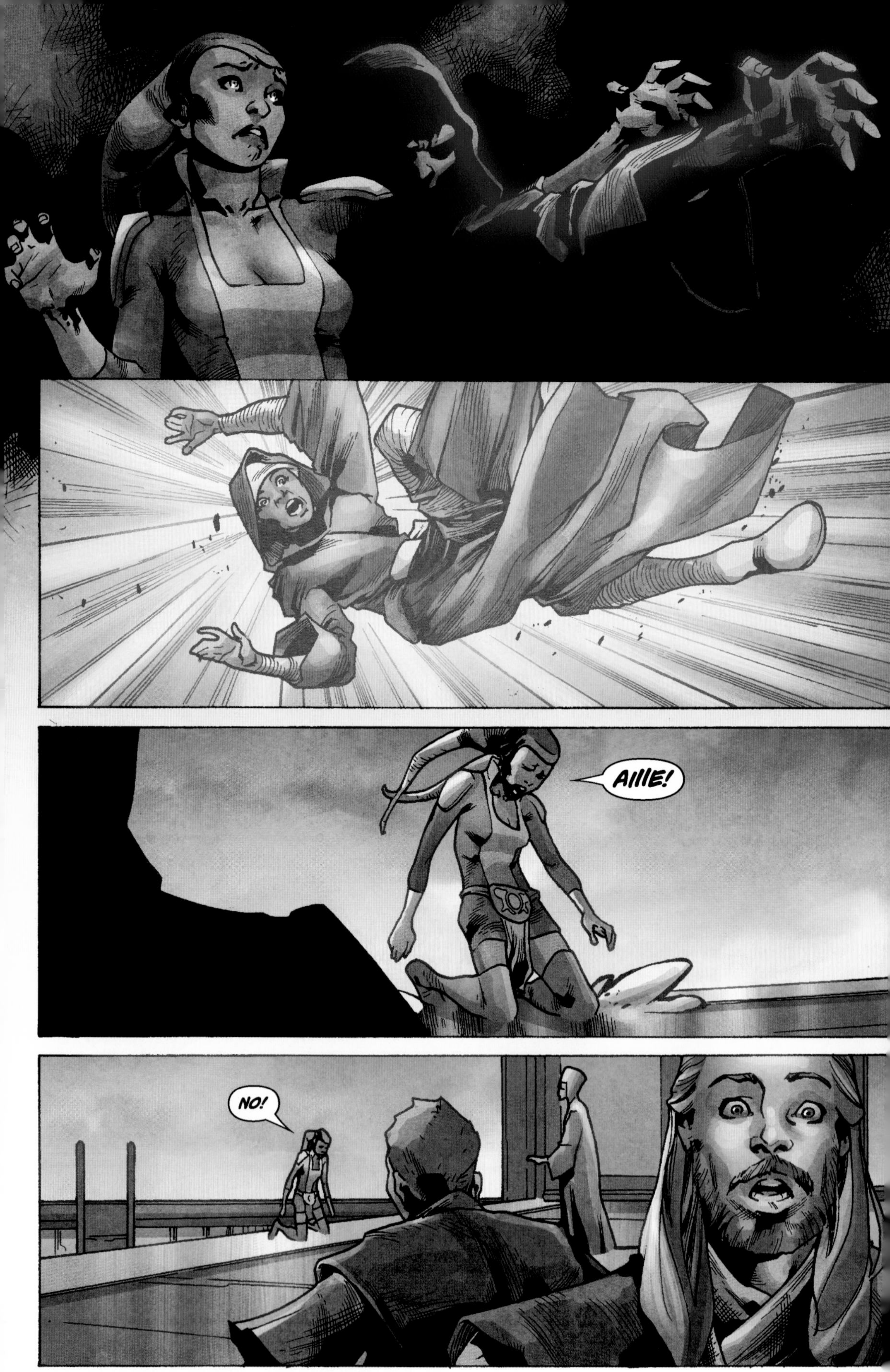
AIIIE!
NO!

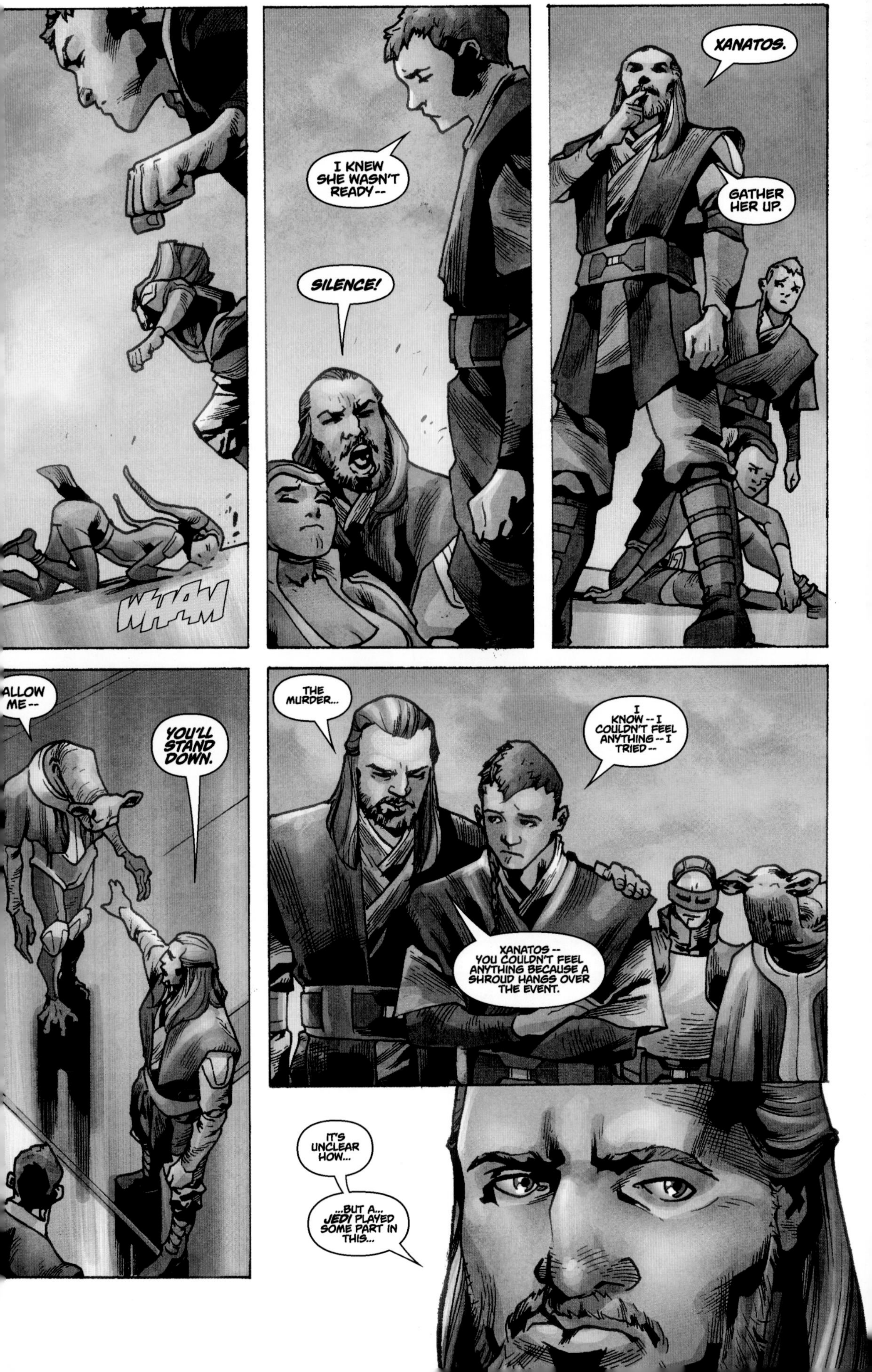
WHAM
I KNEW SHE WASN'T READY --
SILENCE!
XANATOS.
GATHER HER UP.
ALLOW ME --
YOU'LL STAND DOWN.
THE MURDER...
I KNOW -- I COULDN'T FEEL ANYTHING -- I TRIED --
XANATOS -- YOU COULDN'T FEEL ANYTHING BECAUSE A SHROUD HANGS OVER THE EVENT.
IT'S UNCLEAR HOW...
...BUT A... JEDI PLAYED SOME PART IN THIS...

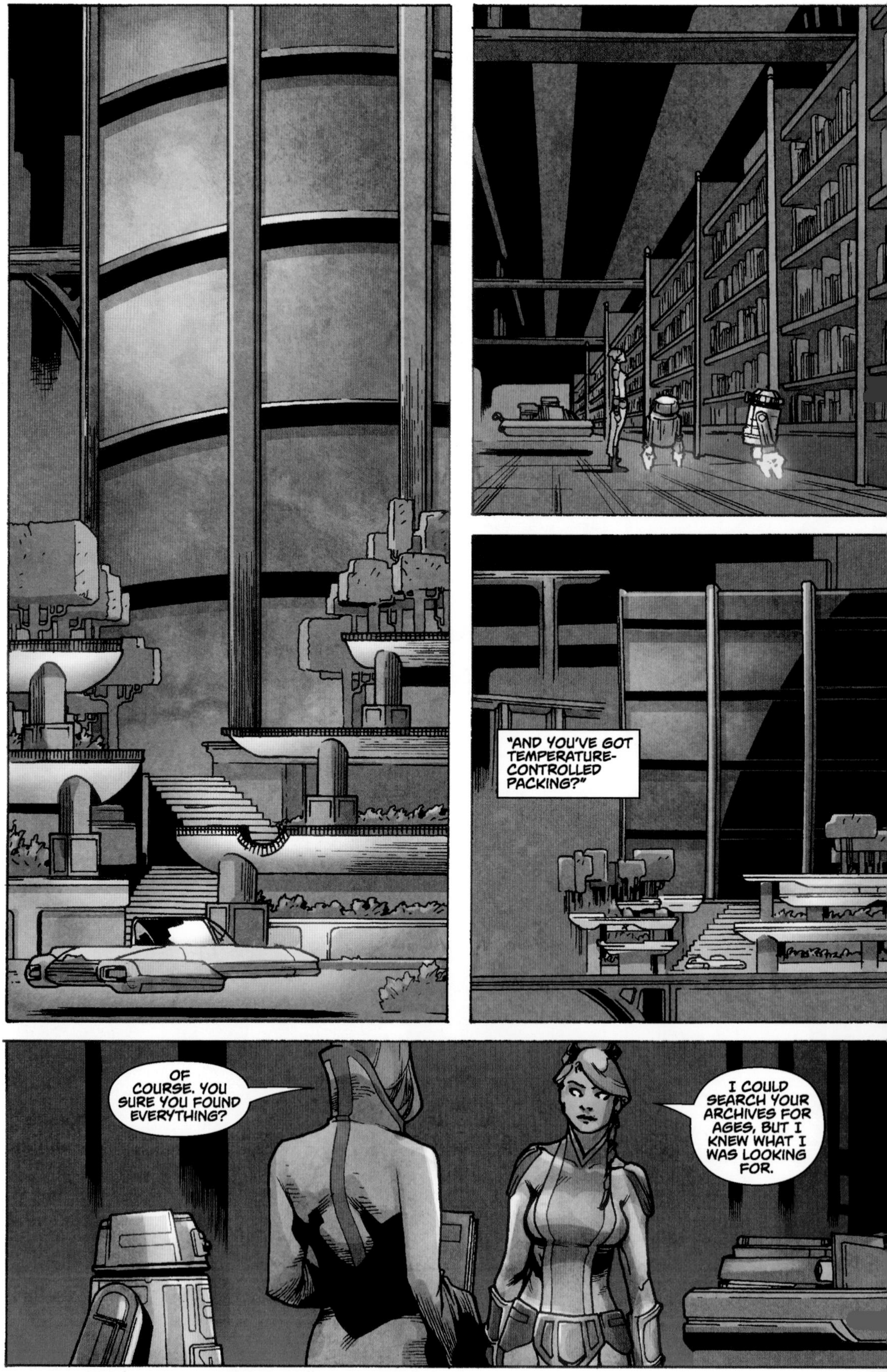
"AND YOU'VE GOT TEMPERATURE-CONTROLLED PACKING?"
OF COURSE. YOU SURE YOU FOUND EVERYTHING?
I COULD SEARCH YOUR ARCHIVES FOR AGES, BUT I KNEW WHAT I WAS LOOKING FOR.

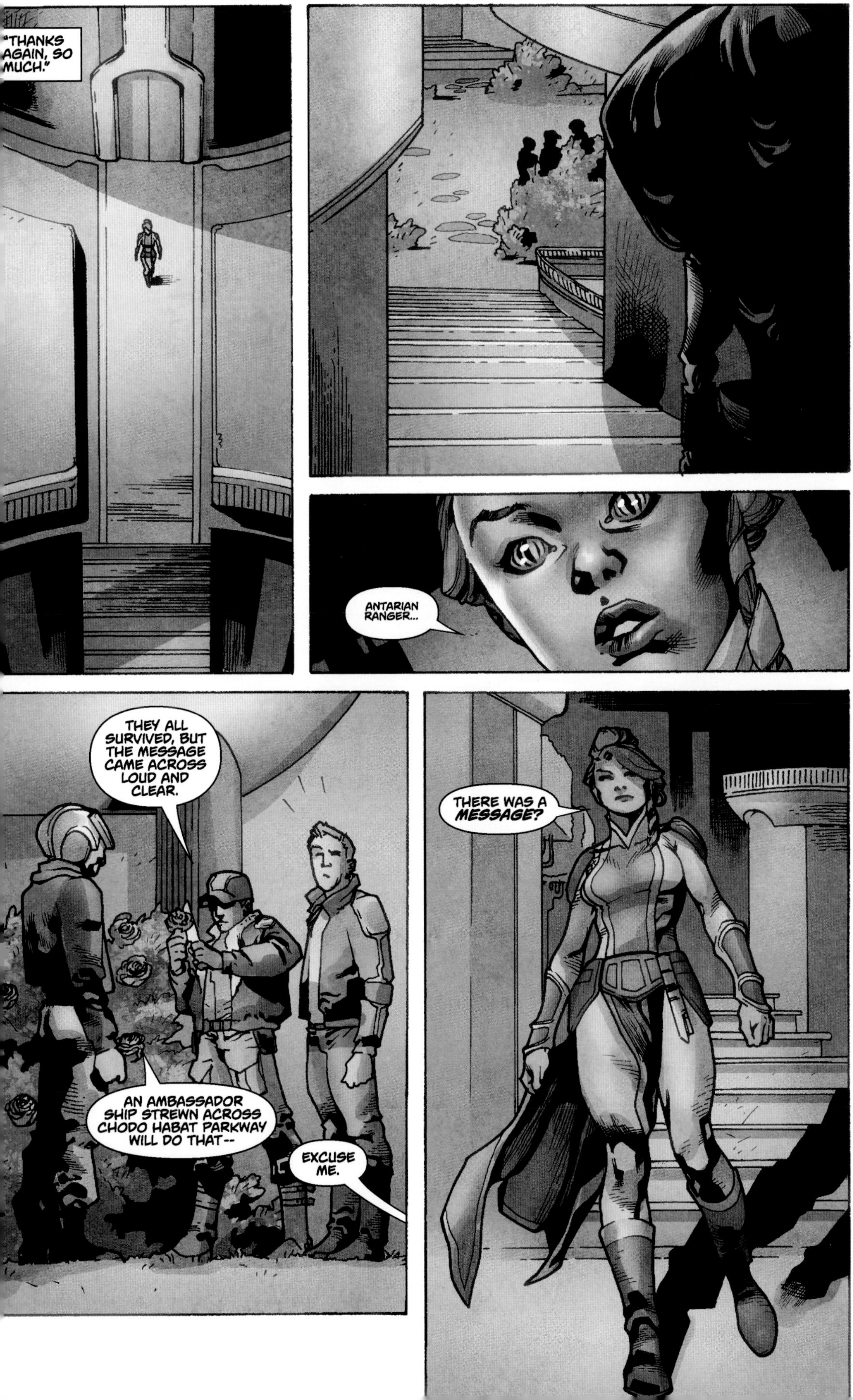
"THANKS AGAIN, SO MUCH."
ANTARIAN RANGER...
THEY ALL SURVIVED, BUT THE MESSAGE CAME ACROSS LOUD AND CLEAR.
AN AMBASSADOR SHIP STREWN ACROSS CHODO HABAT PARKWAY WILL DO THAT--
EXCUSE ME.
THERE WAS A *MESSAGE?*

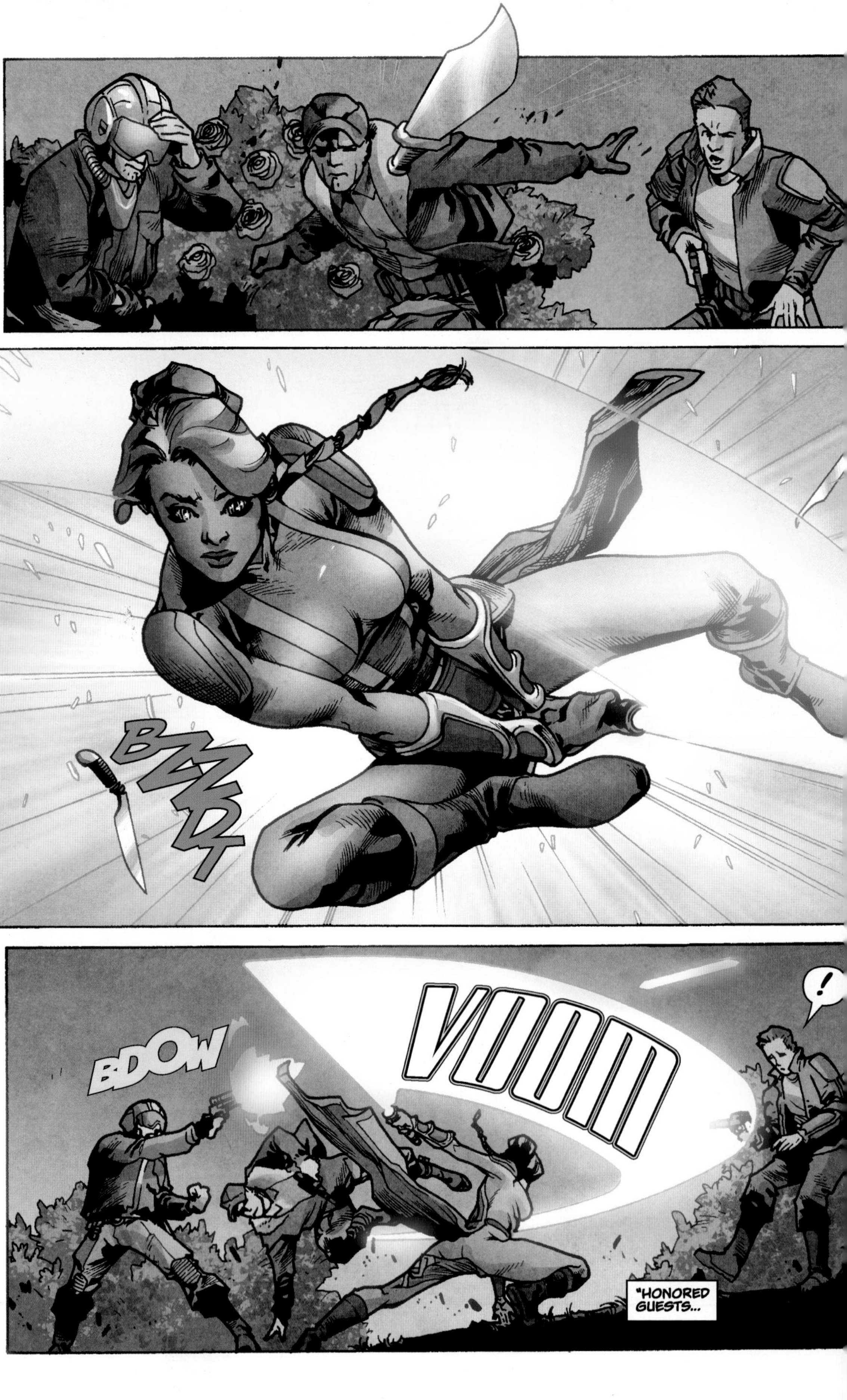
BMMDT
BDOW
VOOM
!
"HONORED GUESTS...

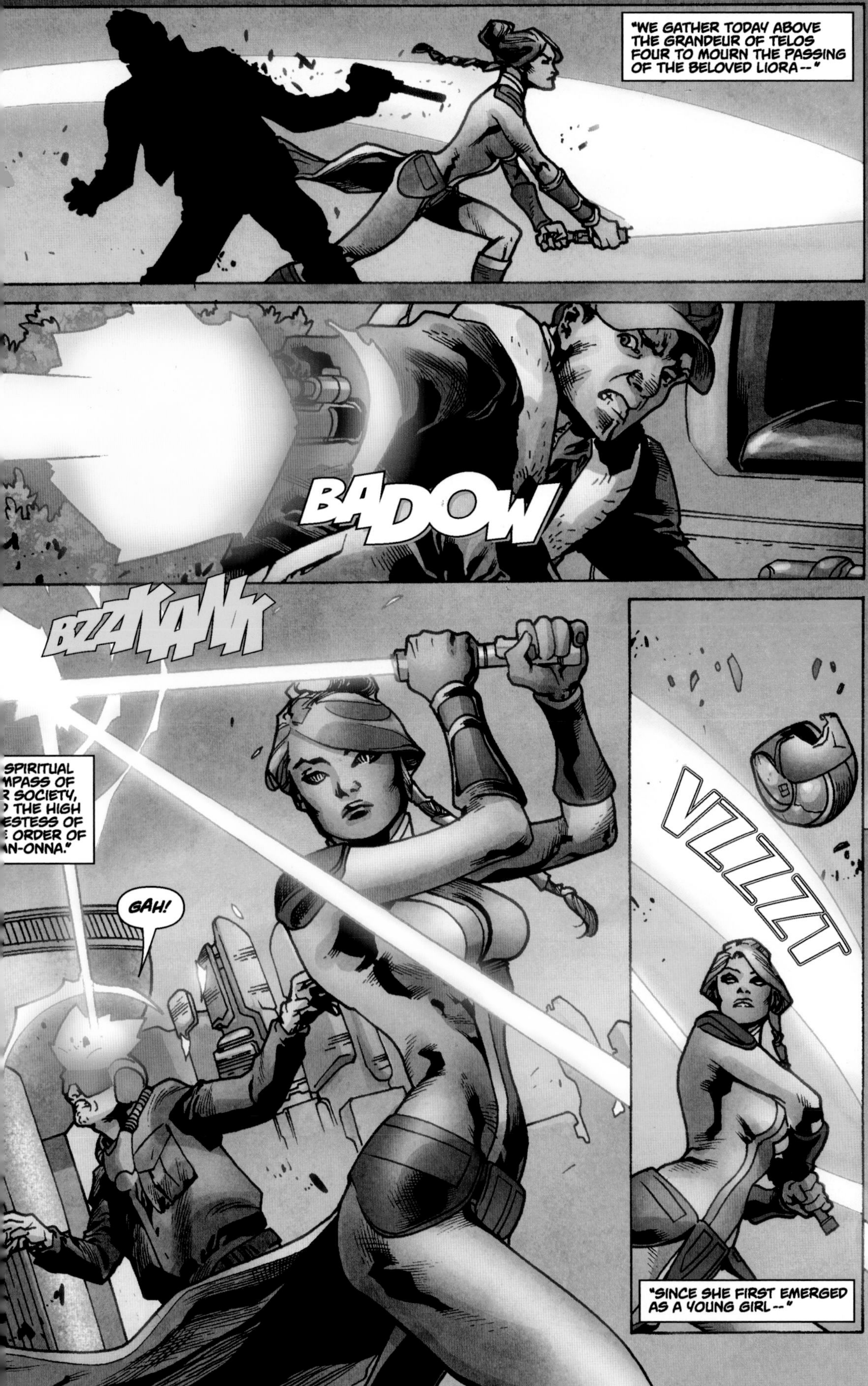
"WE GATHER TODAY ABOVE THE GRANDEUR OF TELOS FOUR TO MOURN THE PASSING OF THE BELOVED LIORA--"
BADOW
BZZAKANK
SPIRITUAL MPASS OF R SOCIETY, D THE HIGH ESTESS OF E ORDER OF AN-ONNA."
GAH!
VZZZZT
"SINCE SHE FIRST EMERGED AS A YOUNG GIRL--"

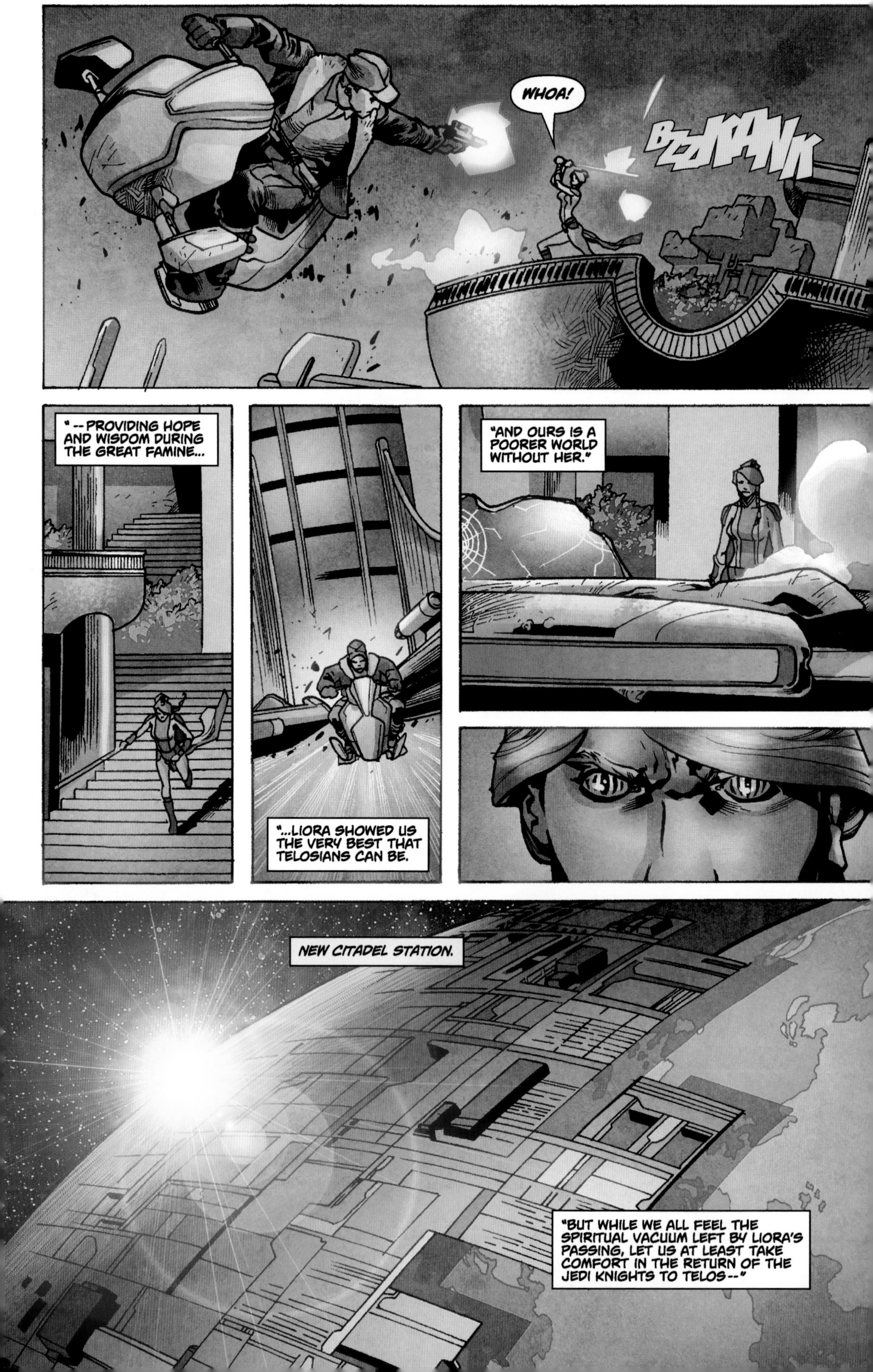
WHOA!
BZZKRANK
" --PROVIDING HOPE AND WISDOM DURING THE GREAT FAMINE...
"...LIORA SHOWED US THE VERY BEST THAT TELOSIANS CAN BE.
"AND OURS IS A POORER WORLD WITHOUT HER."
NEW CITADEL STATION.
"BUT WHILE WE ALL FEEL THE SPIRITUAL VACUUM LEFT BY LIORA'S PASSING, LET US AT LEAST TAKE COMFORT IN THE RETURN OF THE JEDI KNIGHTS TO TELOS--"

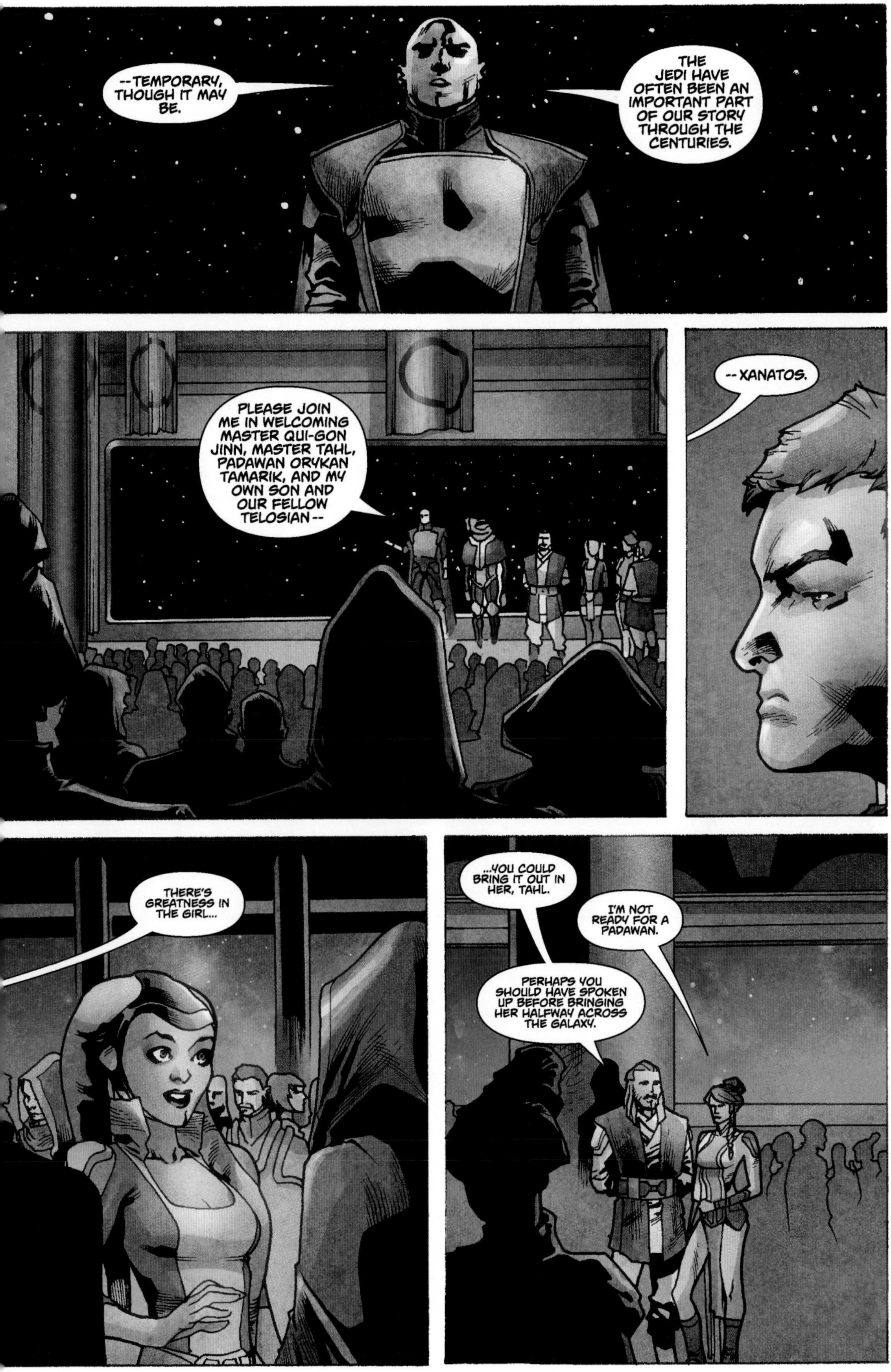

--TEMPORARY, THOUGH IT MAY BE.
THE JEDI HAVE OFTEN BEEN AN IMPORTANT PART OF OUR STORY THROUGH THE CENTURIES.
PLEASE JOIN ME IN WELCOMING MASTER QUI-GON JINN, MASTER TAHL, PADAWAN ORYKAN TAMARIK, AND MY OWN SON AND OUR FELLOW TELOSIAN--
--XANATOS.
THERE'S GREATNESS IN THE GIRL...
...YOU COULD BRING IT OUT IN HER, TAHL.
I'M NOT READY FOR A PADAWAN.
PERHAPS YOU SHOULD HAVE SPOKEN UP BEFORE BRINGING HER HALFWAY ACROSS THE GALAXY.

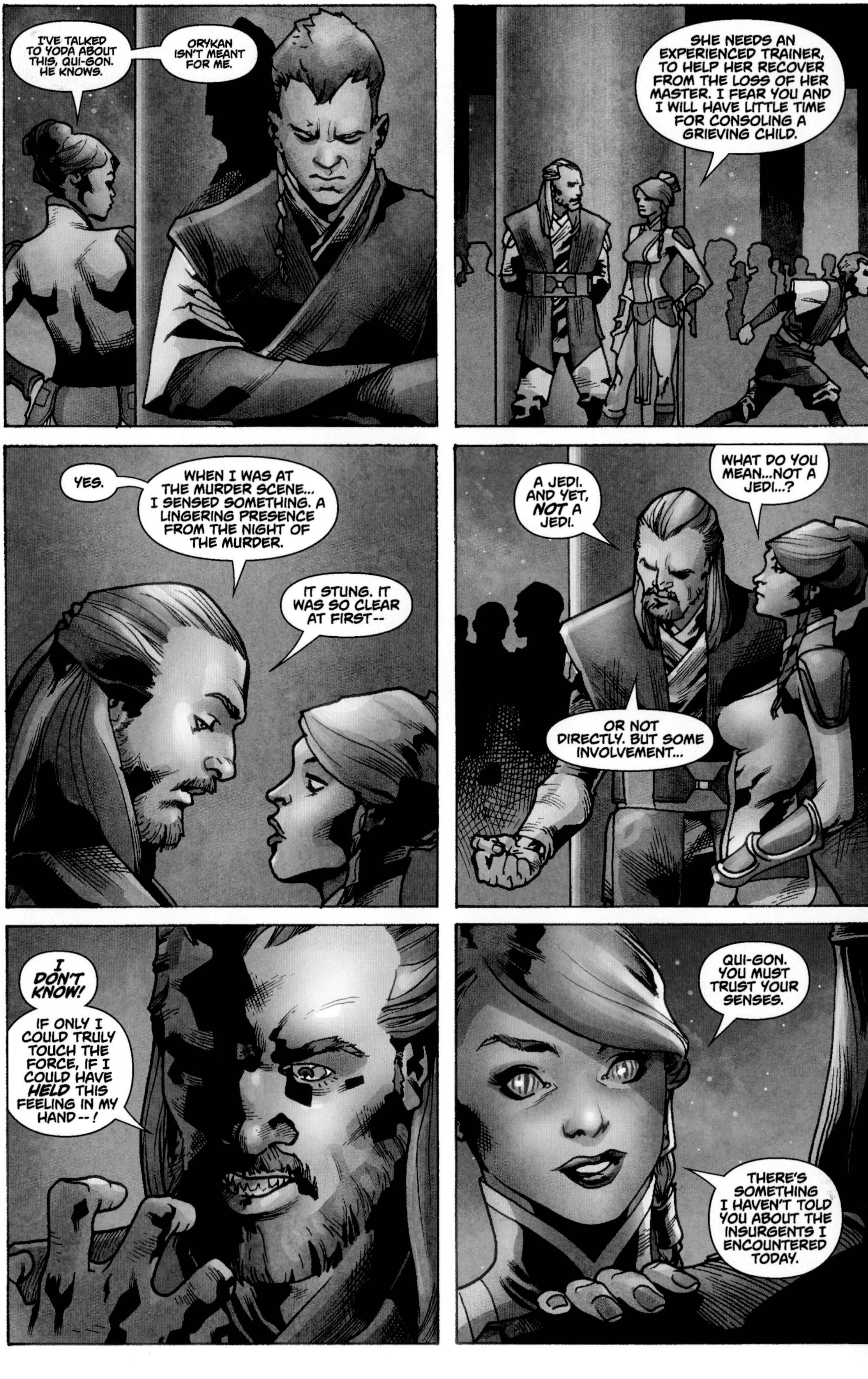
I'VE TALKED TO YODA ABOUT THIS, QUI-GON. HE KNOWS.
ORYKAN ISN'T MEANT FOR ME.
SHE NEEDS AN EXPERIENCED TRAINER, TO HELP HER RECOVER FROM THE LOSS OF HER MASTER. I FEAR YOU AND I WILL HAVE LITTLE TIME FOR CONSOLING A GRIEVING CHILD.
YES.
WHEN I WAS AT THE MURDER SCENE... I SENSED SOMETHING. A LINGERING PRESENCE FROM THE NIGHT OF THE MURDER.
IT STUNG. IT WAS SO CLEAR AT FIRST--
A JEDI. AND YET, *NOT* A JEDI.
WHAT DO YOU MEAN...NOT A JEDI...?
OR NOT DIRECTLY. BUT SOME INVOLVEMENT...
I DON'T KNOW!
IF ONLY I COULD TRULY TOUCH THE FORCE, IF I COULD HAVE *HELD* THIS FEELING IN MY HAND--!
QUI-GON. YOU MUST TRUST YOUR SENSES.
THERE'S SOMETHING I HAVEN'T TOLD YOU ABOUT THE INSURGENTS I ENCOUNTERED TODAY.

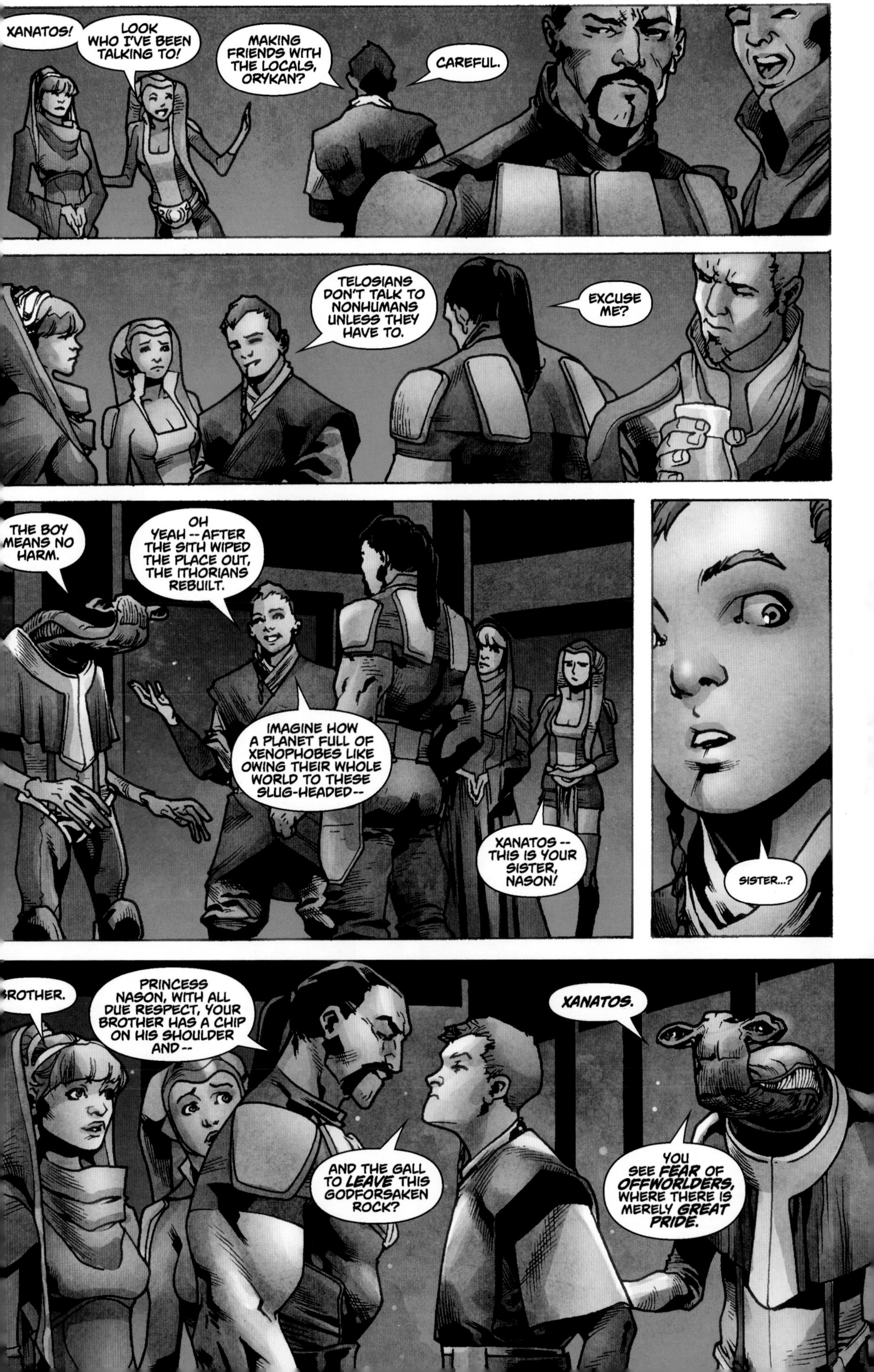
XANATOS!
LOOK WHO I'VE BEEN TALKING TO!
MAKING FRIENDS WITH THE LOCALS, ORYKAN?
CAREFUL.
TELOSIANS DON'T TALK TO NONHUMANS UNLESS THEY HAVE TO.
EXCUSE ME?
THE BOY MEANS NO HARM.
OH YEAH -- AFTER THE SITH WIPED THE PLACE OUT, THE ITHORIANS REBUILT.
IMAGINE HOW A PLANET FULL OF XENOPHOBES LIKE OWING THEIR WHOLE WORLD TO THESE SLUG-HEADED--
XANATOS -- THIS IS YOUR SISTER, NASON!
SISTER...?
ROTHER.
PRINCESS NASON, WITH ALL DUE RESPECT, YOUR BROTHER HAS A CHIP ON HIS SHOULDER AND --
AND THE GALL TO LEAVE THIS GODFORSAKEN ROCK?
XANATOS.
YOU SEE FEAR OF OFFWORLDERS, WHERE THERE IS MERELY GREAT PRIDE.

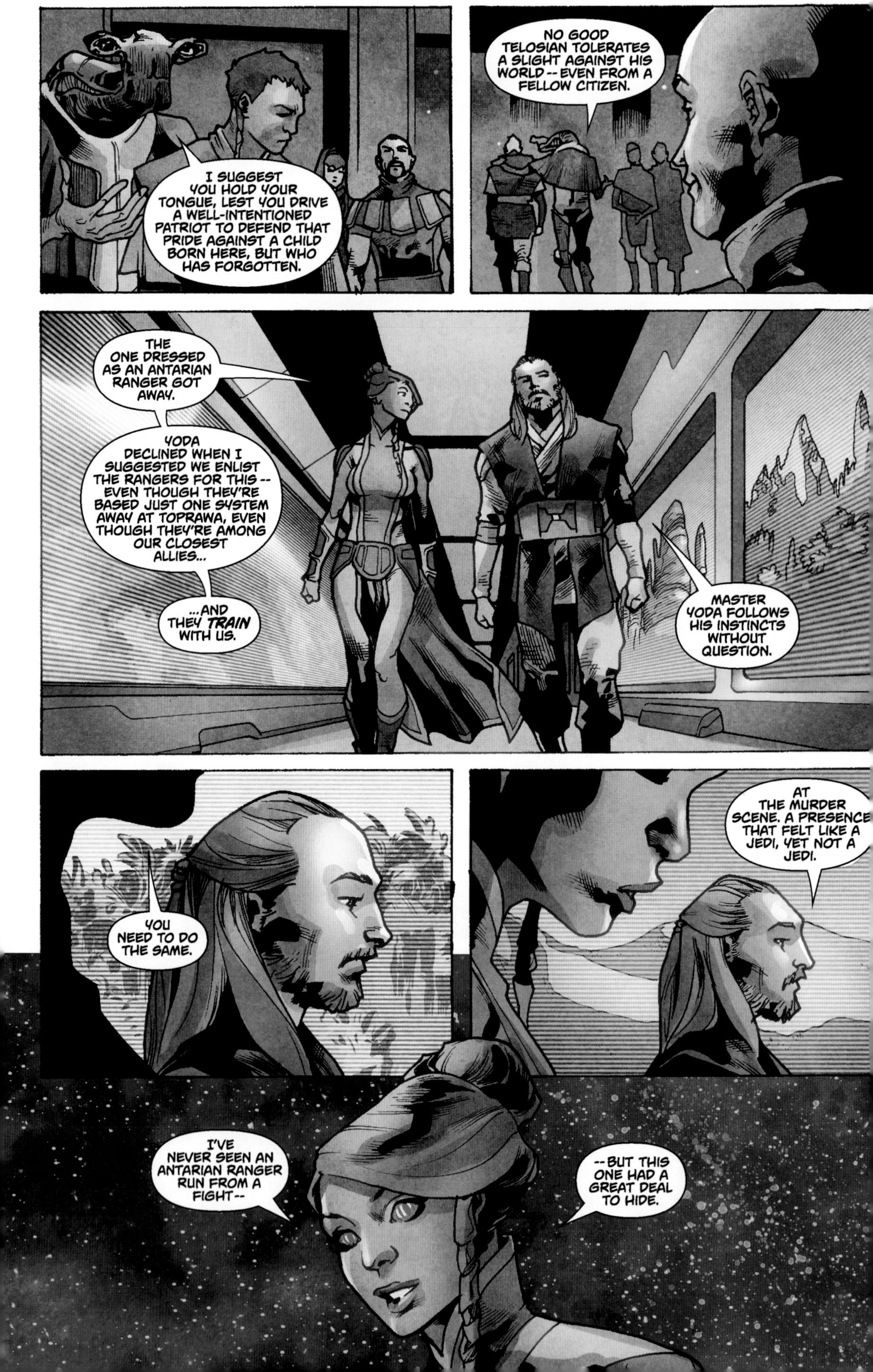
I SUGGEST YOU HOLD YOUR TONGUE, LEST YOU DRIVE A WELL-INTENTIONED PATRIOT TO DEFEND THAT PRIDE AGAINST A CHILD BORN HERE, BUT WHO HAS FORGOTTEN.
NO GOOD TELOSIAN TOLERATES A SLIGHT AGAINST HIS WORLD -- EVEN FROM A FELLOW CITIZEN.
THE ONE DRESSED AS AN ANTARIAN RANGER GOT AWAY.
YODA DECLINED WHEN I SUGGESTED WE ENLIST THE RANGERS FOR THIS -- EVEN THOUGH THEY'RE BASED JUST ONE SYSTEM AWAY AT TOPRAWA, EVEN THOUGH THEY'RE AMONG OUR CLOSEST ALLIES...
...AND THEY *TRAIN* WITH US.
MASTER YODA FOLLOWS HIS INSTINCTS WITHOUT QUESTION.
YOU NEED TO DO THE SAME.
AT THE MURDER SCENE. A PRESENCE THAT FELT LIKE A JEDI, YET NOT A JEDI.
I'VE NEVER SEEN AN ANTARIAN RANGER RUN FROM A FIGHT--
--BUT THIS ONE HAD A GREAT DEAL TO HIDE.

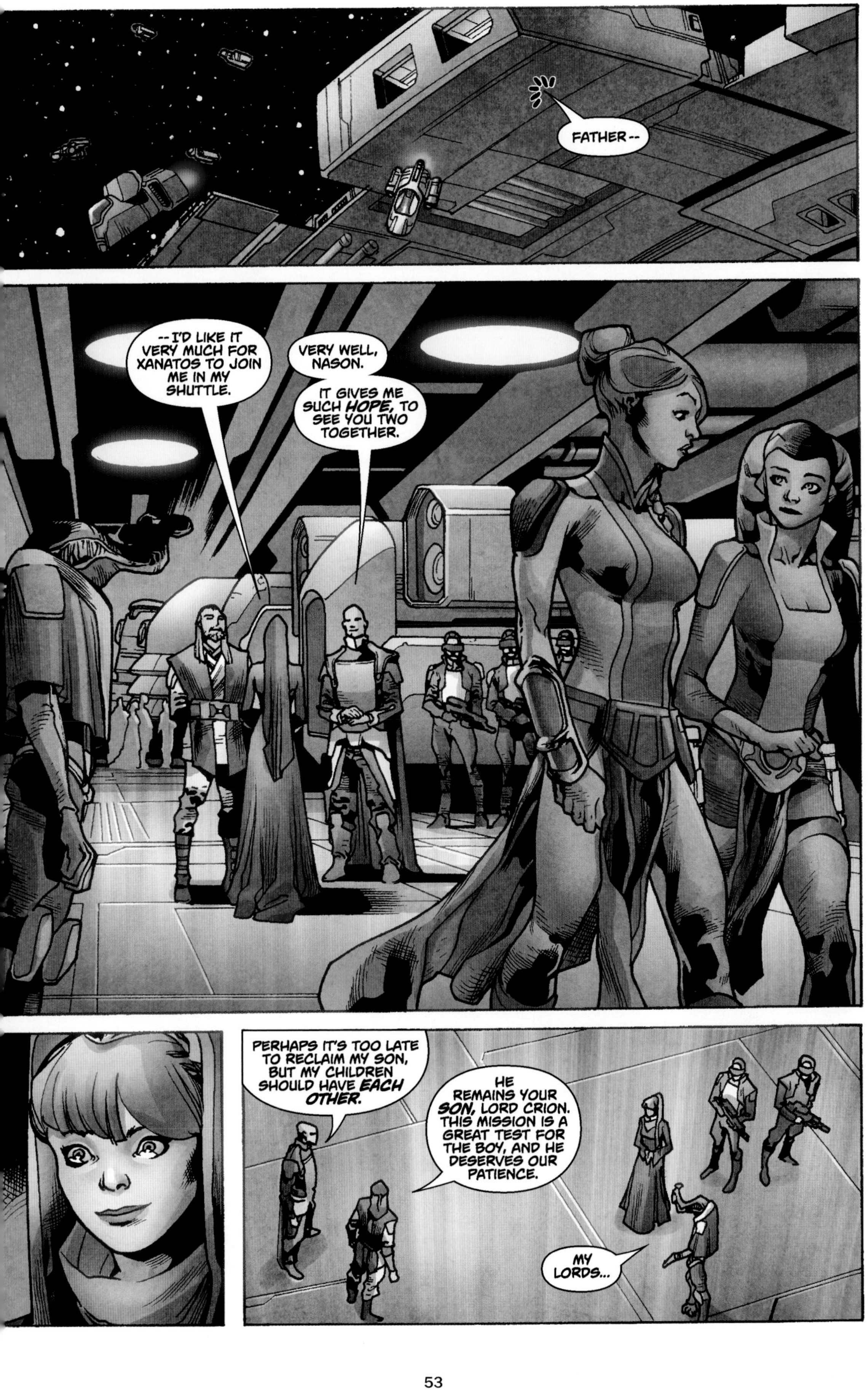
FATHER--
--I'D LIKE IT VERY MUCH FOR XANATOS TO JOIN ME IN MY SHUTTLE.
VERY WELL, NASON.
IT GIVES ME SUCH HOPE, TO SEE YOU TWO TOGETHER.
PERHAPS IT'S TOO LATE TO RECLAIM MY SON, BUT MY CHILDREN SHOULD HAVE EACH OTHER.
HE REMAINS YOUR SON, LORD CRION. THIS MISSION IS A GREAT TEST FOR THE BOY, AND HE DESERVES OUR PATIENCE.
MY LORDS...

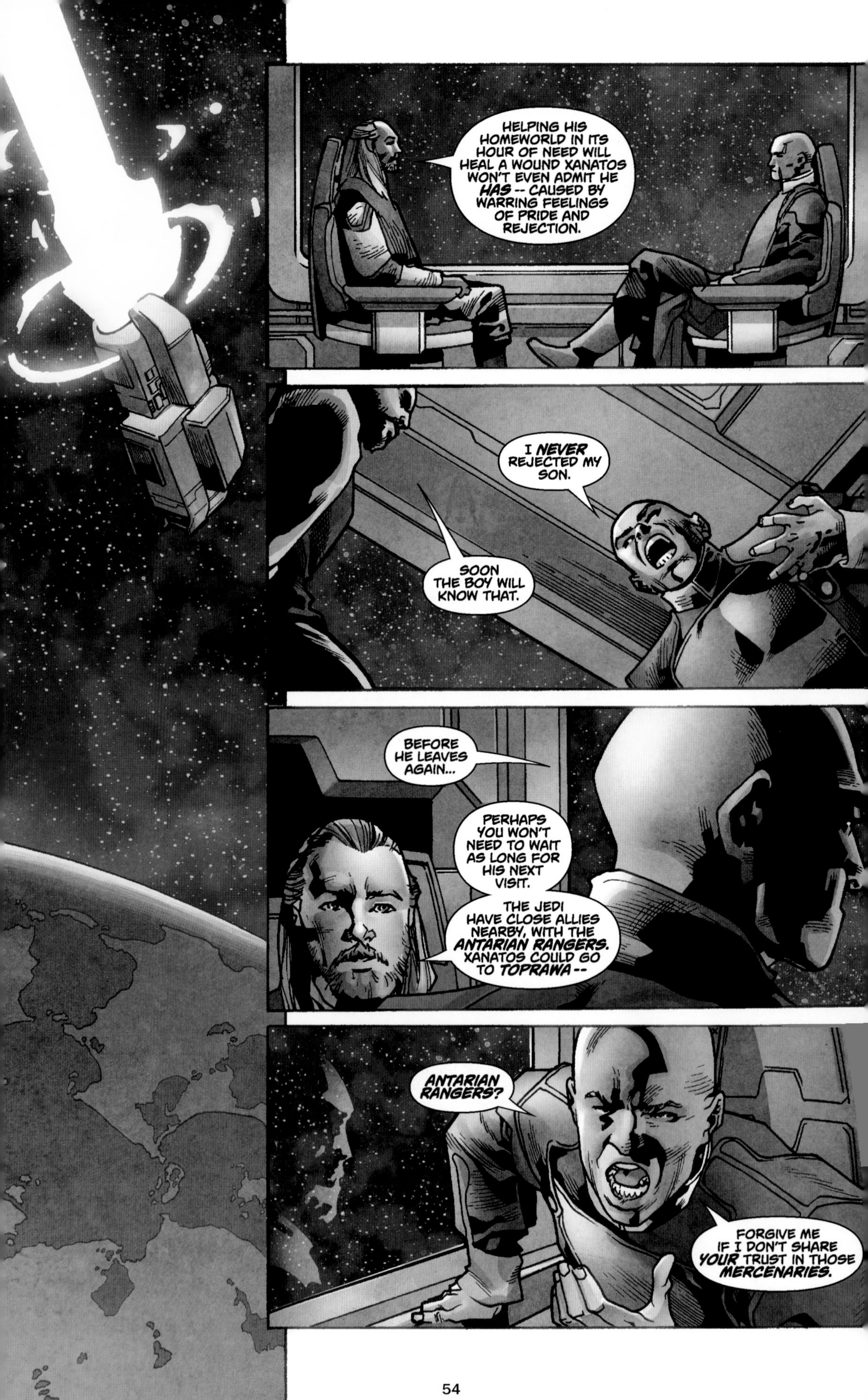
HELPING HIS HOMEWORLD IN ITS HOUR OF NEED WILL HEAL A WOUND XANATOS WON'T EVEN ADMIT HE *HAS* -- CAUSED BY WARRING FEELINGS OF PRIDE AND REJECTION.
I *NEVER* REJECTED MY SON.
SOON THE BOY WILL KNOW THAT.
BEFORE HE LEAVES AGAIN...
PERHAPS YOU WON'T NEED TO WAIT AS LONG FOR HIS NEXT VISIT.
THE JEDI HAVE CLOSE ALLIES NEARBY, WITH THE *ANTARIAN RANGERS*. XANATOS COULD GO TO *TOPRAWA* --
ANTARIAN RANGERS?
FORGIVE ME IF I DON'T SHARE *YOUR* TRUST IN THOSE *MERCENARIES*.

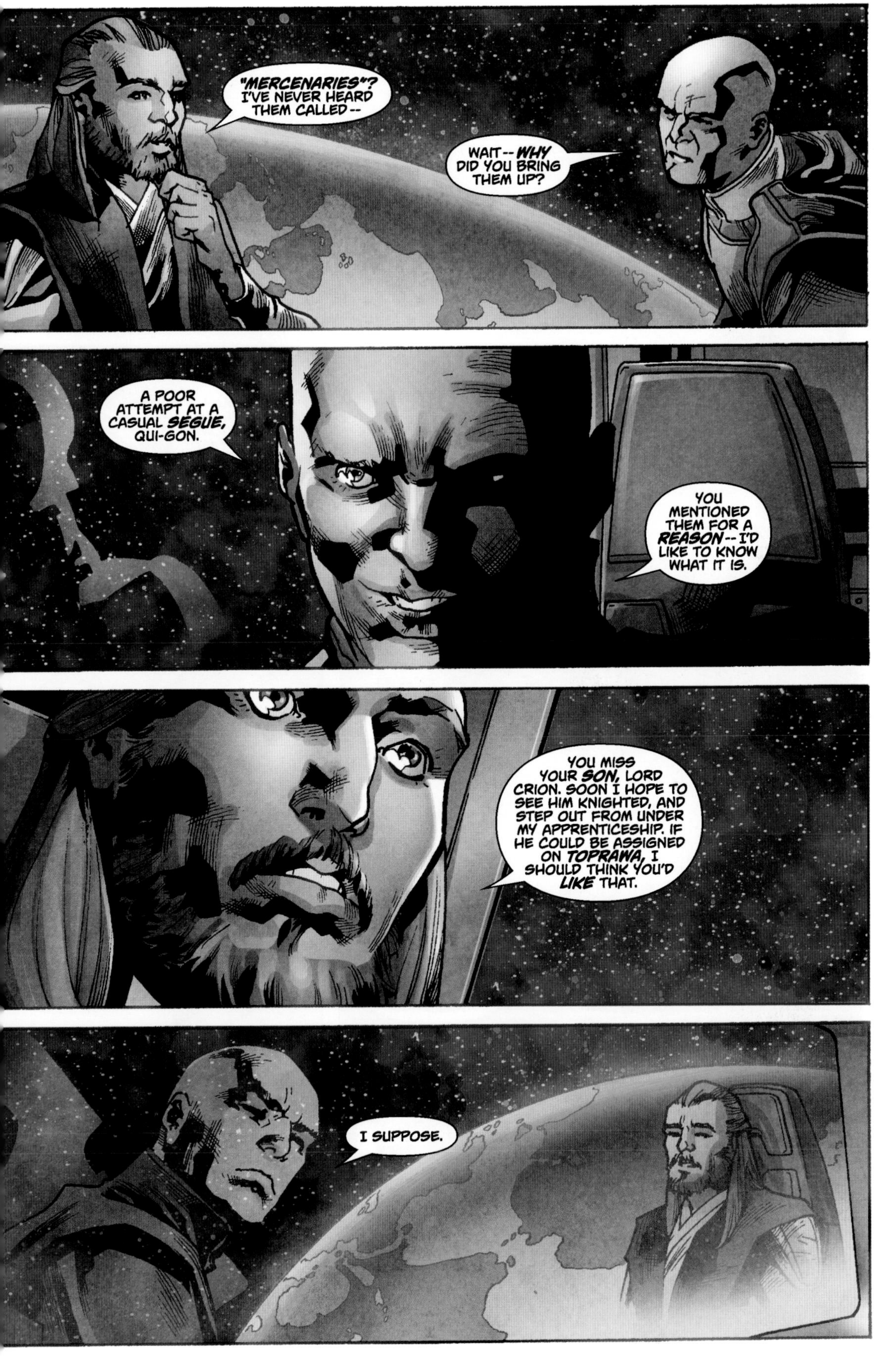
"MERCENARIES"? I'VE NEVER HEARD THEM CALLED --
WAIT -- WHY DID YOU BRING THEM UP?
A POOR ATTEMPT AT A CASUAL SEGUE, QUI-GON.
YOU MENTIONED THEM FOR A REASON -- I'D LIKE TO KNOW WHAT IT IS.
YOU MISS YOUR SON, LORD CRION. SOON I HOPE TO SEE HIM KNIGHTED, AND STEP OUT FROM UNDER MY APPRENTICESHIP. IF HE COULD BE ASSIGNED ON TOPRAWA, I SHOULD THINK YOU'D LIKE THAT.
I SUPPOSE.

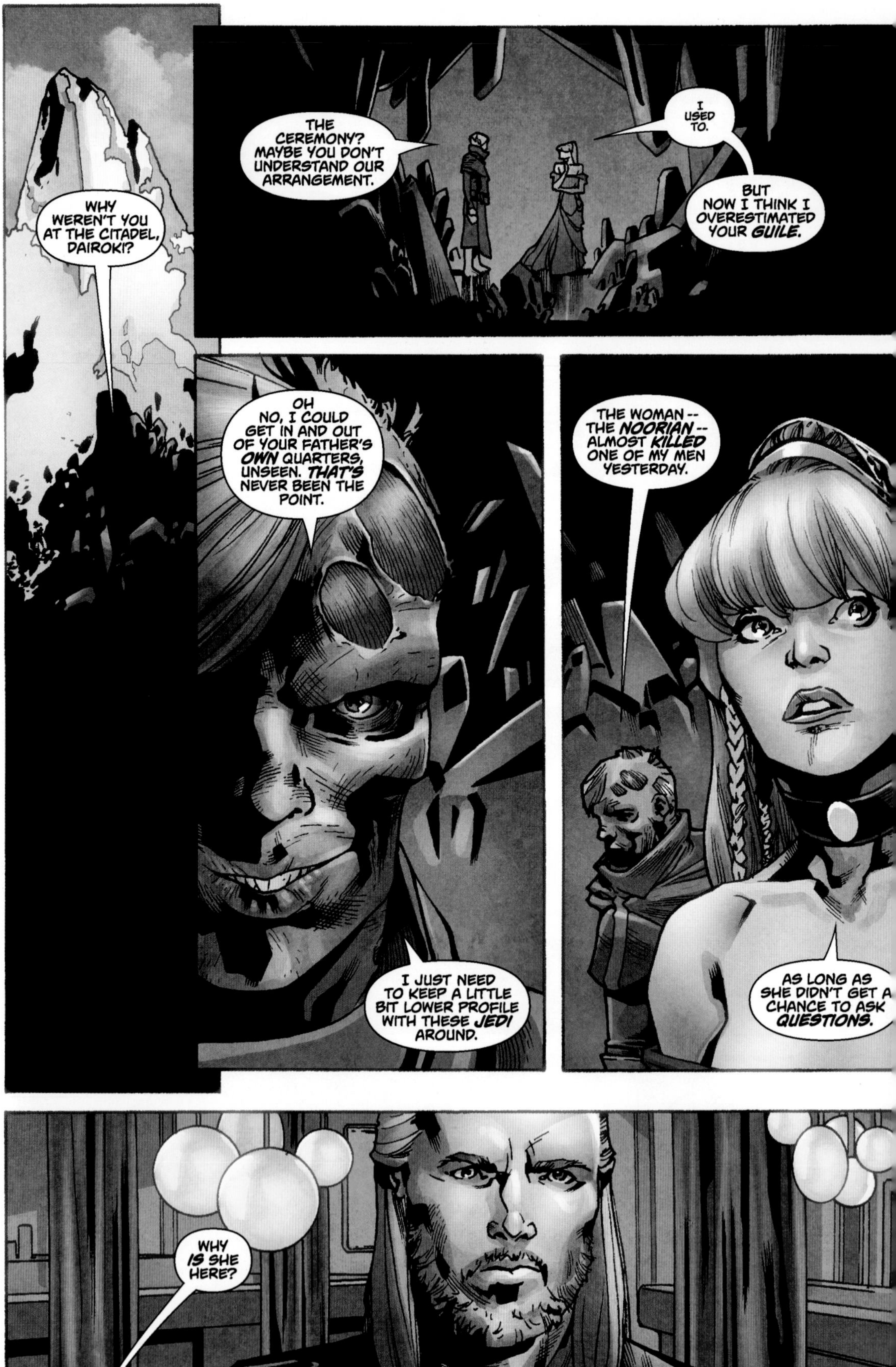
WHY WEREN'T YOU AT THE CITADEL, DAIROKI?
THE CEREMONY? MAYBE YOU DON'T UNDERSTAND OUR ARRANGEMENT.
I USED TO.
BUT NOW I THINK I OVERESTIMATED YOUR GUILE.
OH NO, I COULD GET IN AND OUT OF YOUR FATHER'S OWN QUARTERS, UNSEEN. THAT'S NEVER BEEN THE POINT.
I JUST NEED TO KEEP A LITTLE BIT LOWER PROFILE WITH THESE JEDI AROUND.
THE WOMAN -- THE NOORIAN -- ALMOST KILLED ONE OF MY MEN YESTERDAY.
AS LONG AS SHE DIDN'T GET A CHANCE TO ASK QUESTIONS.
WHY IS SHE HERE?

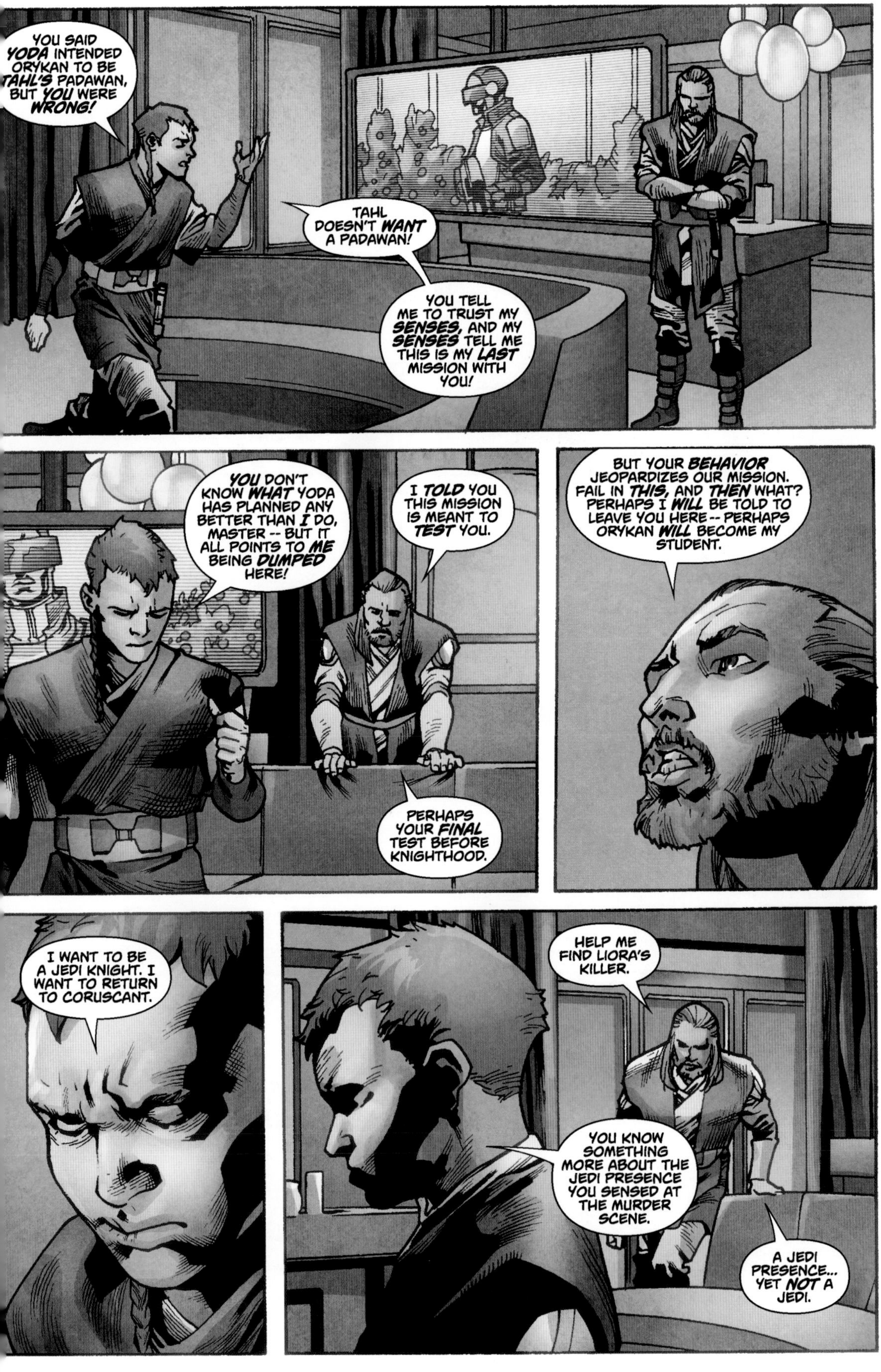
YOU SAID YODA INTENDED ORYKAN TO BE TAHL'S PADAWAN, BUT YOU WERE WRONG!
TAHL DOESN'T WANT A PADAWAN!
YOU TELL ME TO TRUST MY SENSES, AND MY SENSES TELL ME THIS IS MY LAST MISSION WITH YOU!
YOU DON'T KNOW WHAT YODA HAS PLANNED ANY BETTER THAN I DO, MASTER -- BUT IT ALL POINTS TO ME BEING DUMPED HERE!
I TOLD YOU THIS MISSION IS MEANT TO TEST YOU.
PERHAPS YOUR FINAL TEST BEFORE KNIGHTHOOD.
BUT YOUR BEHAVIOR JEOPARDIZES OUR MISSION. FAIL IN THIS, AND THEN WHAT? PERHAPS I WILL BE TOLD TO LEAVE YOU HERE -- PERHAPS ORYKAN WILL BECOME MY STUDENT.
I WANT TO BE A JEDI KNIGHT. I WANT TO RETURN TO CORUSCANT.
HELP ME FIND LIORA'S KILLER.
YOU KNOW SOMETHING MORE ABOUT THE JEDI PRESENCE YOU SENSED AT THE MURDER SCENE.
A JEDI PRESENCE... YET NOT A JEDI.

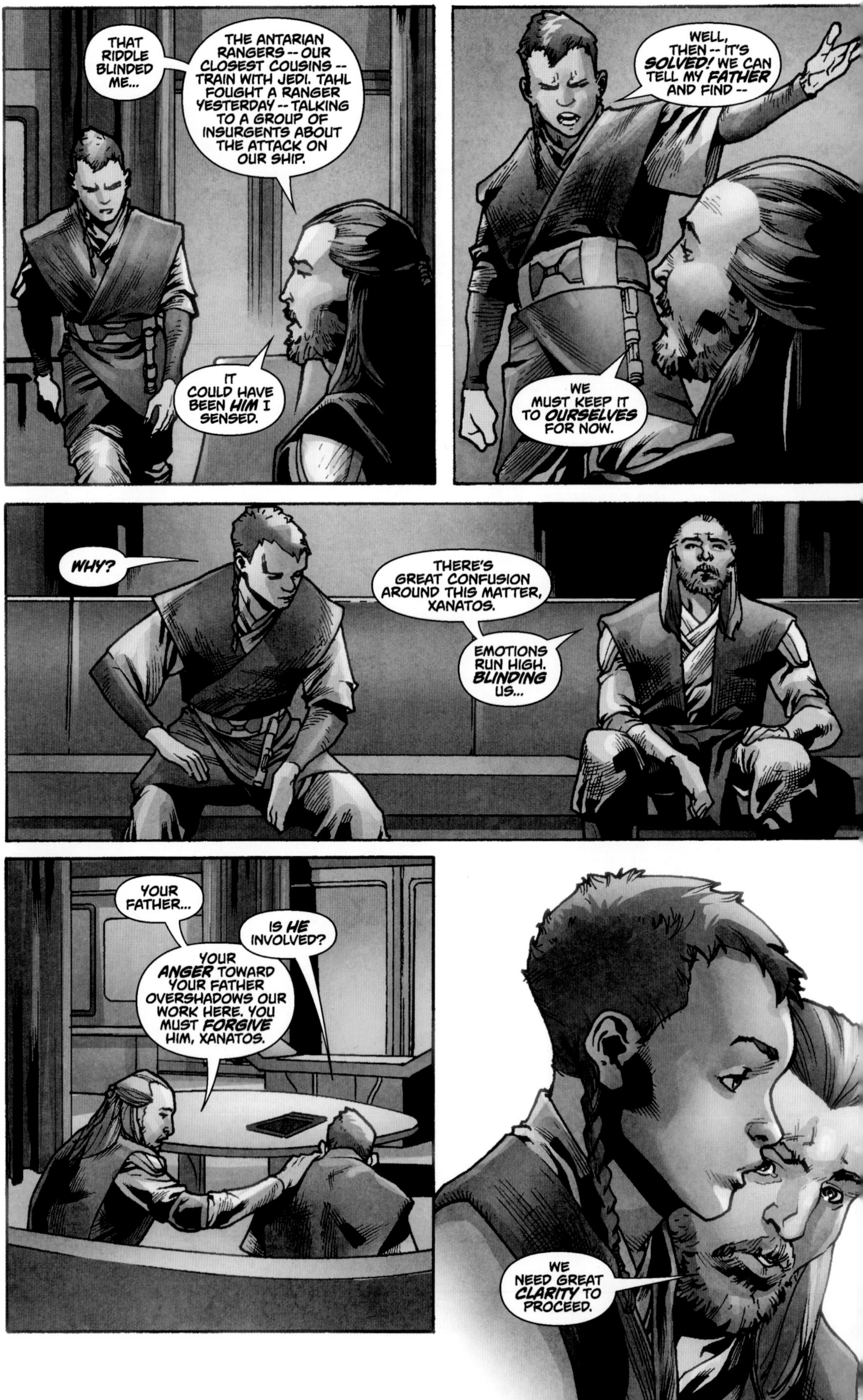
THAT RIDDLE BLINDED ME...
THE ANTARIAN RANGERS -- OUR CLOSEST COUSINS -- TRAIN WITH JEDI. TAHL FOUGHT A RANGER YESTERDAY -- TALKING TO A GROUP OF INSURGENTS ABOUT THE ATTACK ON OUR SHIP.
IT COULD HAVE BEEN HIM I SENSED.
WELL, THEN -- IT'S SOLVED! WE CAN TELL MY FATHER AND FIND --
WE MUST KEEP IT TO OURSELVES FOR NOW.
WHY?
THERE'S GREAT CONFUSION AROUND THIS MATTER, XANATOS.
EMOTIONS RUN HIGH. BLINDING US...
YOUR FATHER...
IS HE INVOLVED?
YOUR ANGER TOWARD YOUR FATHER OVERSHADOWS OUR WORK HERE. YOU MUST FORGIVE HIM, XANATOS.
WE NEED GREAT CLARITY TO PROCEED.

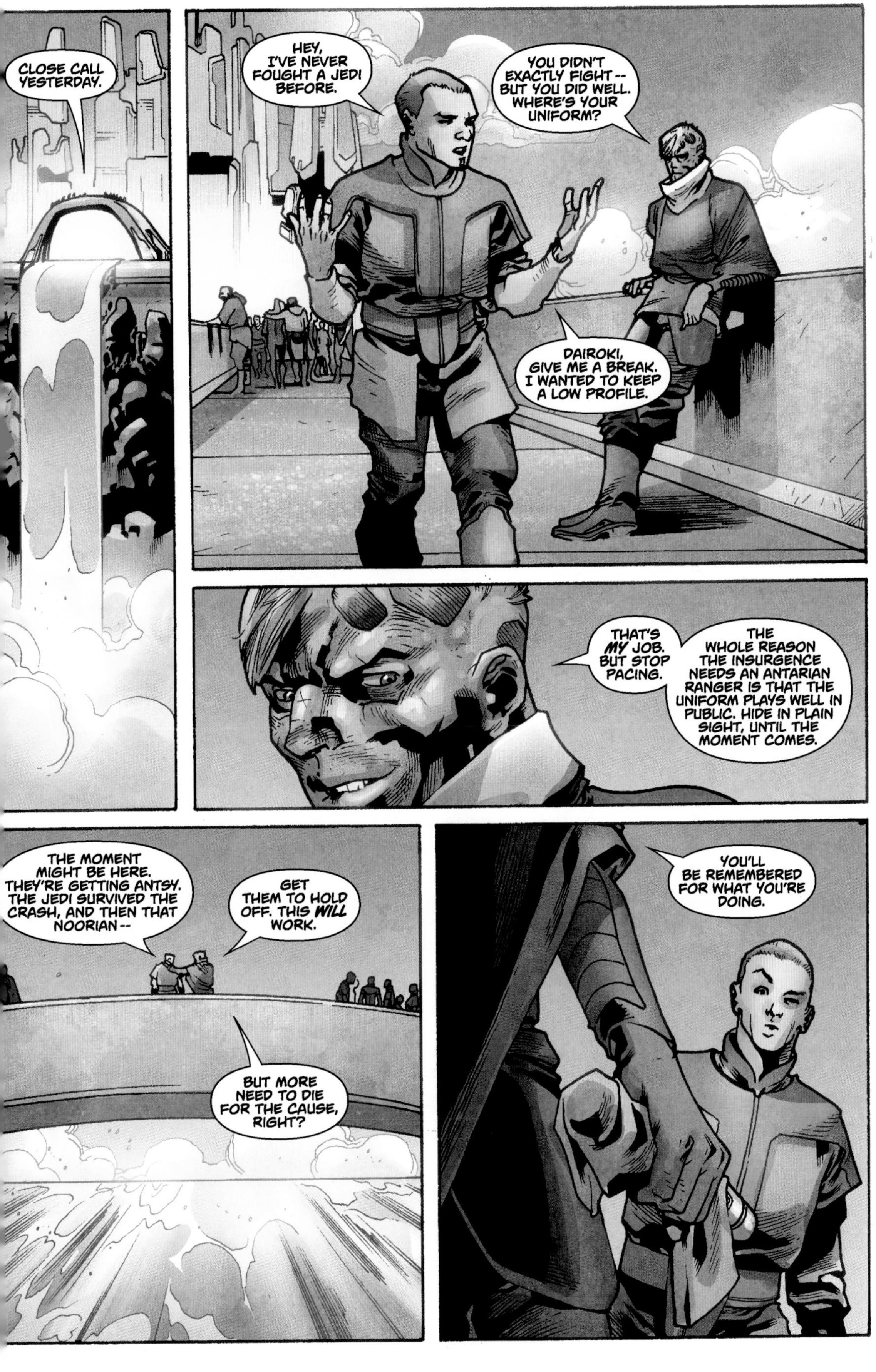
CLOSE CALL YESTERDAY.
HEY, I'VE NEVER FOUGHT A JEDI BEFORE.
YOU DIDN'T EXACTLY FIGHT -- BUT YOU DID WELL. WHERE'S YOUR UNIFORM?
DAIROKI, GIVE ME A BREAK. I WANTED TO KEEP A LOW PROFILE.
THAT'S *MY* JOB. BUT STOP PACING.
THE WHOLE REASON THE INSURGENCE NEEDS AN ANTARIAN RANGER IS THAT THE UNIFORM PLAYS WELL IN PUBLIC. HIDE IN PLAIN SIGHT, UNTIL THE MOMENT COMES.
THE MOMENT MIGHT BE HERE. THEY'RE GETTING ANTSY. THE JEDI SURVIVED THE CRASH, AND THEN THAT NOORIAN --
GET THEM TO HOLD OFF. THIS *WILL* WORK.
BUT MORE NEED TO DIE FOR THE CAUSE, RIGHT?
YOU'LL BE REMEMBERED FOR WHAT YOU'RE DOING.

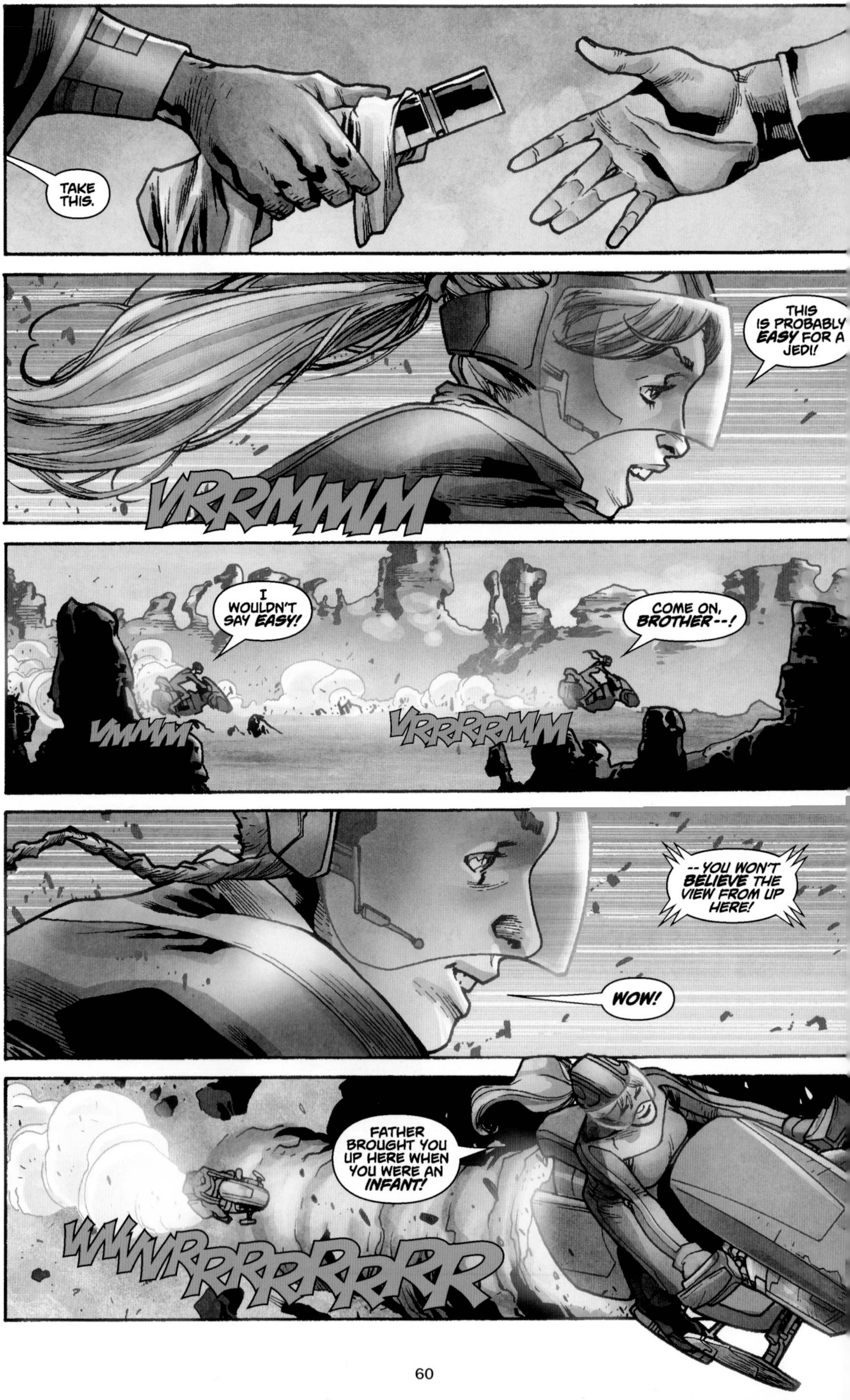
TAKE THIS.
THIS IS PROBABLY EASY FOR A JEDI!
VRRMMM
I WOULDN'T SAY EASY!
COME ON, BROTHER--!
VMMM
VRRRRMM
--YOU WON'T BELIEVE THE VIEW FROM UP HERE!
WOW!
FATHER BROUGHT YOU UP HERE WHEN YOU WERE AN INFANT!
WWWRRRRRRRRR

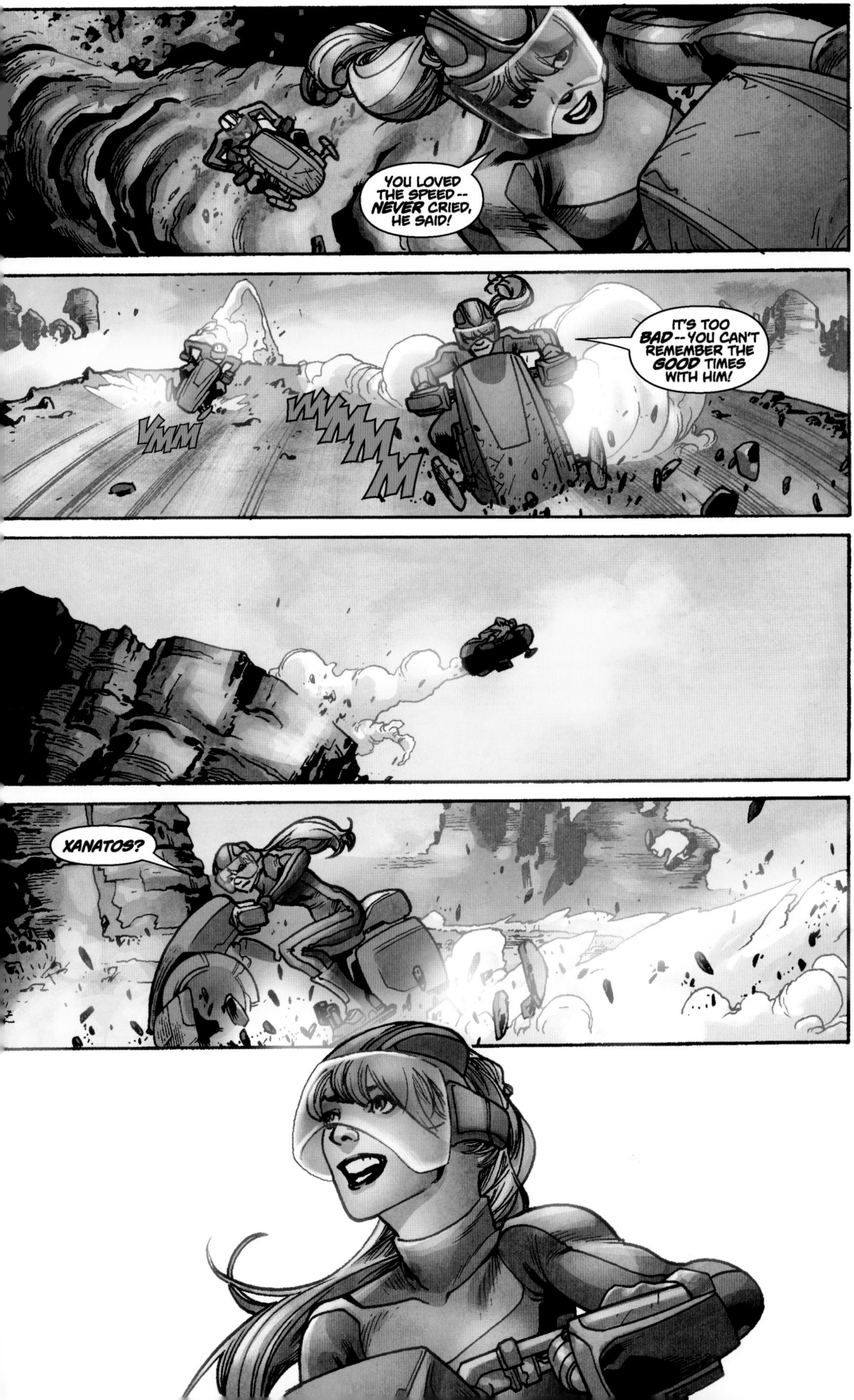
YOU LOVED THE SPEED -- NEVER CRIED, HE SAID!
IT'S TOO BAD -- YOU CAN'T REMEMBER THE GOOD TIMES WITH HIM!
VMM
VVVMMMM
XANATOS?

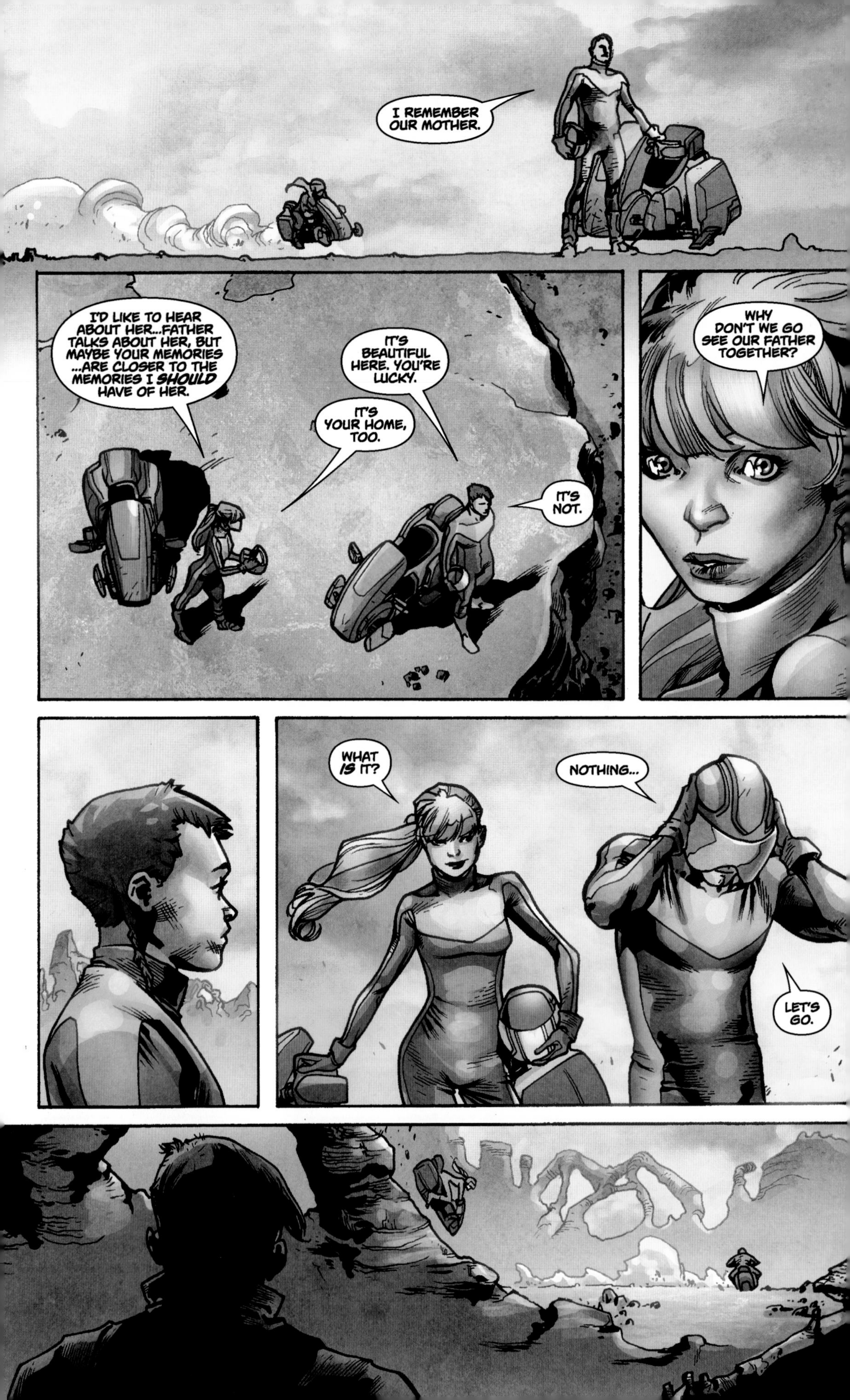
I REMEMBER OUR MOTHER.
I'D LIKE TO HEAR ABOUT HER...FATHER TALKS ABOUT HER, BUT MAYBE YOUR MEMORIES ...ARE CLOSER TO THE MEMORIES I SHOULD HAVE OF HER.
IT'S BEAUTIFUL HERE. YOU'RE LUCKY.
IT'S YOUR HOME, TOO.
IT'S NOT.
WHY DON'T WE GO SEE OUR FATHER TOGETHER?
WHAT IS IT?
NOTHING...
LET'S GO.

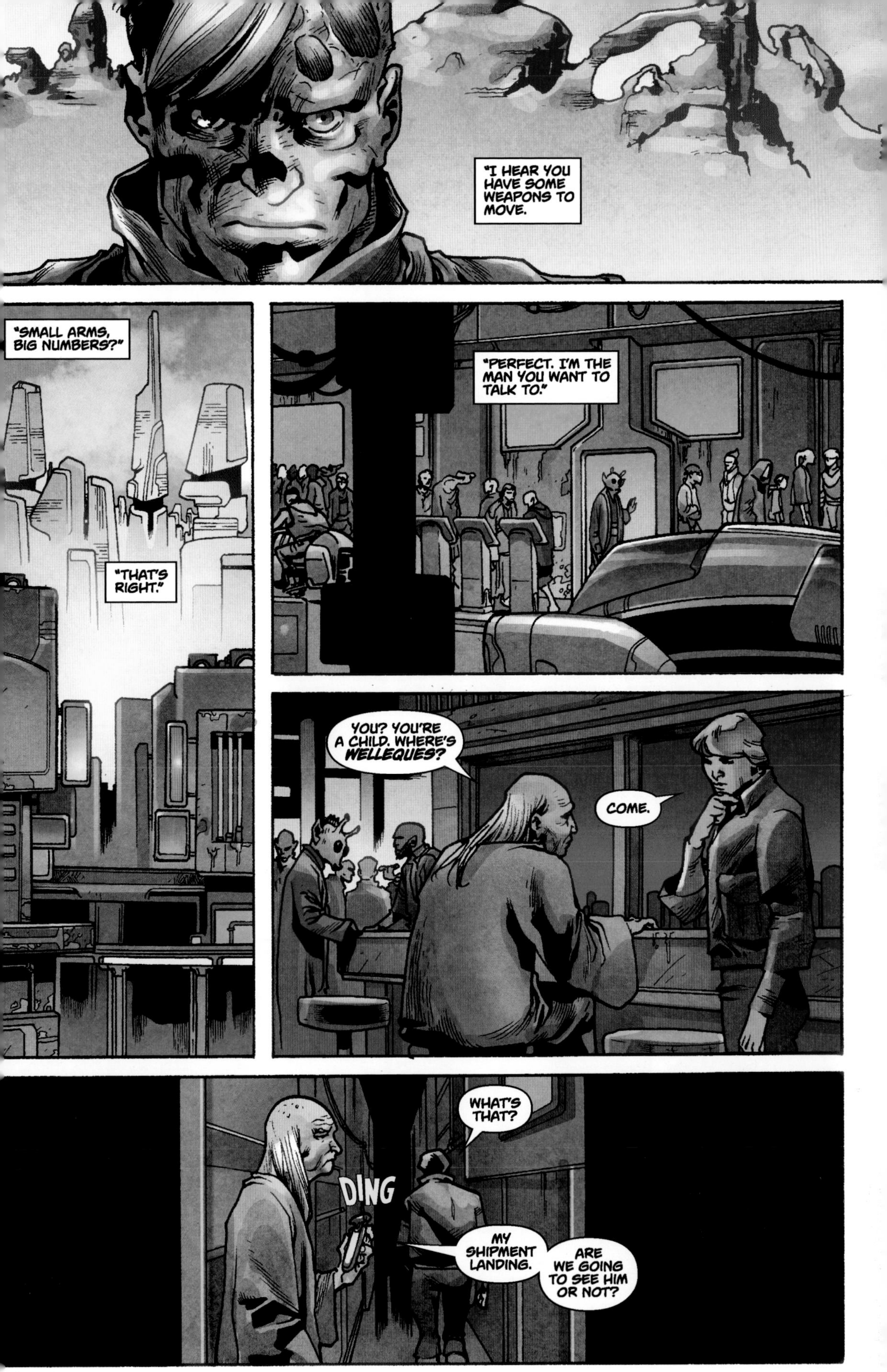
"I HEAR YOU HAVE SOME WEAPONS TO MOVE.
"SMALL ARMS, BIG NUMBERS?"
"THAT'S RIGHT."
"PERFECT. I'M THE MAN YOU WANT TO TALK TO."
YOU? YOU'RE A CHILD. WHERE'S *WELLEQUES?*
COME.
WHAT'S THAT?
DING
MY SHIPMENT LANDING.
ARE WE GOING TO SEE HIM OR NOT?

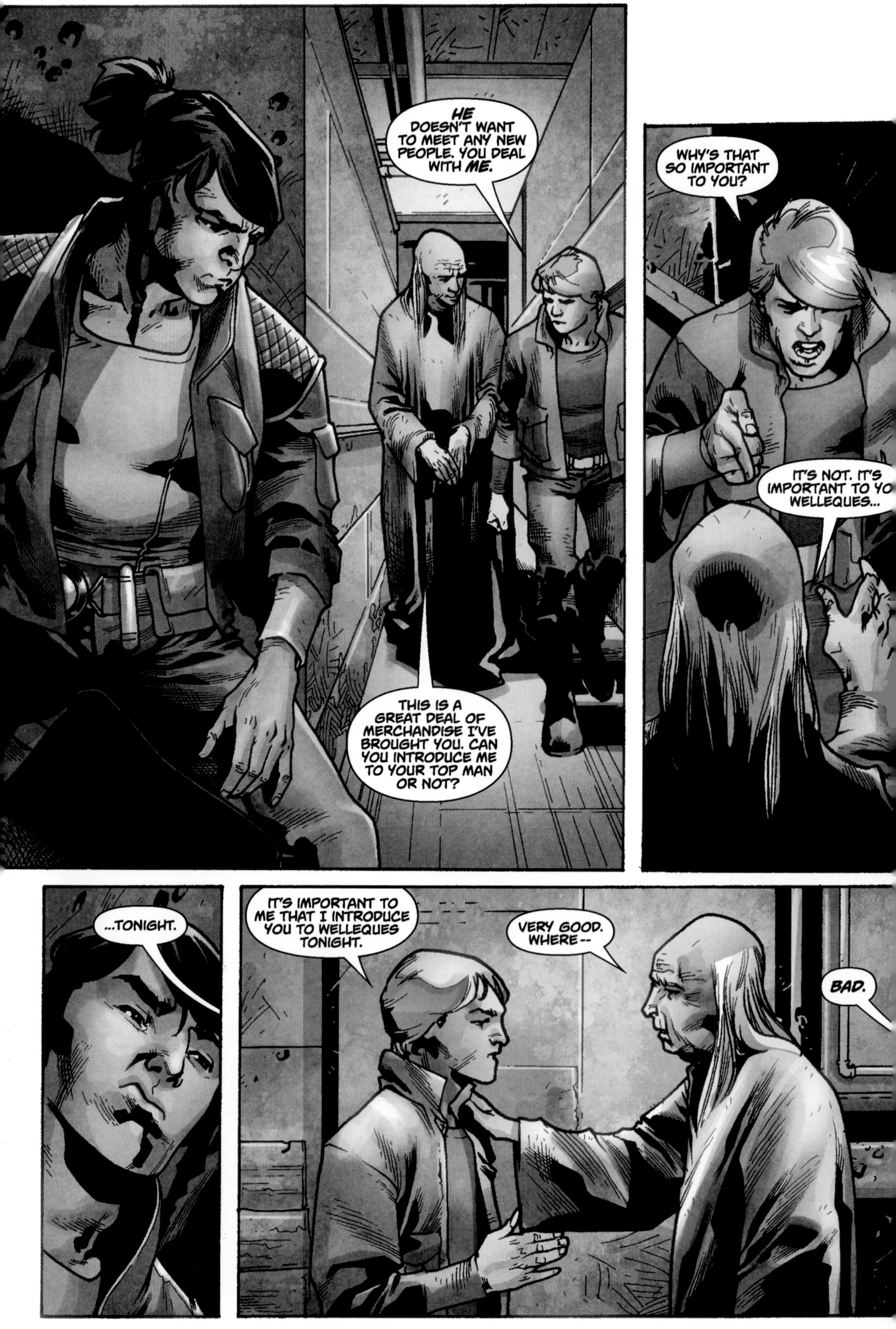
HE DOESN'T WANT TO MEET ANY NEW PEOPLE. YOU DEAL WITH ME.
THIS IS A GREAT DEAL OF MERCHANDISE I'VE BROUGHT YOU. CAN YOU INTRODUCE ME TO YOUR TOP MAN OR NOT?
WHY'S THAT SO IMPORTANT TO YOU?
IT'S NOT. IT'S IMPORTANT TO YO WELLEQUES...
...TONIGHT.
IT'S IMPORTANT TO ME THAT I INTRODUCE YOU TO WELLEQUES TONIGHT.
VERY GOOD. WHERE--
BAD.

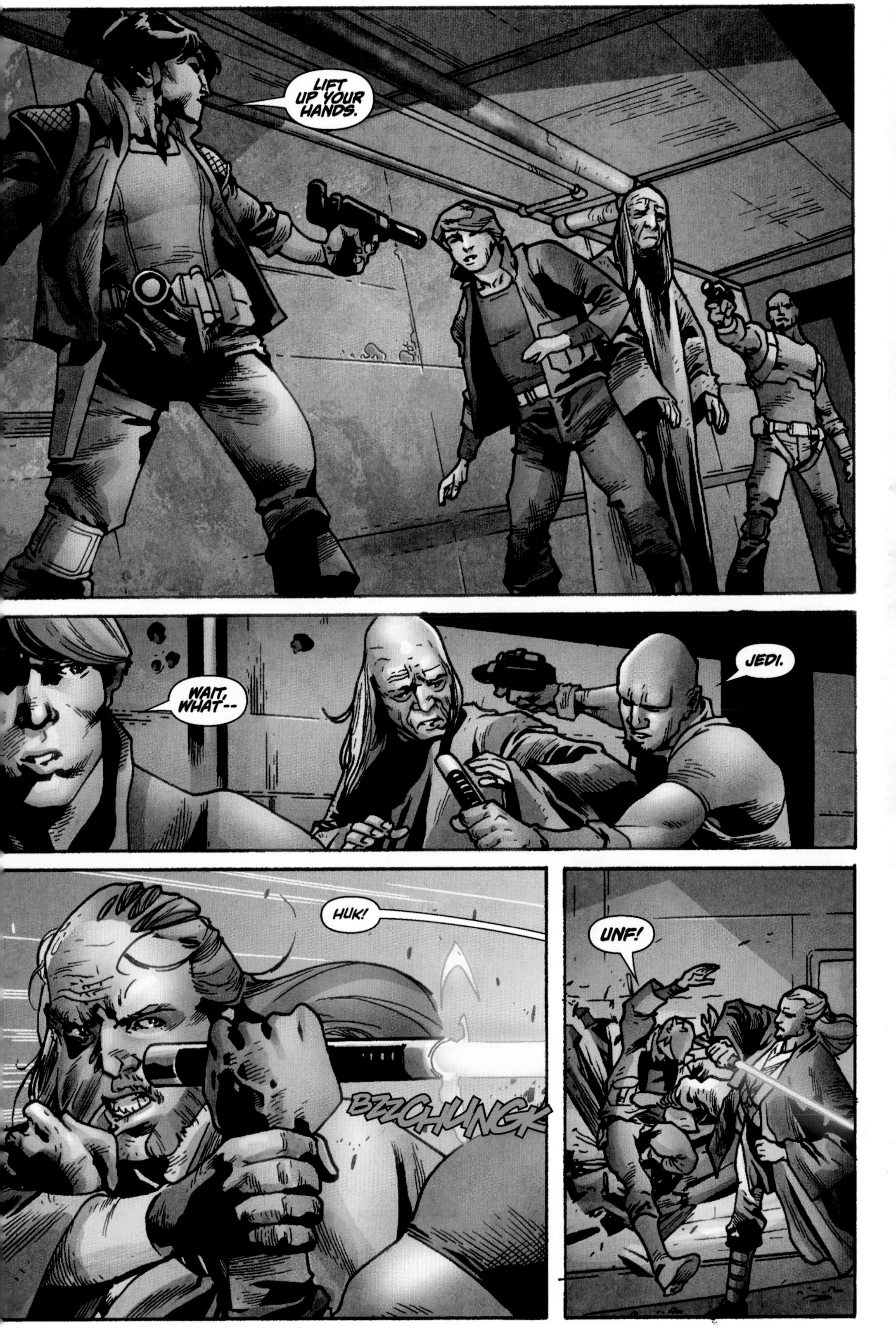
LIFT UP YOUR HANDS.
WAIT, WHAT--
JEDI.
HUK!
BZZCHUNGK
UNF!

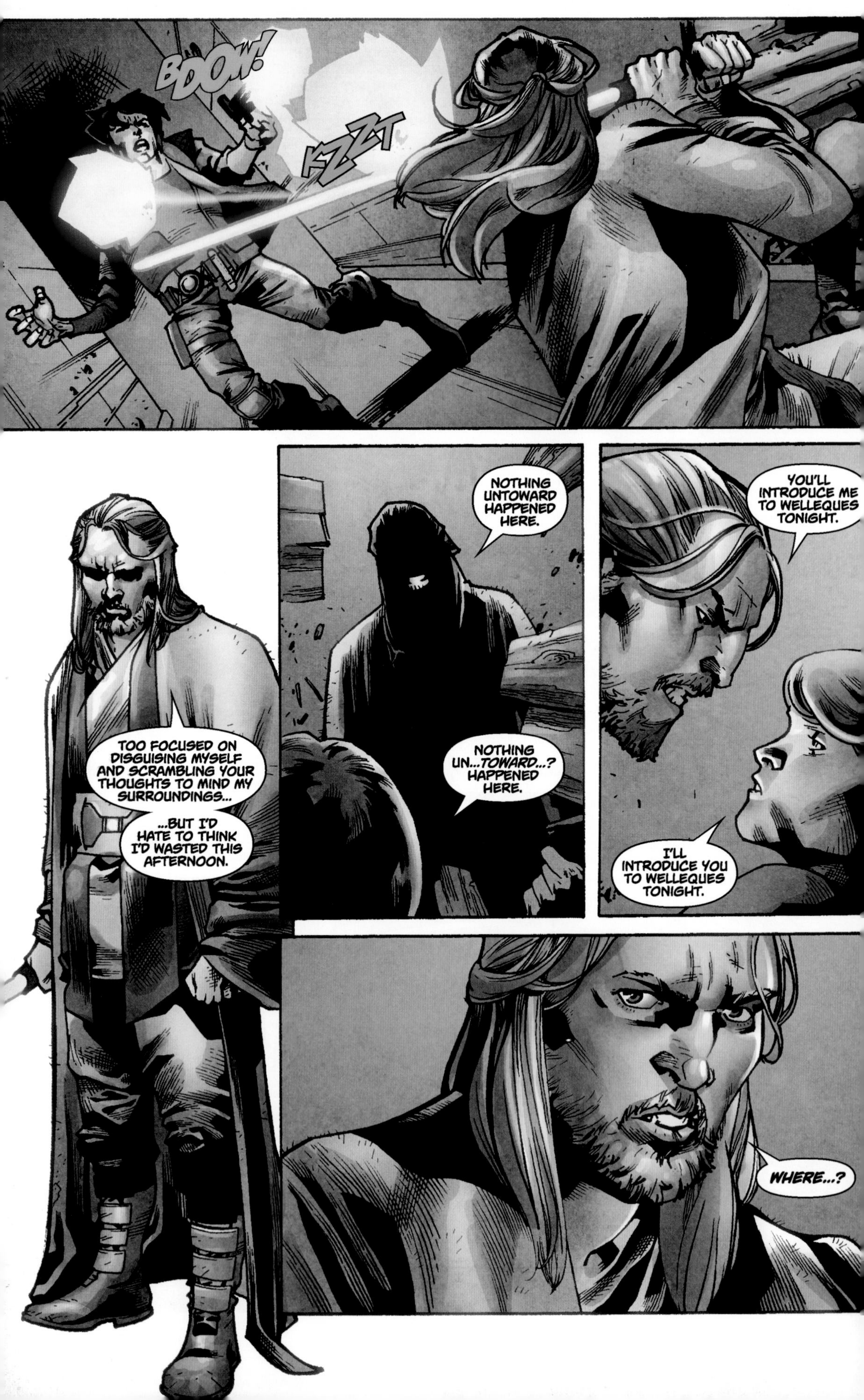
BDOW!
KZZZT
TOO FOCUSED ON DISGUISING MYSELF AND SCRAMBLING YOUR THOUGHTS TO MIND MY SURROUNDINGS...
...BUT I'D HATE TO THINK I'D WASTED THIS AFTERNOON.
NOTHING UNTOWARD HAPPENED HERE.
NOTHING UN...TOWARD...? HAPPENED HERE.
YOU'LL INTRODUCE ME TO WELLEQUES TONIGHT.
I'LL INTRODUCE YOU TO WELLEQUES TONIGHT.
WHERE...?

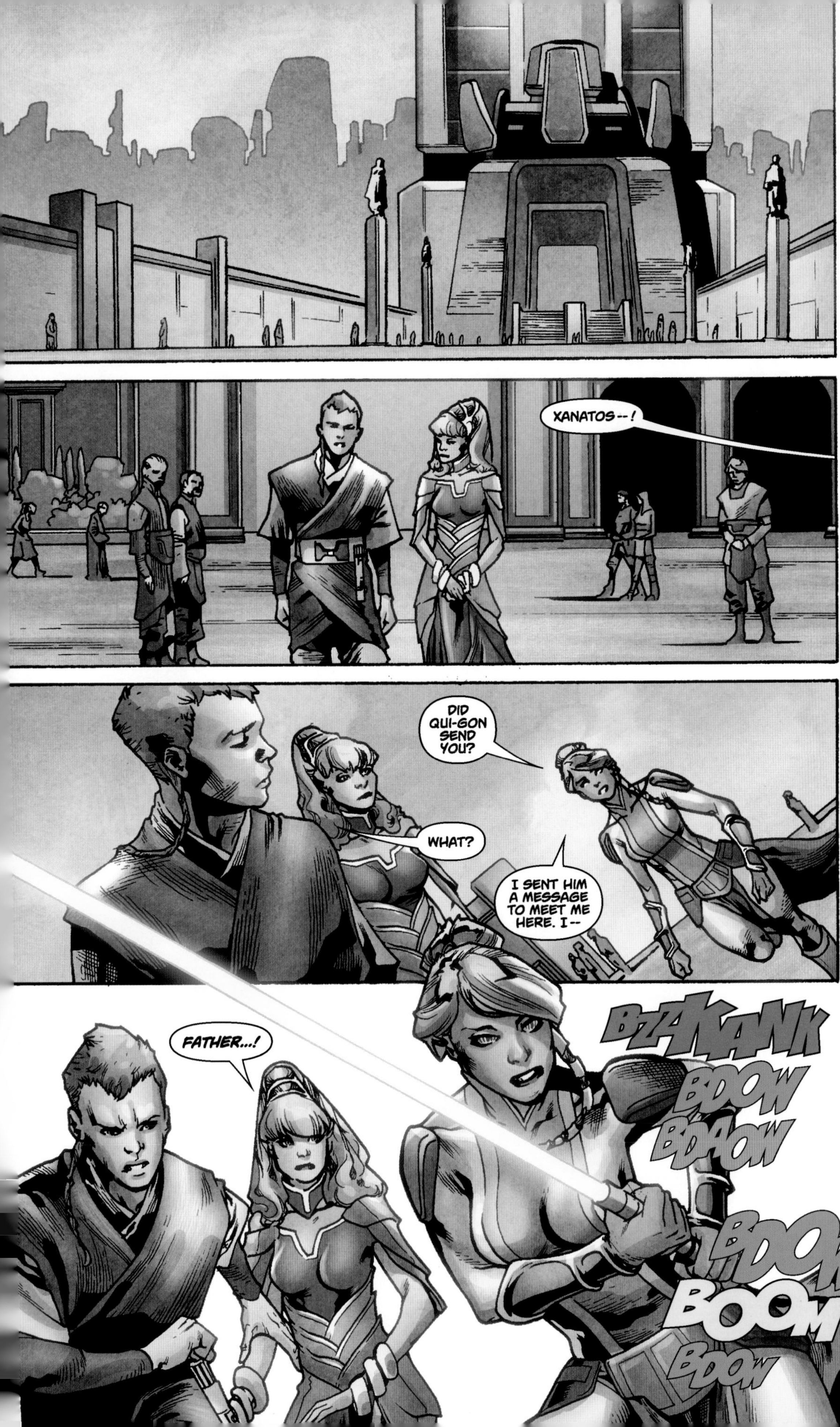
XANATOS--!
DID QUI-GON SEND YOU?
WHAT?
I SENT HIM A MESSAGE TO MEET ME HERE. I--
FATHER...!
BZZKANK
BDOW
BDAOW
BDOW
BOOM
BDOW

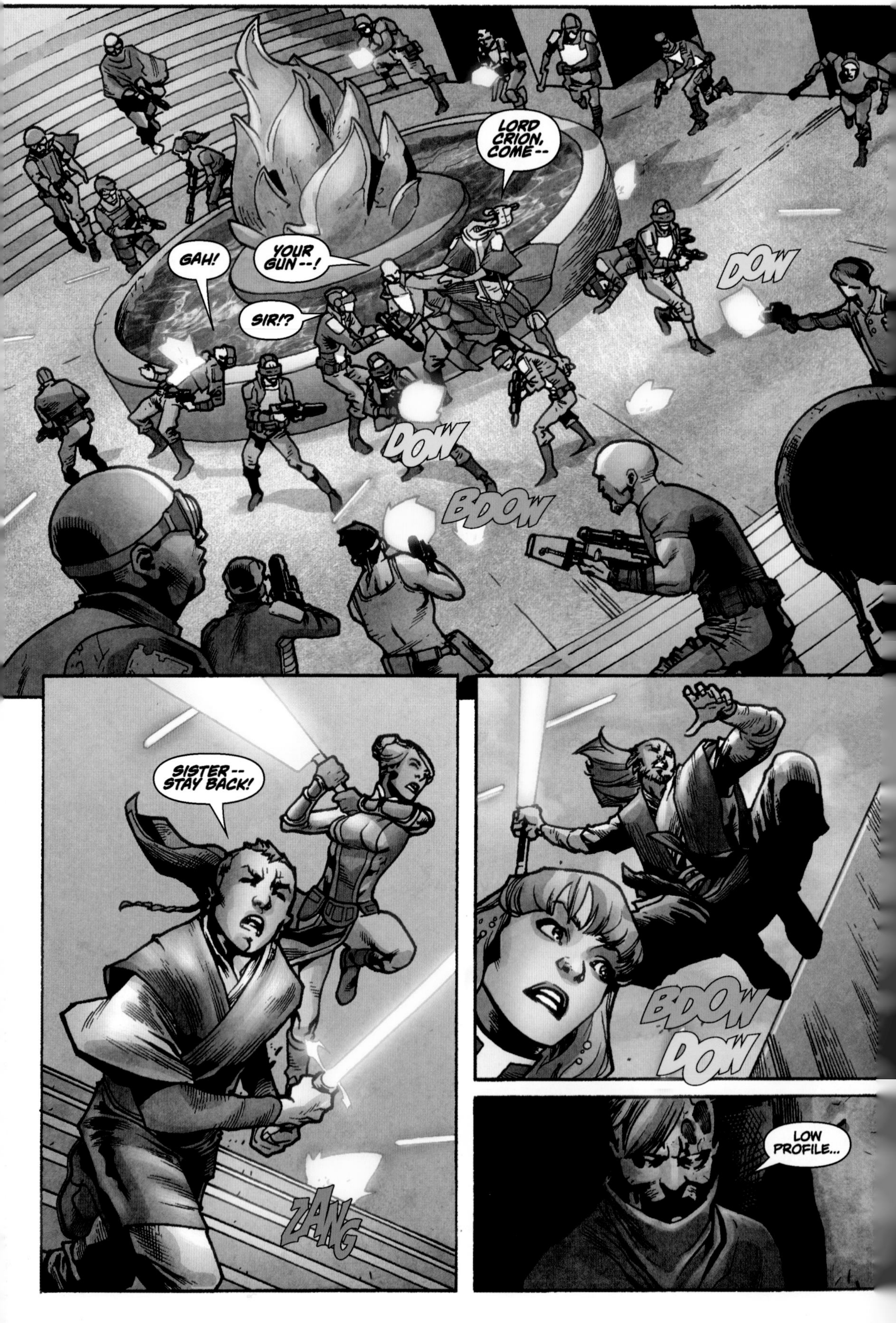
LORD CRION, COME--
GAH!
YOUR GUN--!
SIR!?
DOW
DOW
BDOW
SISTER-- STAY BACK!
ZANG
BDOW
DOW
LOW PROFILE...

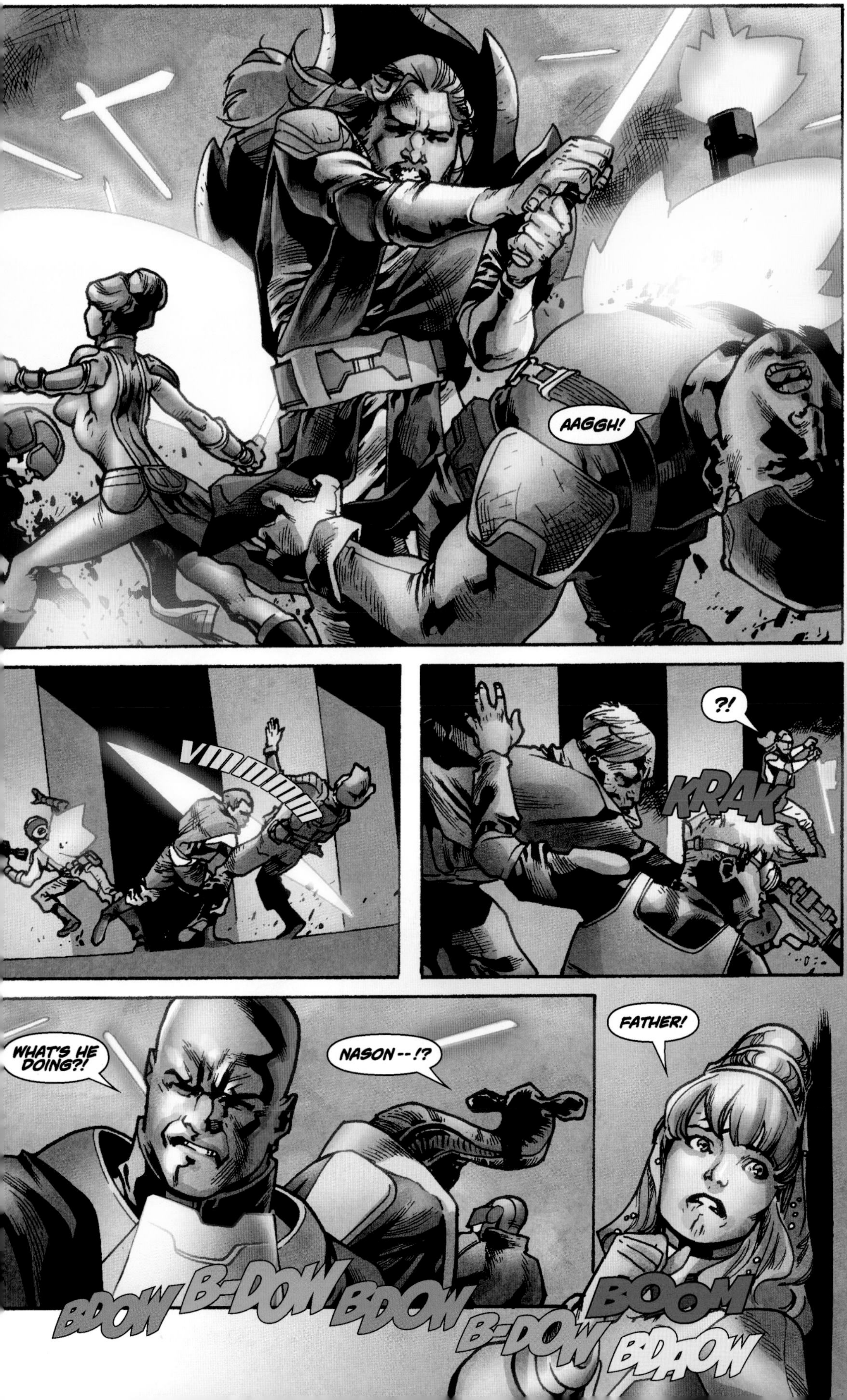
AAGGH!
VMMMMMM
?!
KRAK
WHAT'S HE DOING?!
NASON--!?
FATHER!
BDOW B-DOW BDOW B-DOW BOOM BDAOW

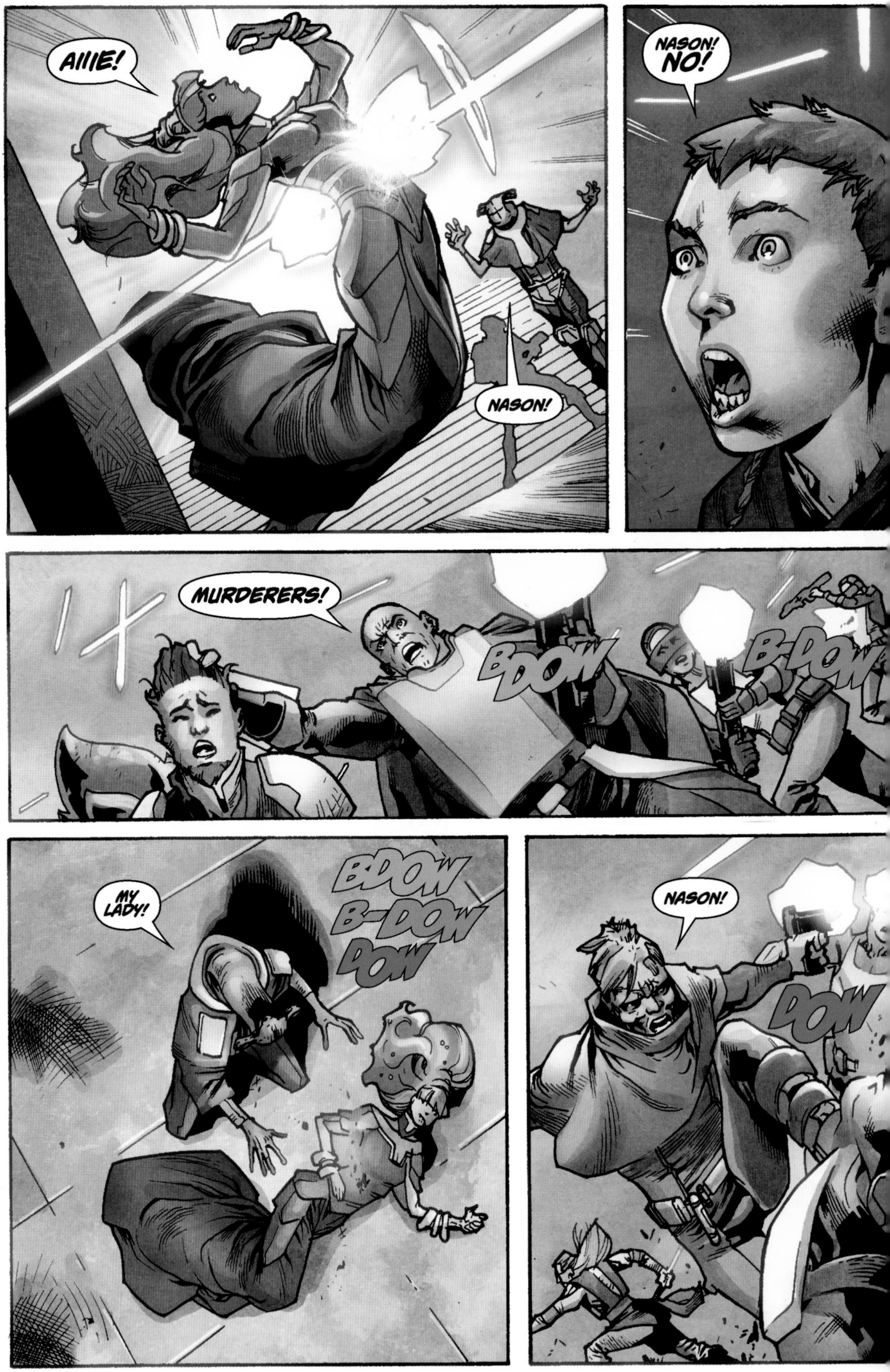
AIIIE!
NASON!
NASON! NO!
MURDERERS!
BDOW
B-DOW
MY LADY!
BDOW
B-DOW
DOW
NASON!
DOW

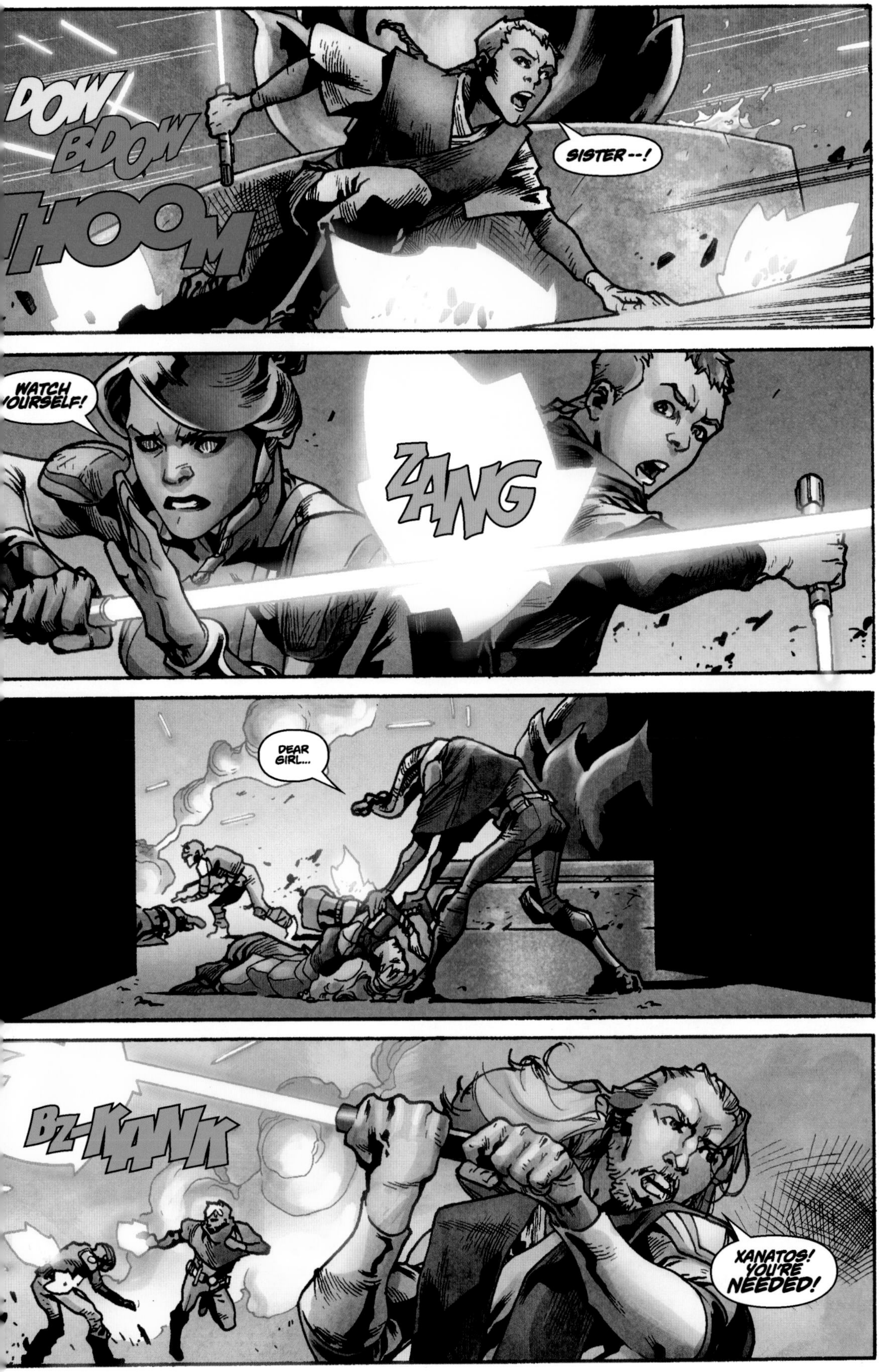
DOW
BDOW
THOOM
SISTER--!
WATCH YOURSELF!
ZZANG
DEAR GIRL...
BZ-KANK
XANATOS! YOU'RE NEEDED!

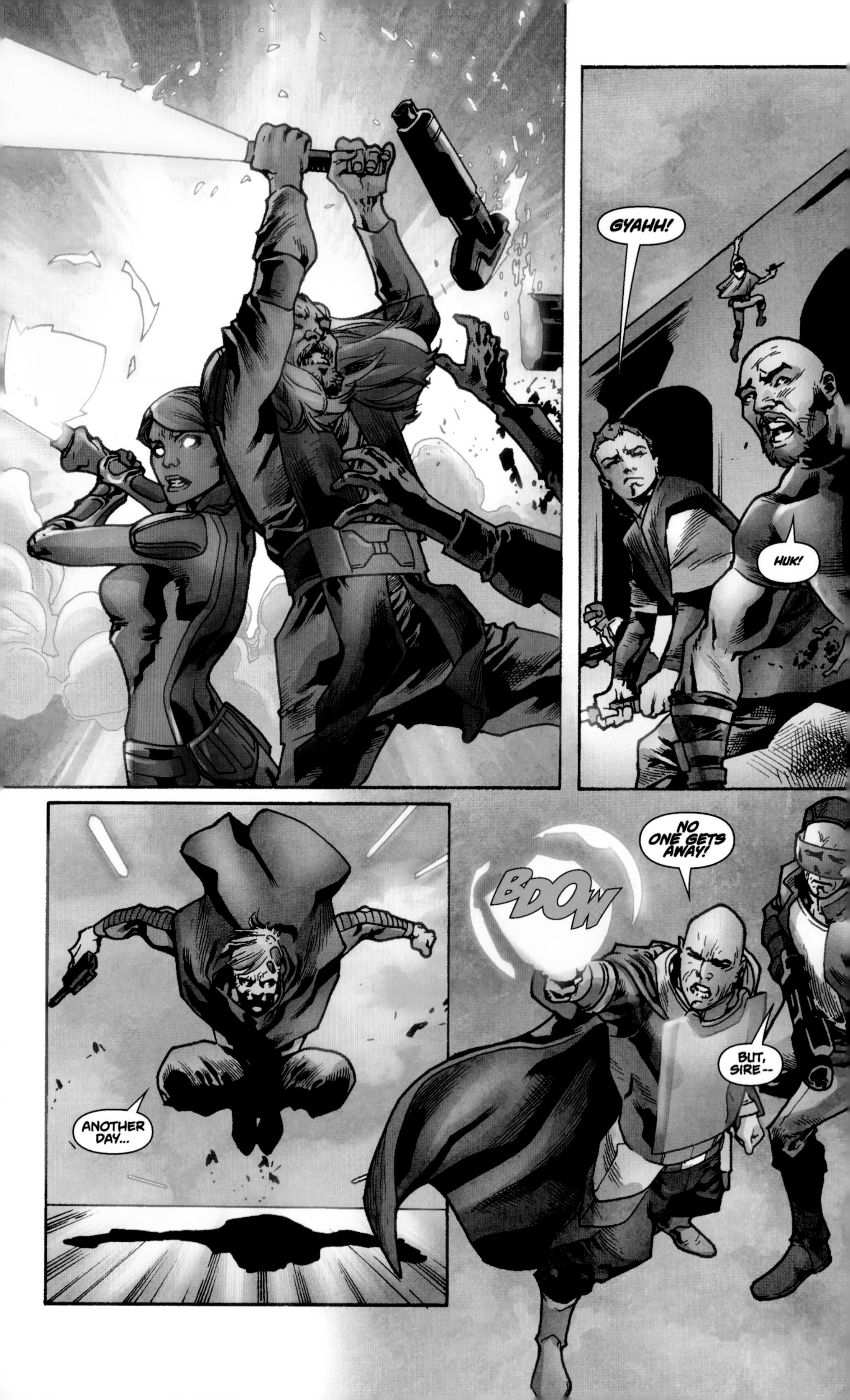
GYAHH!
HUK!
ANOTHER DAY...
BDOW
NO ONE GETS AWAY!
BUT, SIRE--

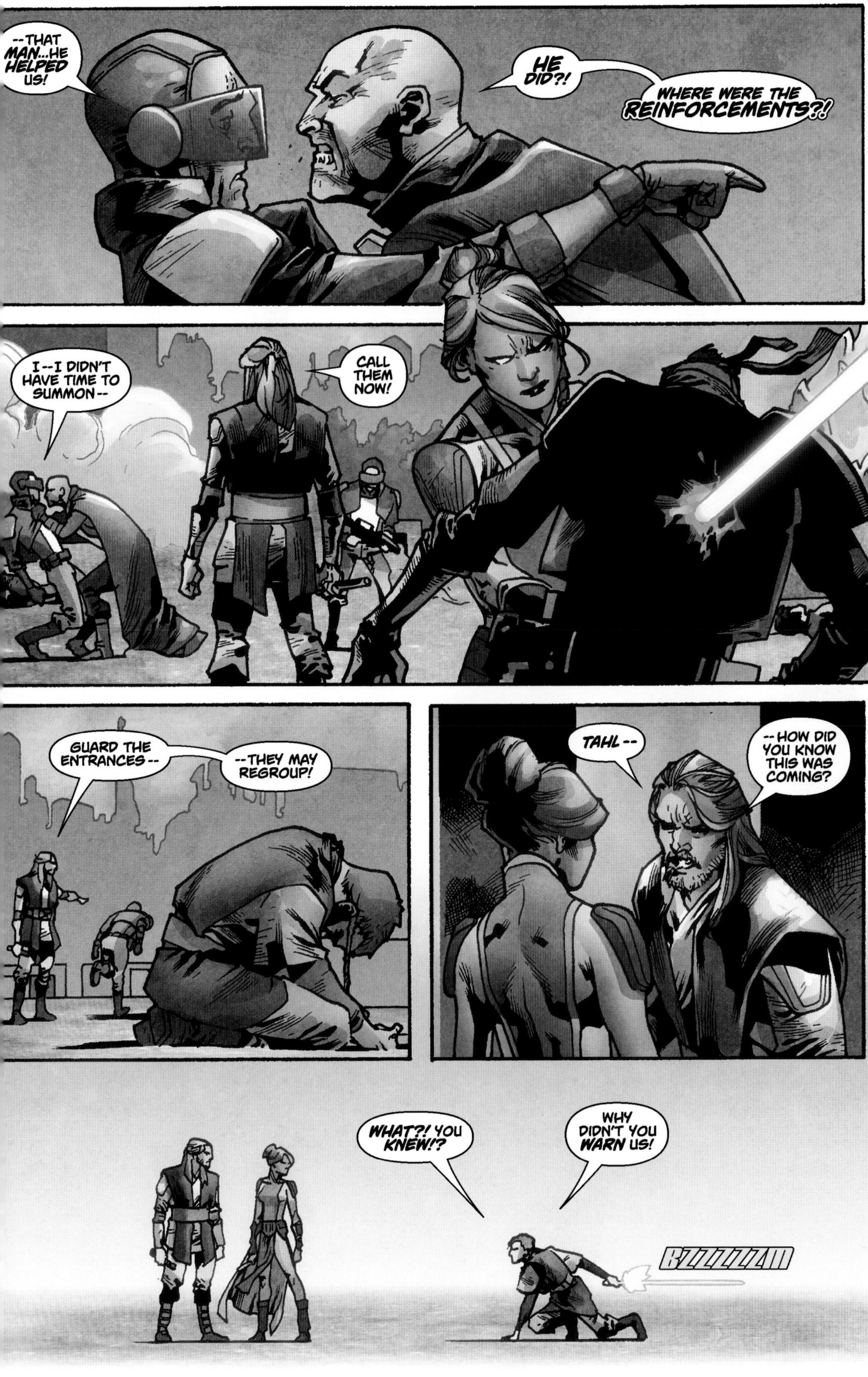
--THAT MAN...HE HELPED US!
HE DID?!
WHERE WERE THE REINFORCEMENTS?!
I--I DIDN'T HAVE TIME TO SUMMON--
CALL THEM NOW!
GUARD THE ENTRANCES--
--THEY MAY REGROUP!
TAHL--
--HOW DID YOU KNOW THIS WAS COMING?
WHAT?! YOU KNEW!?
WHY DIDN'T YOU WARN US!
BZZZZZZM

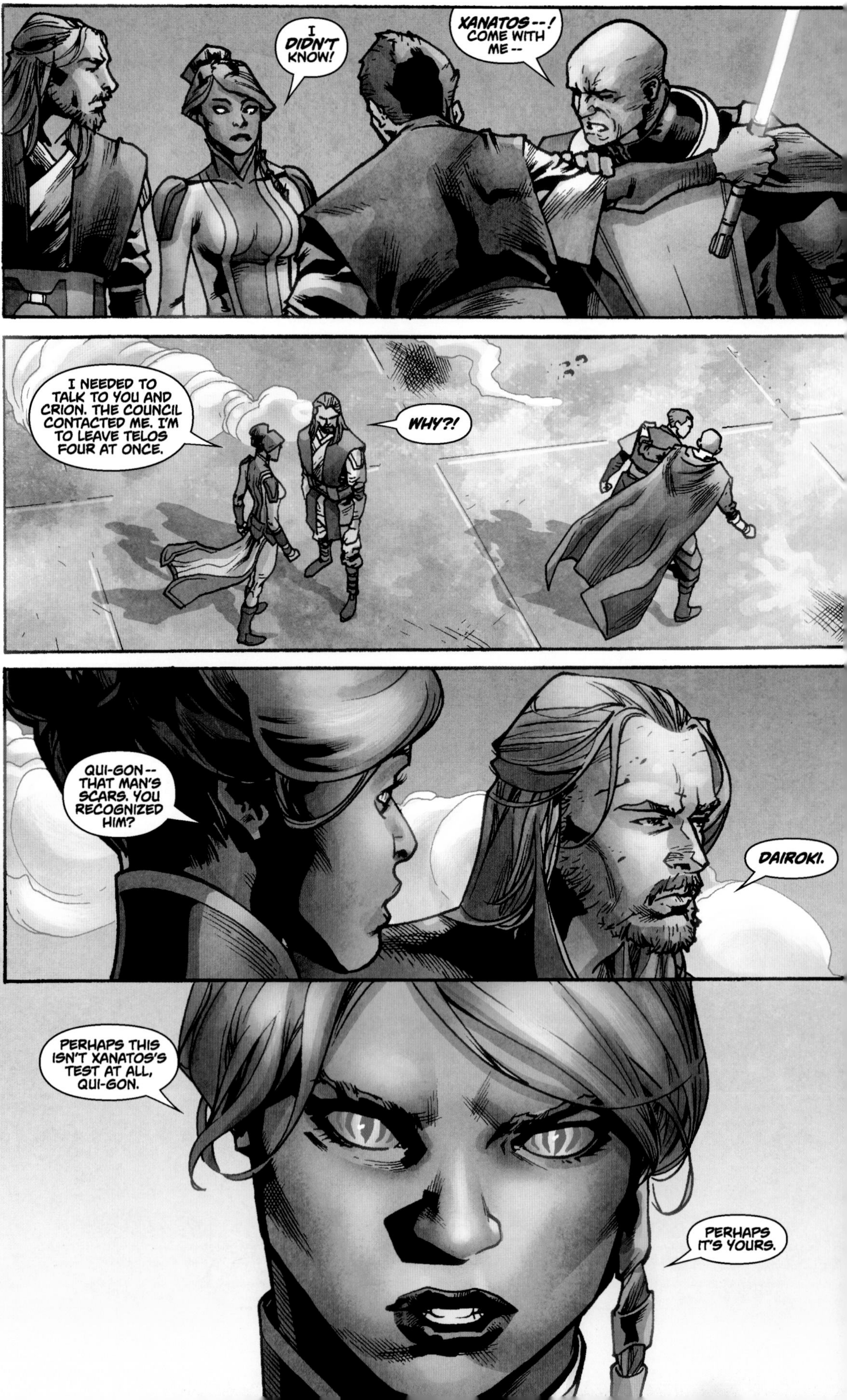
I DIDN'T KNOW!
XANATOS--! COME WITH ME--
I NEEDED TO TALK TO YOU AND CRION. THE COUNCIL CONTACTED ME. I'M TO LEAVE TELOS FOUR AT ONCE.
WHY?!
QUI-GON--THAT MAN'S SCARS. YOU RECOGNIZED HIM?
DAIROKI.
PERHAPS THIS ISN'T XANATOS'S TEST AT ALL, QUI-GON.
PERHAPS IT'S YOURS.

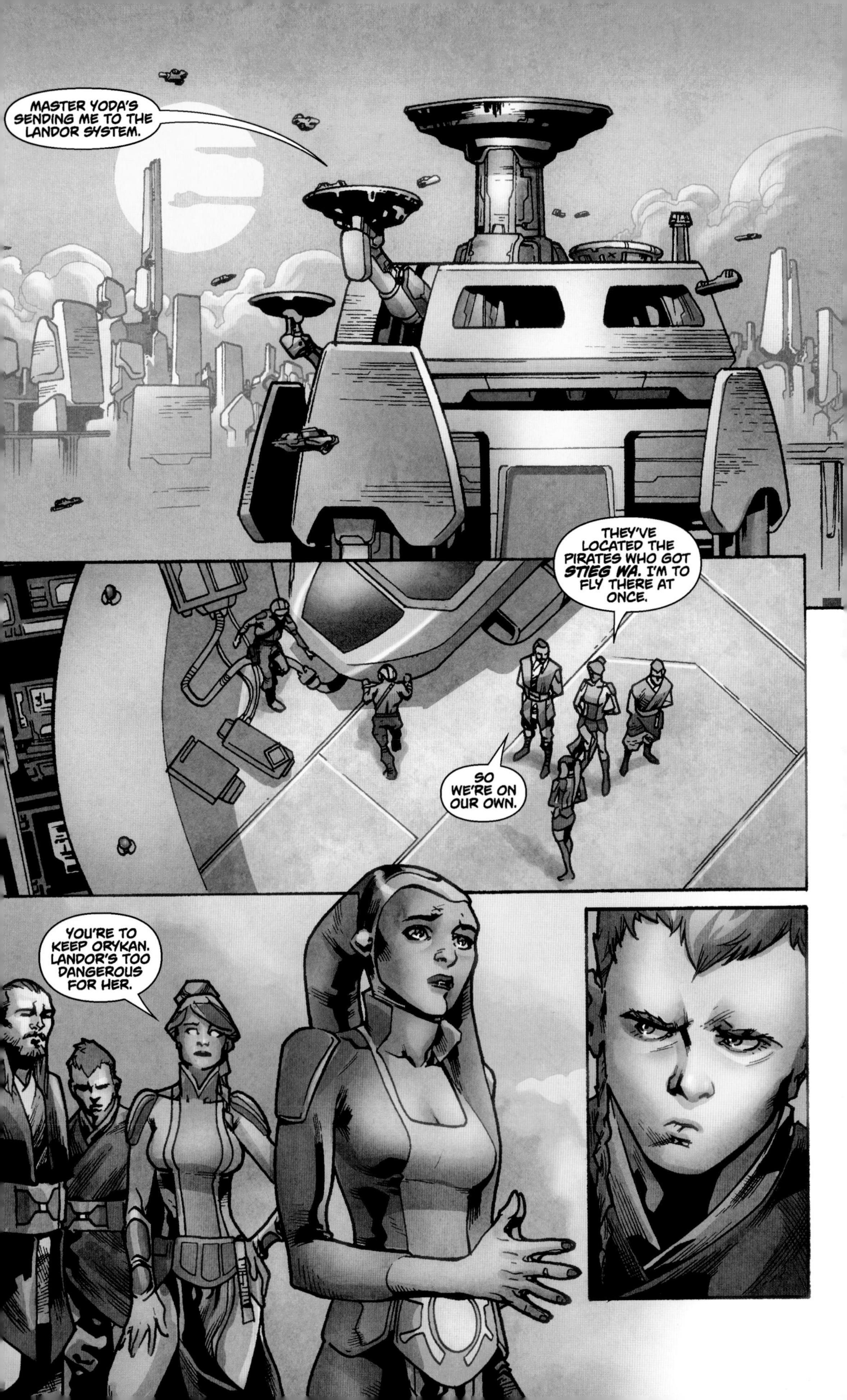
MASTER YODA'S SENDING ME TO THE LANDOR SYSTEM.
THEY'VE LOCATED THE PIRATES WHO GOT STIEG WA. I'M TO FLY THERE AT ONCE.
SO WE'RE ON OUR OWN.
YOU'RE TO KEEP ORYKAN. LANDOR'S TOO DANGEROUS FOR HER.

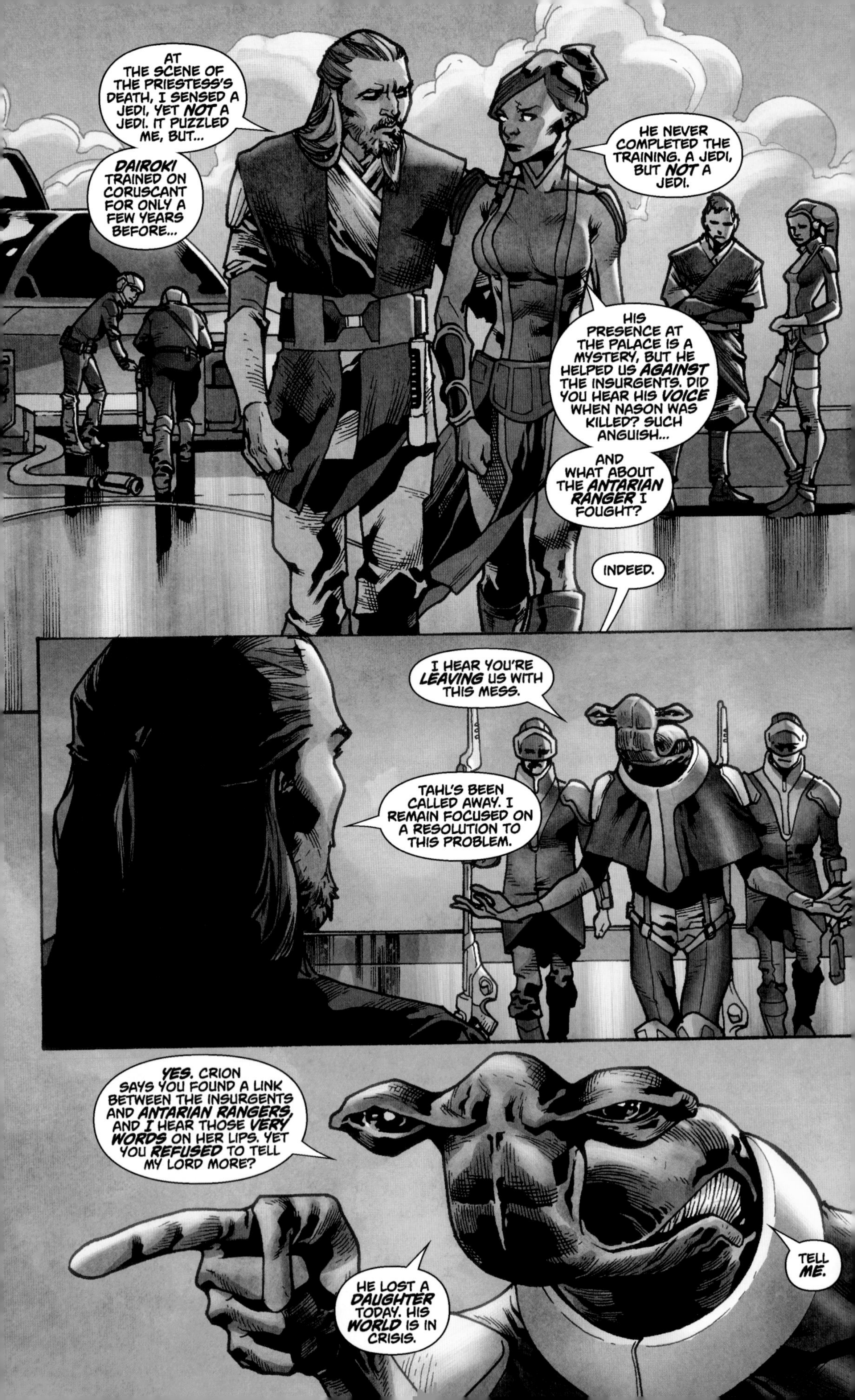
AT THE SCENE OF THE PRIESTESS'S DEATH, I SENSED A JEDI, YET NOT A JEDI. IT PUZZLED ME, BUT...
DAIROKI TRAINED ON CORUSCANT FOR ONLY A FEW YEARS BEFORE...
HE NEVER COMPLETED THE TRAINING. A JEDI, BUT NOT A JEDI.
HIS PRESENCE AT THE PALACE IS A MYSTERY, BUT HE HELPED US AGAINST THE INSURGENTS. DID YOU HEAR HIS VOICE WHEN NASON WAS KILLED? SUCH ANGUISH...
AND WHAT ABOUT THE ANTARIAN RANGER I FOUGHT?
INDEED.
I HEAR YOU'RE LEAVING US WITH THIS MESS.
TAHL'S BEEN CALLED AWAY. I REMAIN FOCUSED ON A RESOLUTION TO THIS PROBLEM.
YES. CRION SAYS YOU FOUND A LINK BETWEEN THE INSURGENTS AND ANTARIAN RANGERS, AND I HEAR THOSE VERY WORDS ON HER LIPS. YET YOU REFUSED TO TELL MY LORD MORE?
HE LOST A DAUGHTER TODAY. HIS WORLD IS IN CRISIS.
TELL ME.

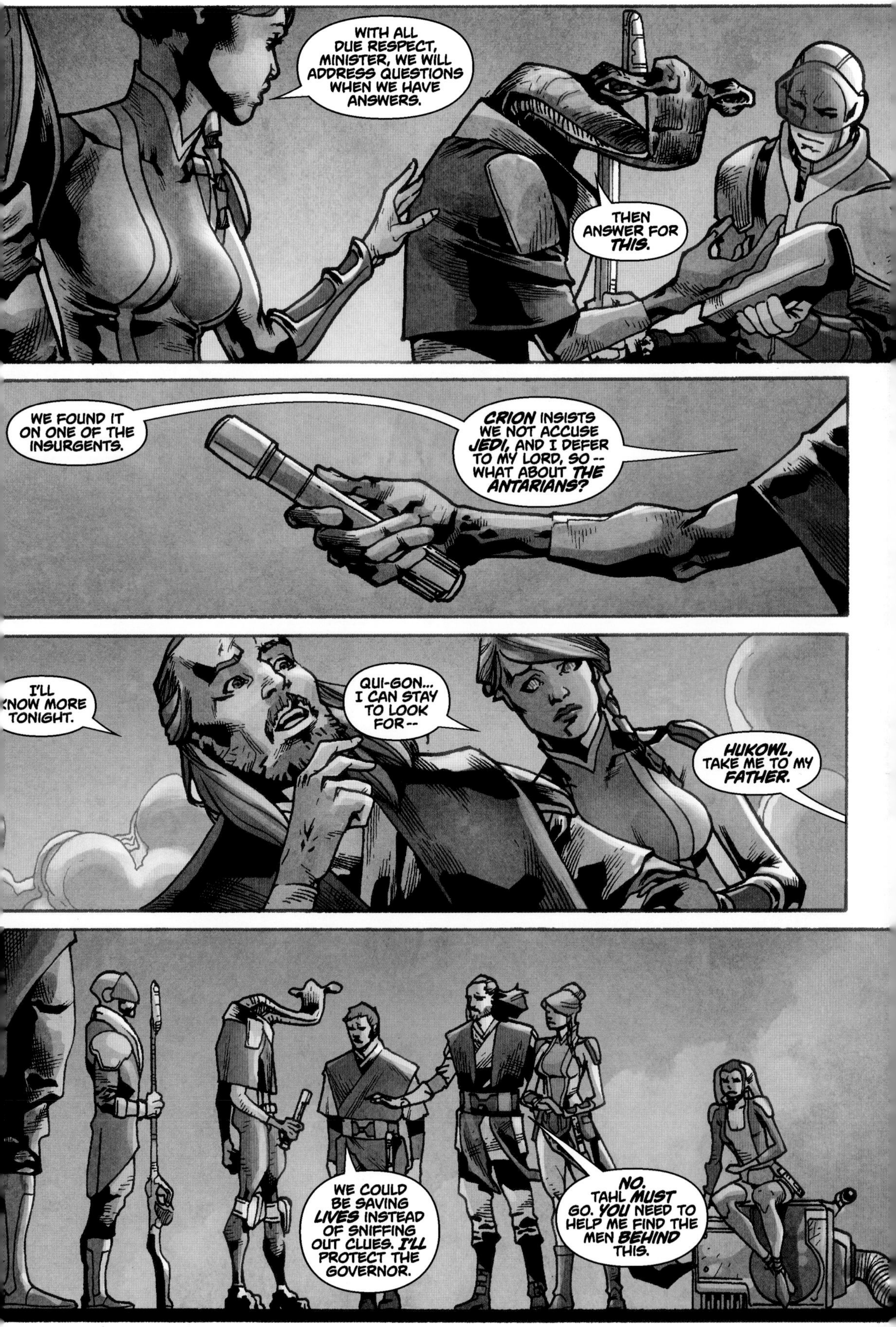
WITH ALL DUE RESPECT, MINISTER, WE WILL ADDRESS QUESTIONS WHEN WE HAVE ANSWERS.
THEN ANSWER FOR *THIS.*
WE FOUND IT ON ONE OF THE INSURGENTS.
CRION INSISTS WE NOT ACCUSE *JEDI,* AND I DEFER TO MY LORD, SO -- WHAT ABOUT *THE ANTARIANS?*
I'LL KNOW MORE TONIGHT.
QUI-GON... I CAN STAY TO LOOK FOR --
HUKOWL, TAKE ME TO MY *FATHER.*
WE COULD BE SAVING *LIVES* INSTEAD OF SNIFFING OUT CLUES. *I'LL* PROTECT THE GOVERNOR.
NO. TAHL *MUST* GO. *YOU* NEED TO HELP ME FIND THE MEN *BEHIND* THIS.

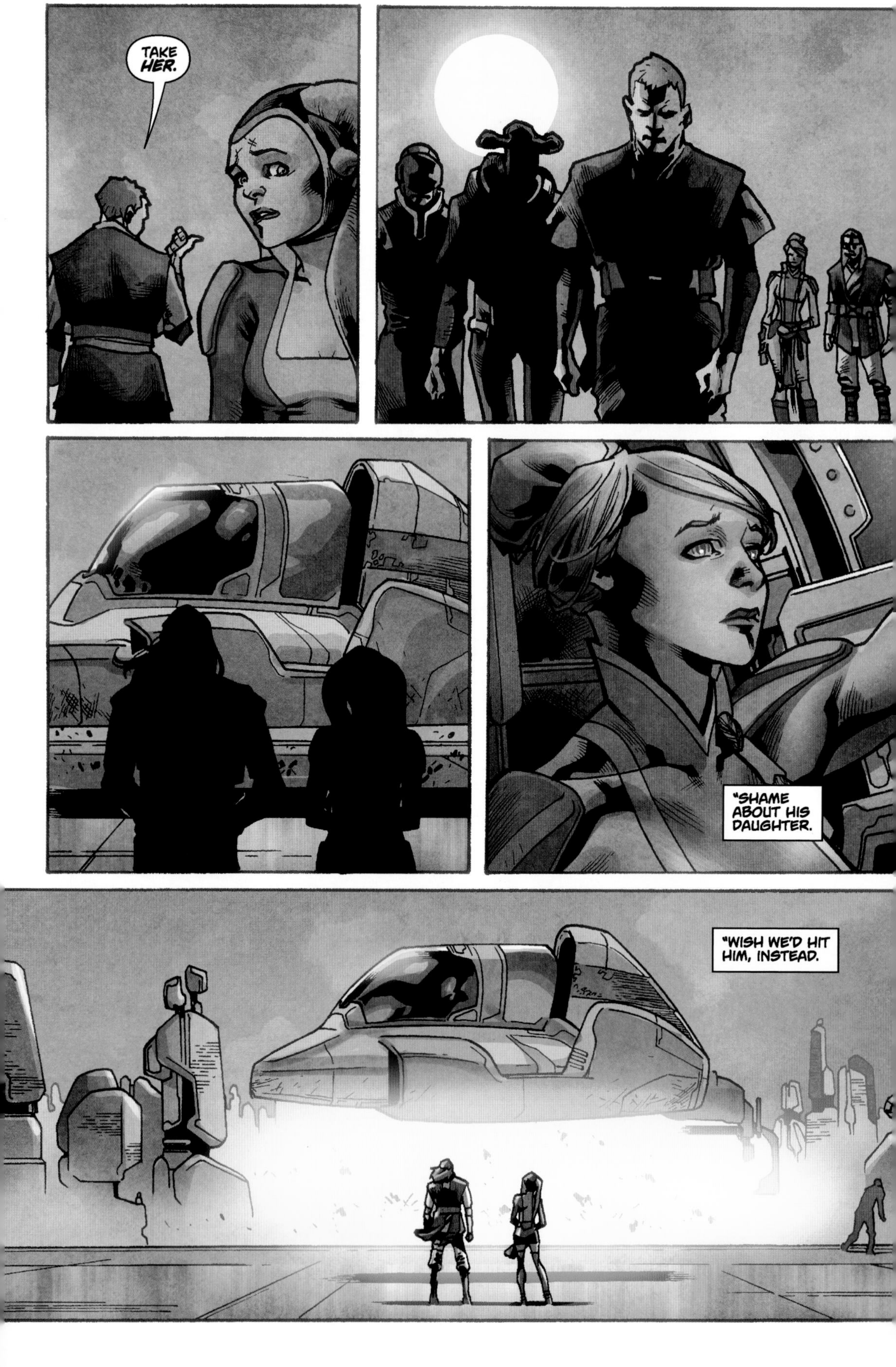
TAKE HER.
"SHAME ABOUT HIS DAUGHTER.
"WISH WE'D HIT HIM, INSTEAD.

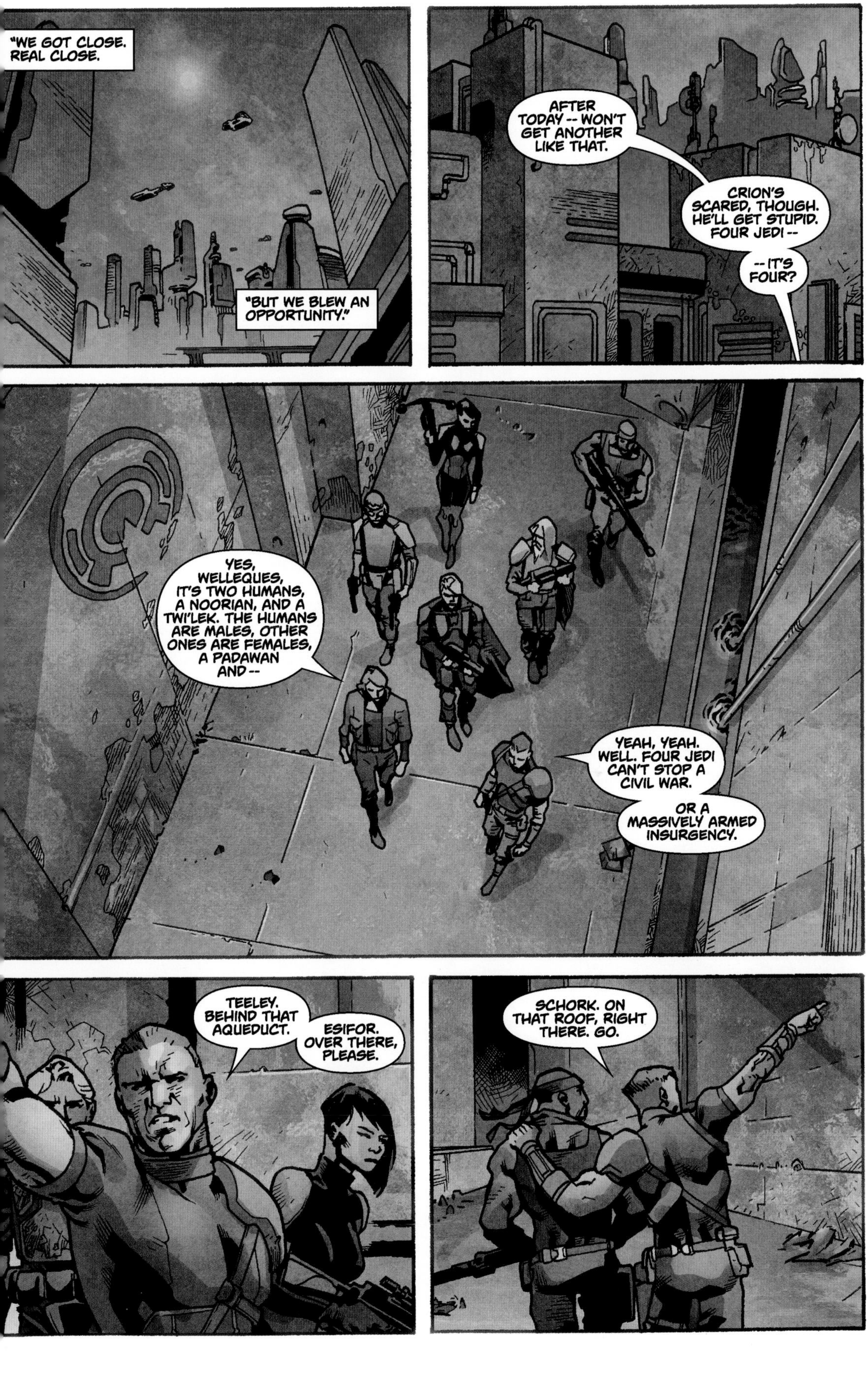
"WE GOT CLOSE. REAL CLOSE.
"BUT WE BLEW AN OPPORTUNITY."
AFTER TODAY -- WON'T GET ANOTHER LIKE THAT.
CRION'S SCARED, THOUGH. HE'LL GET STUPID. FOUR JEDI --
-- IT'S FOUR?
YES, WELLEQUES, IT'S TWO HUMANS, A NOORIAN, AND A TWI'LEK. THE HUMANS ARE MALES, OTHER ONES ARE FEMALES, A PADAWAN AND --
YEAH, YEAH. WELL. FOUR JEDI CAN'T STOP A CIVIL WAR.
OR A MASSIVELY ARMED INSURGENCY.
TEELEY. BEHIND THAT AQUEDUCT.
ESIFOR. OVER THERE, PLEASE.
SCHORK. ON THAT ROOF, RIGHT THERE. GO.

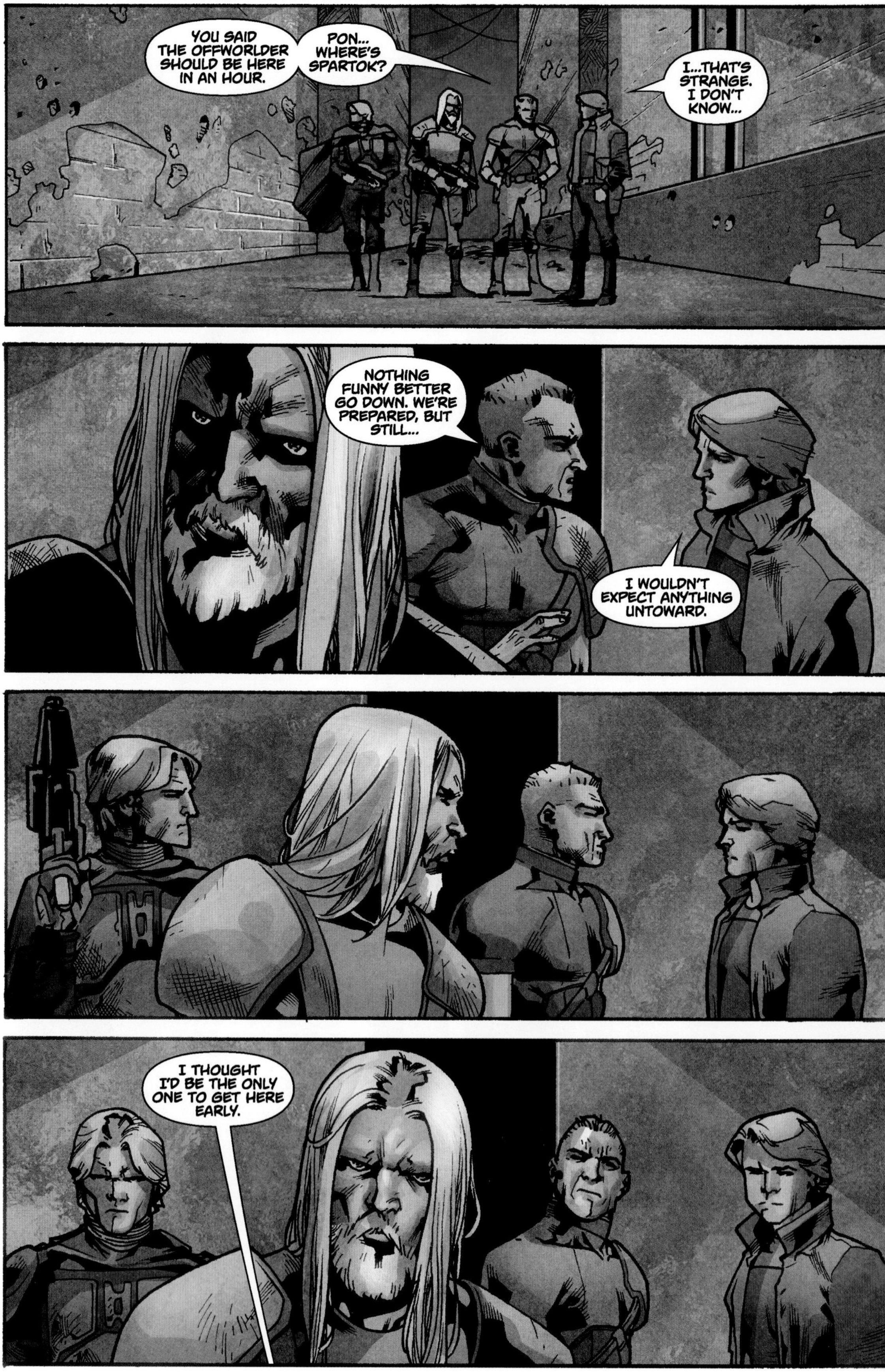

YOU SAID THE OFFWORLDER SHOULD BE HERE IN AN HOUR.
PON... WHERE'S SPARTOK?
I...THAT'S STRANGE. I DON'T KNOW...
NOTHING FUNNY BETTER GO DOWN. WE'RE PREPARED, BUT STILL...
I WOULDN'T EXPECT ANYTHING UNTOWARD.
I THOUGHT I'D BE THE ONLY ONE TO GET HERE EARLY.

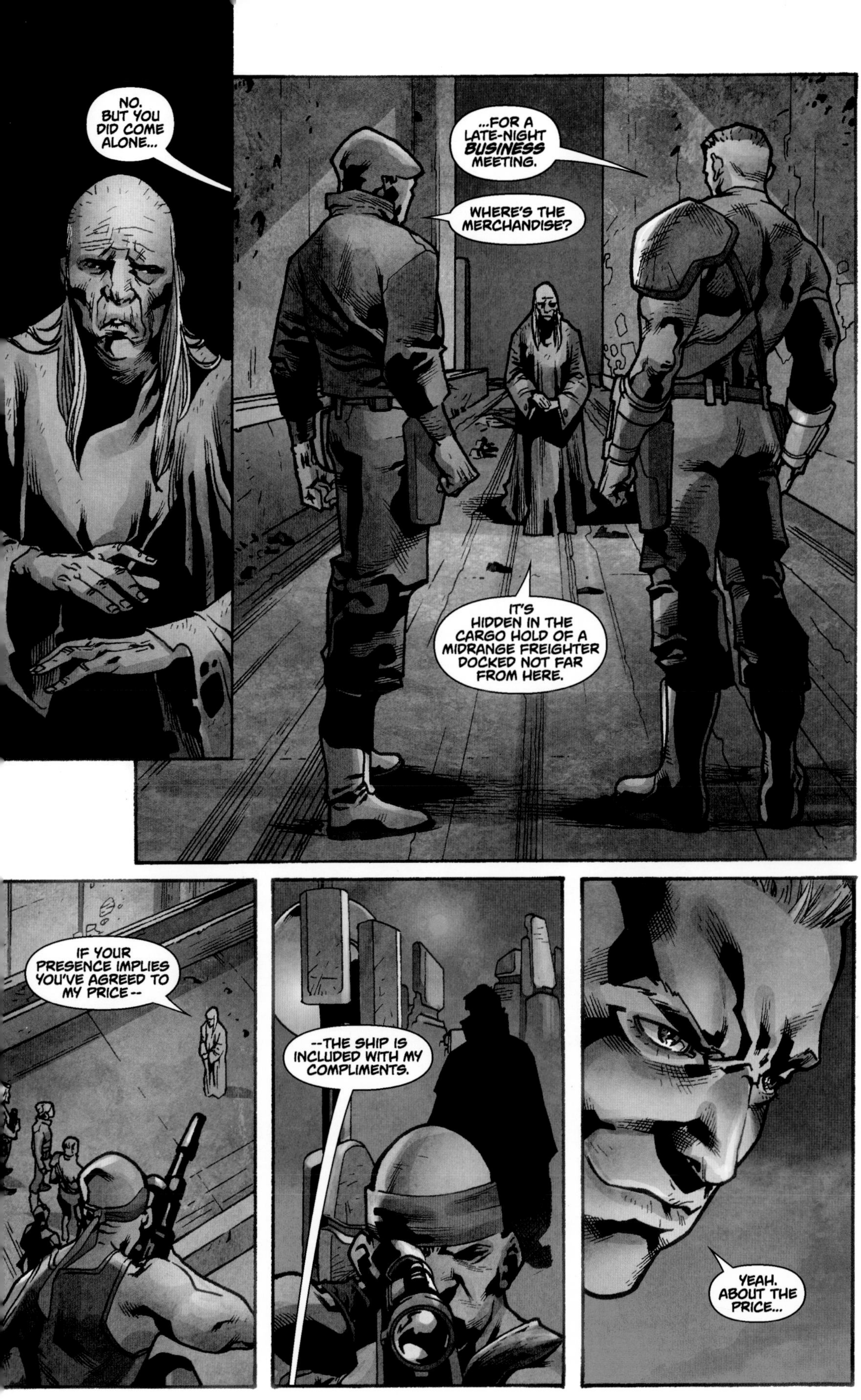
NO. BUT YOU DID COME ALONE...
...FOR A LATE-NIGHT BUSINESS MEETING.
WHERE'S THE MERCHANDISE?
IT'S HIDDEN IN THE CARGO HOLD OF A MIDRANGE FREIGHTER DOCKED NOT FAR FROM HERE.
IF YOUR PRESENCE IMPLIES YOU'VE AGREED TO MY PRICE --
--THE SHIP IS INCLUDED WITH MY COMPLIMENTS.
YEAH. ABOUT THE PRICE...

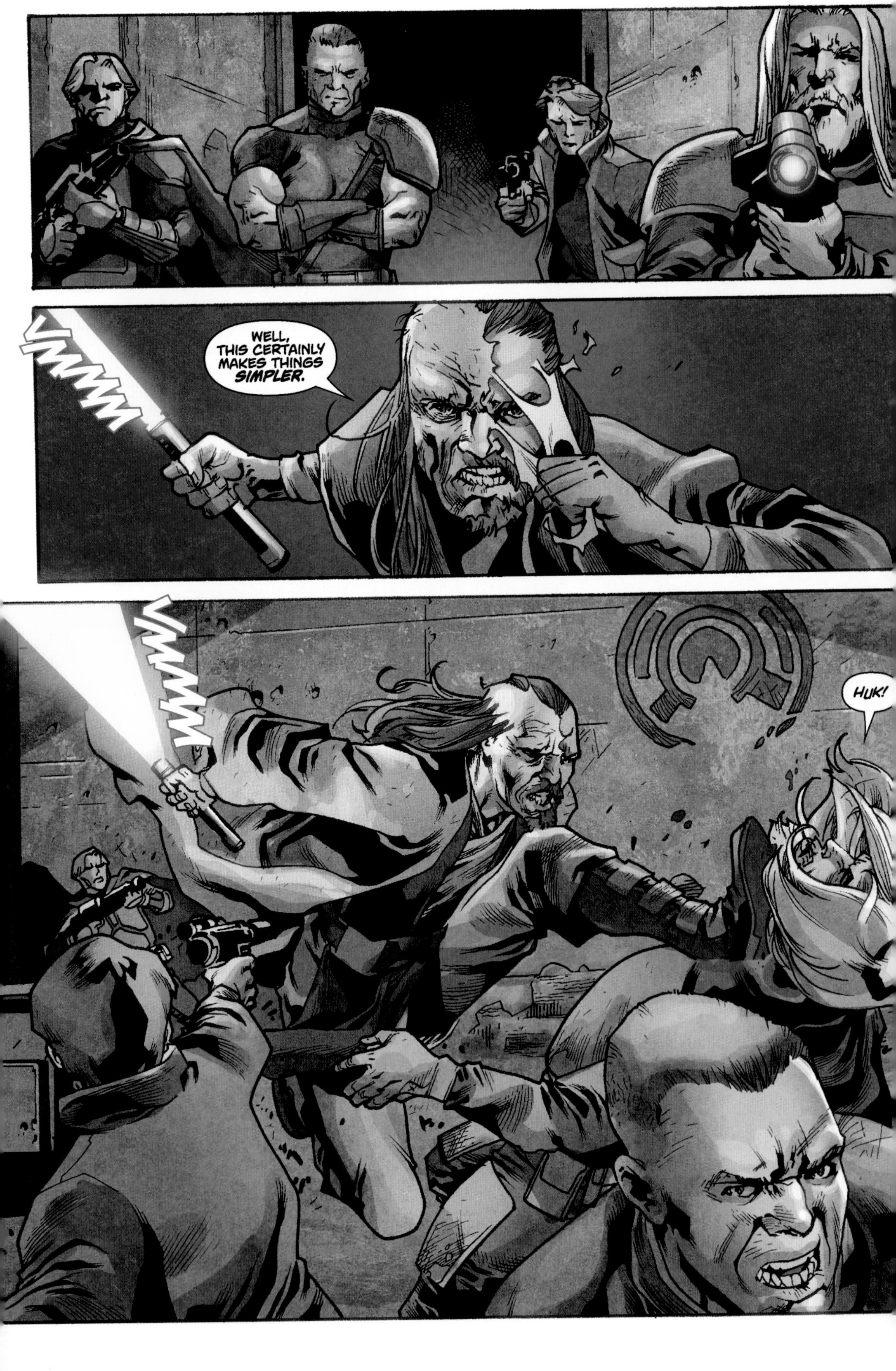

WELL, THIS CERTAINLY MAKES THINGS SIMPLER.
VMMMM
VMMMM
HUK!

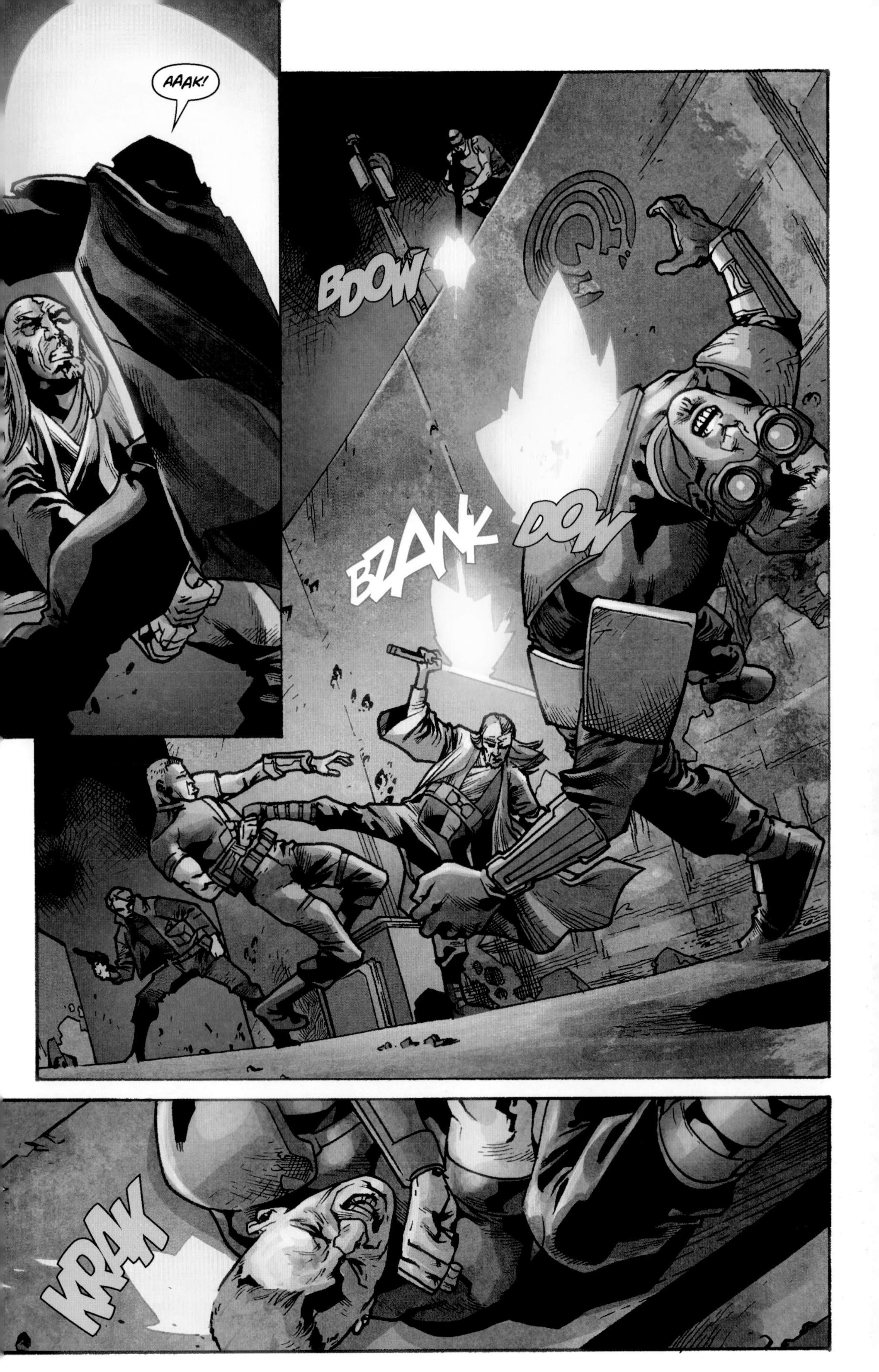
AAAK!
BDOW
BZANK
DOW
KRAK

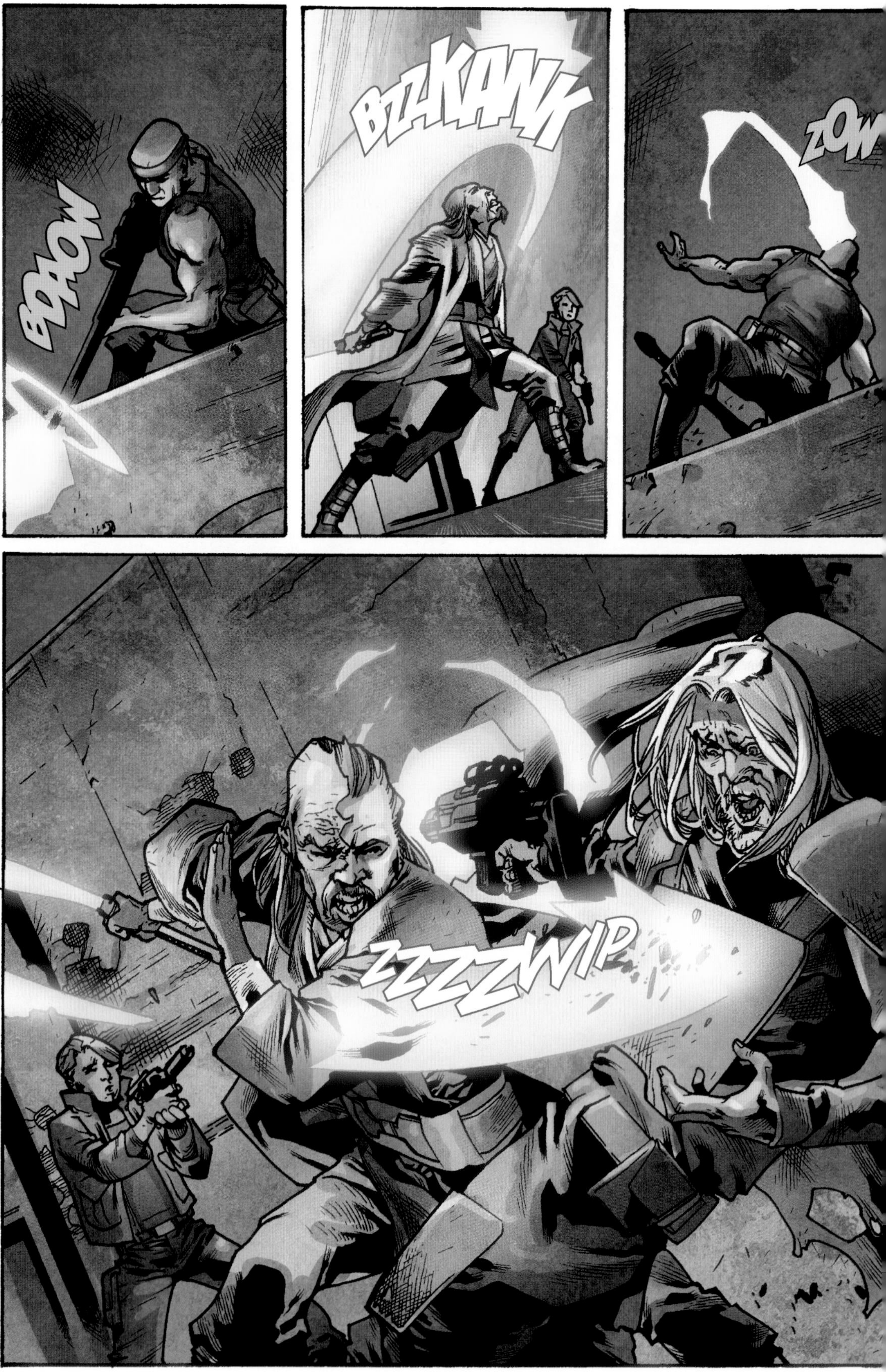
BRAOW
BZZKANK
ZOW
ZZZZWIP

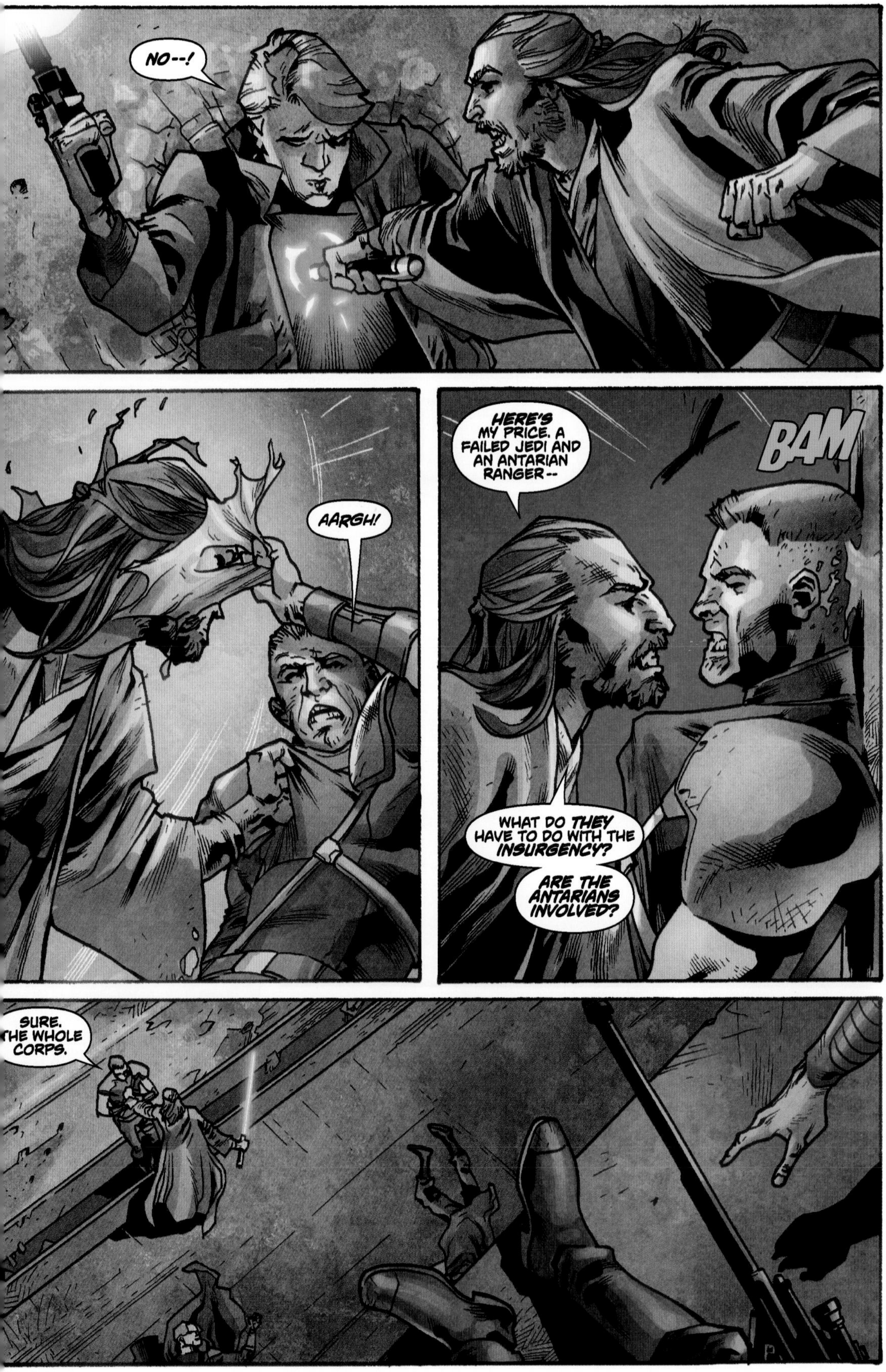
NO--!
AARGH!
HERE'S MY PRICE. A FAILED JEDI AND AN ANTARIAN RANGER--
BAM
WHAT DO THEY HAVE TO DO WITH THE INSURGENCY?
ARE THE ANTARIANS INVOLVED?
SURE. THE WHOLE CORPS.

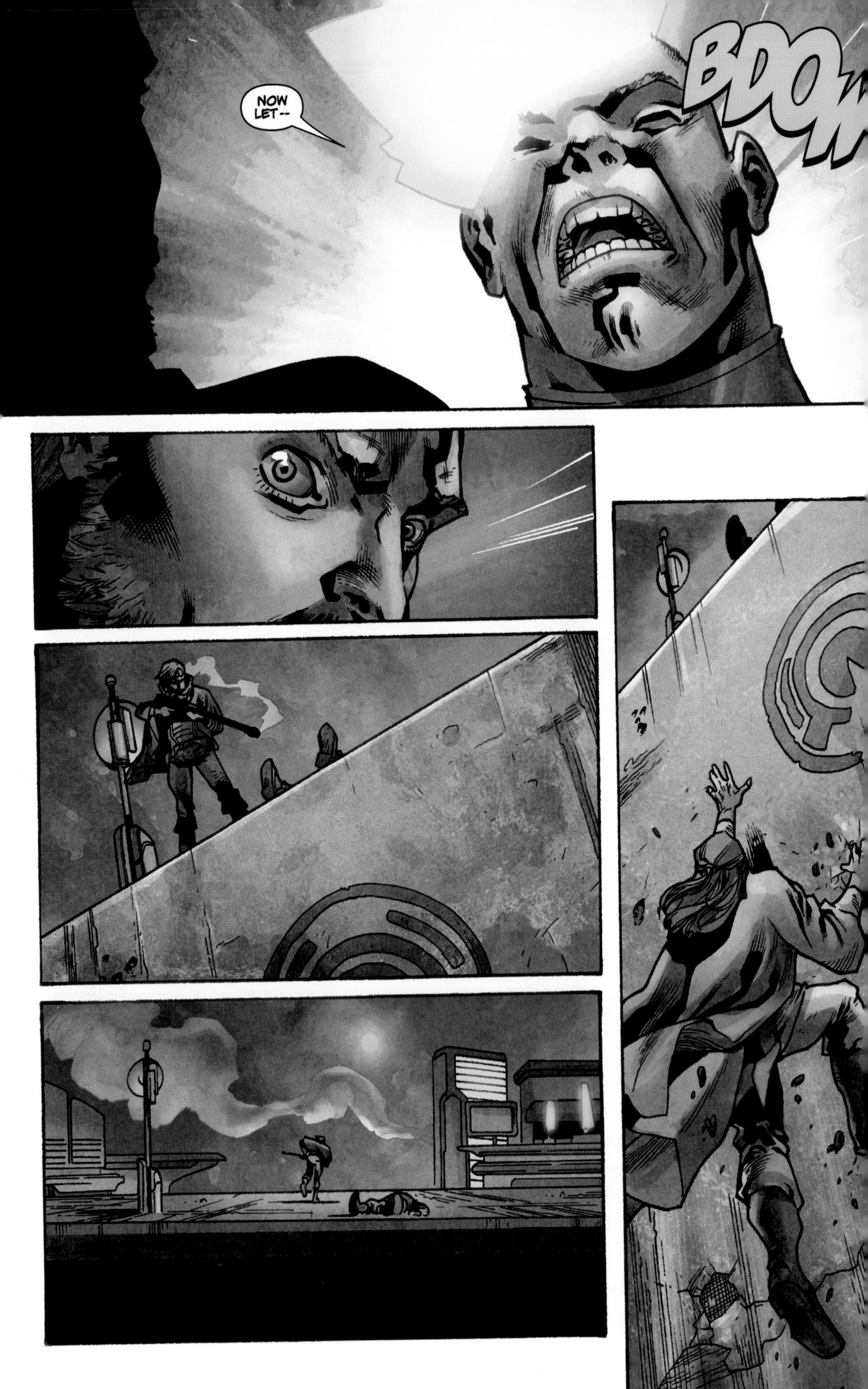
NOW LET--
BDOW

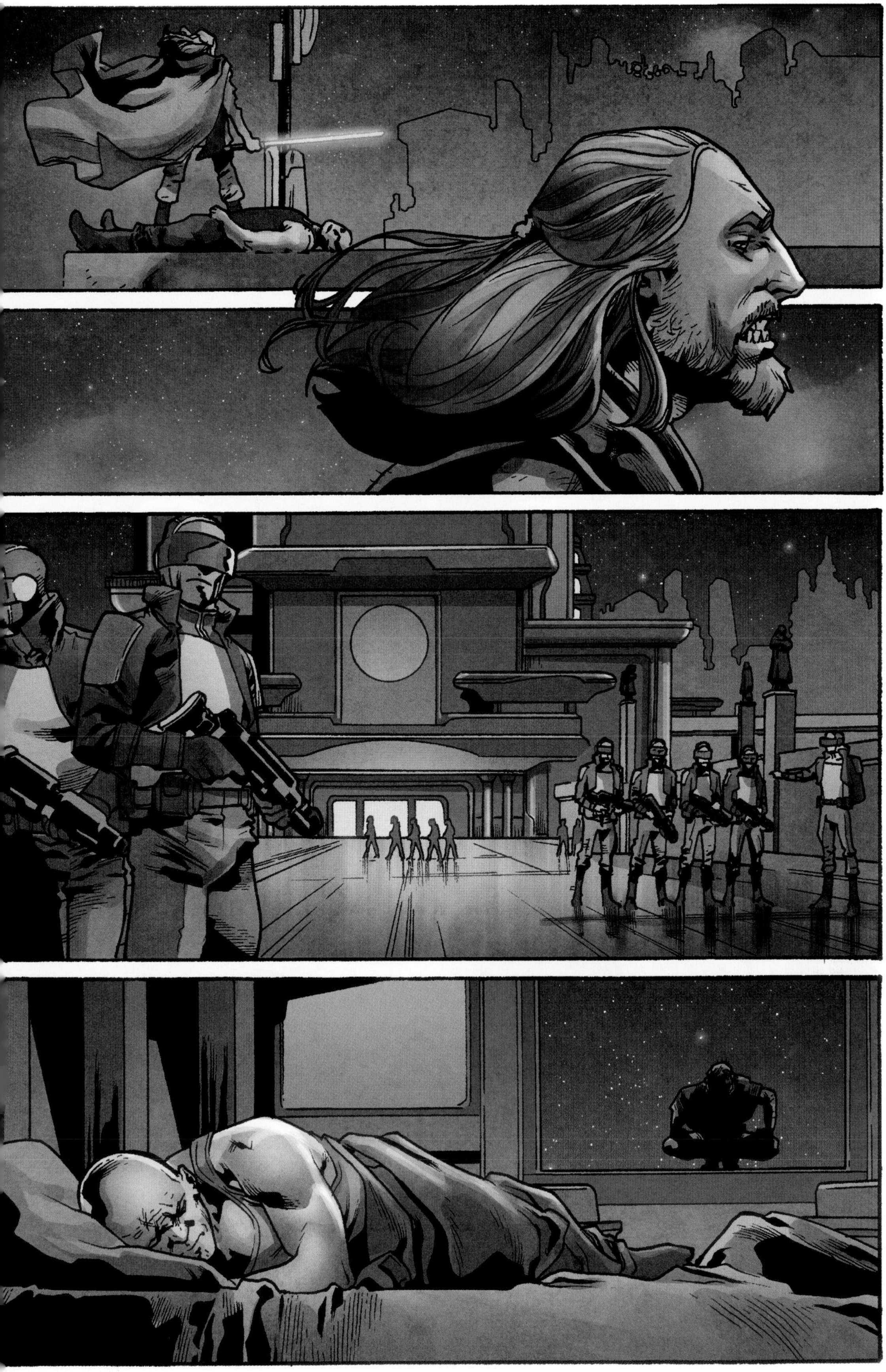

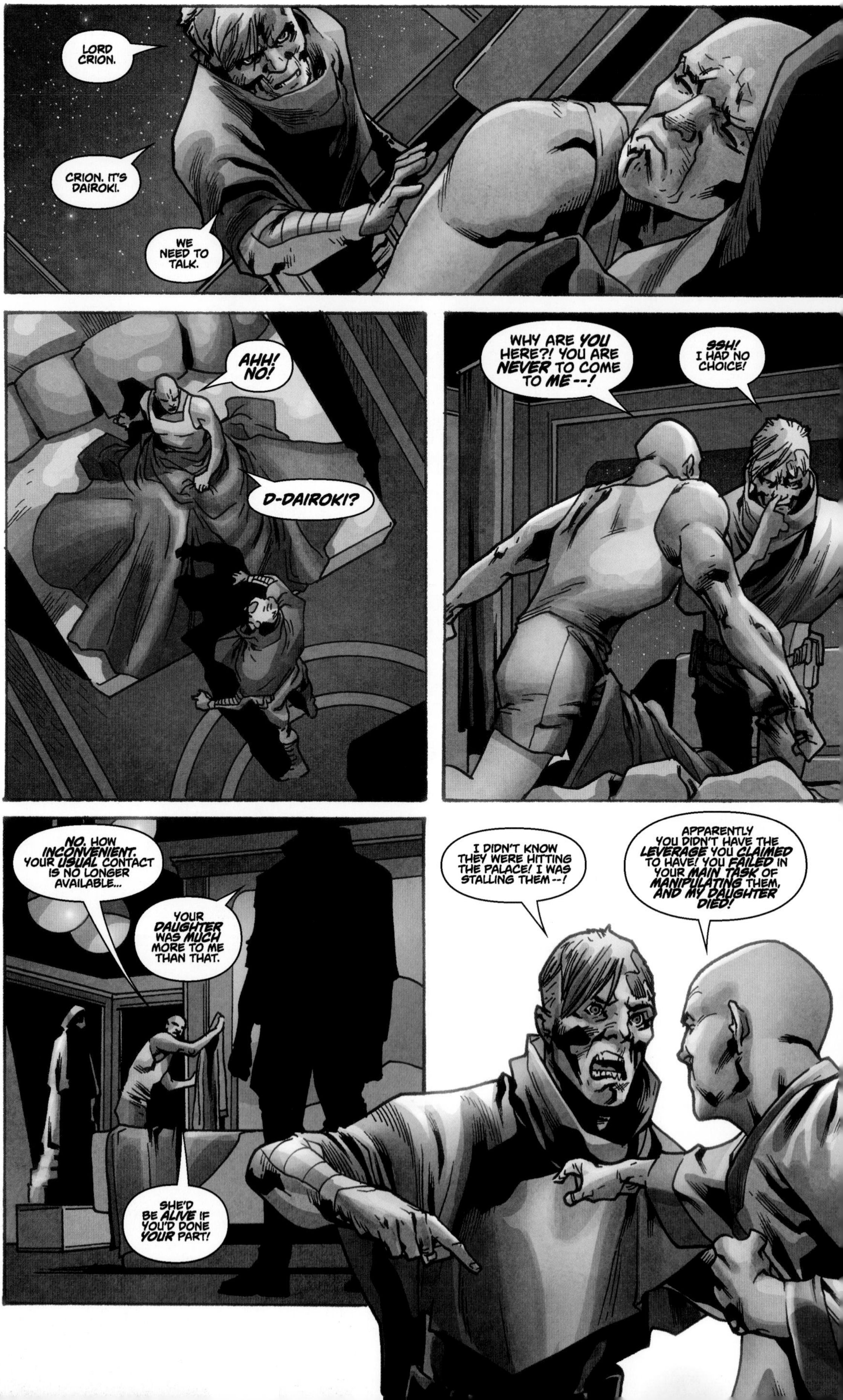
LORD CRION.
CRION. IT'S DAIROKI.
WE NEED TO TALK.
AHH! NO!
D-DAIROKI?
WHY ARE YOU HERE?! YOU ARE NEVER TO COME TO ME--!
SSH! I HAD NO CHOICE!
NO. HOW INCONVENIENT. YOUR USUAL CONTACT IS NO LONGER AVAILABLE...
YOUR DAUGHTER WAS MUCH MORE TO ME THAN THAT.
SHE'D BE ALIVE IF YOU'D DONE YOUR PART!
I DIDN'T KNOW THEY WERE HITTING THE PALACE! I WAS STALLING THEM--!
APPARENTLY YOU DIDN'T HAVE THE LEVERAGE YOU CLAIMED TO HAVE! YOU FAILED IN YOUR MAIN TASK OF MANIPULATING THEM, AND MY DAUGHTER DIED!

"LORD CRION. I CANNOT TELL YOU HOW SORRY I AM ABOUT NASON. I ONLY WANT TO SEE THIS THROUGH NOW."

WE FOUND A LIGHTSABER ON AN INSURGENT.

I DIDN'T THINK IT WOULD COME UP UNTIL LATER -- BUT I GAVE IT TO THEM SO IT WOULD BE FOUND.

IT'S *GOT* TO CONVINCE EVERYONE THAT THE ANTARIAN RANGERS ARE INVOLVED.

UNLESS THEY SAW *YOU.*

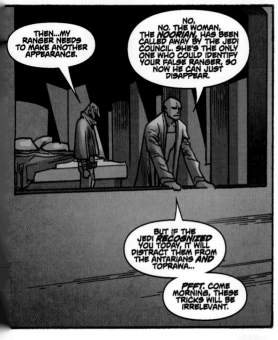

THEN...MY RANGER NEEDS TO MAKE ANOTHER APPEARANCE.

NO. NO, THE WOMAN, THE *NOORIAN,* HAS BEEN CALLED AWAY BY THE JEDI COUNCIL. SHE'S THE ONLY ONE WHO COULD IDENTIFY YOUR FALSE RANGER, SO NOW HE CAN JUST DISAPPEAR.

BUT IF THE JEDI *RECOGNIZED* YOU TODAY, IT WILL DISTRACT THEM FROM THE ANTARIANS *AND* TOPRAWA...

PFFT. COME MORNING, THESE TRICKS WILL BE IRRELEVANT.

BUT BY SHOWING YOURSELF, YOU JEOPARDIZED *EVERYTHING.*

YOU MUST GET OFFWORLD IMMEDIATELY.

MY LORD, WE STILL NEED TO --

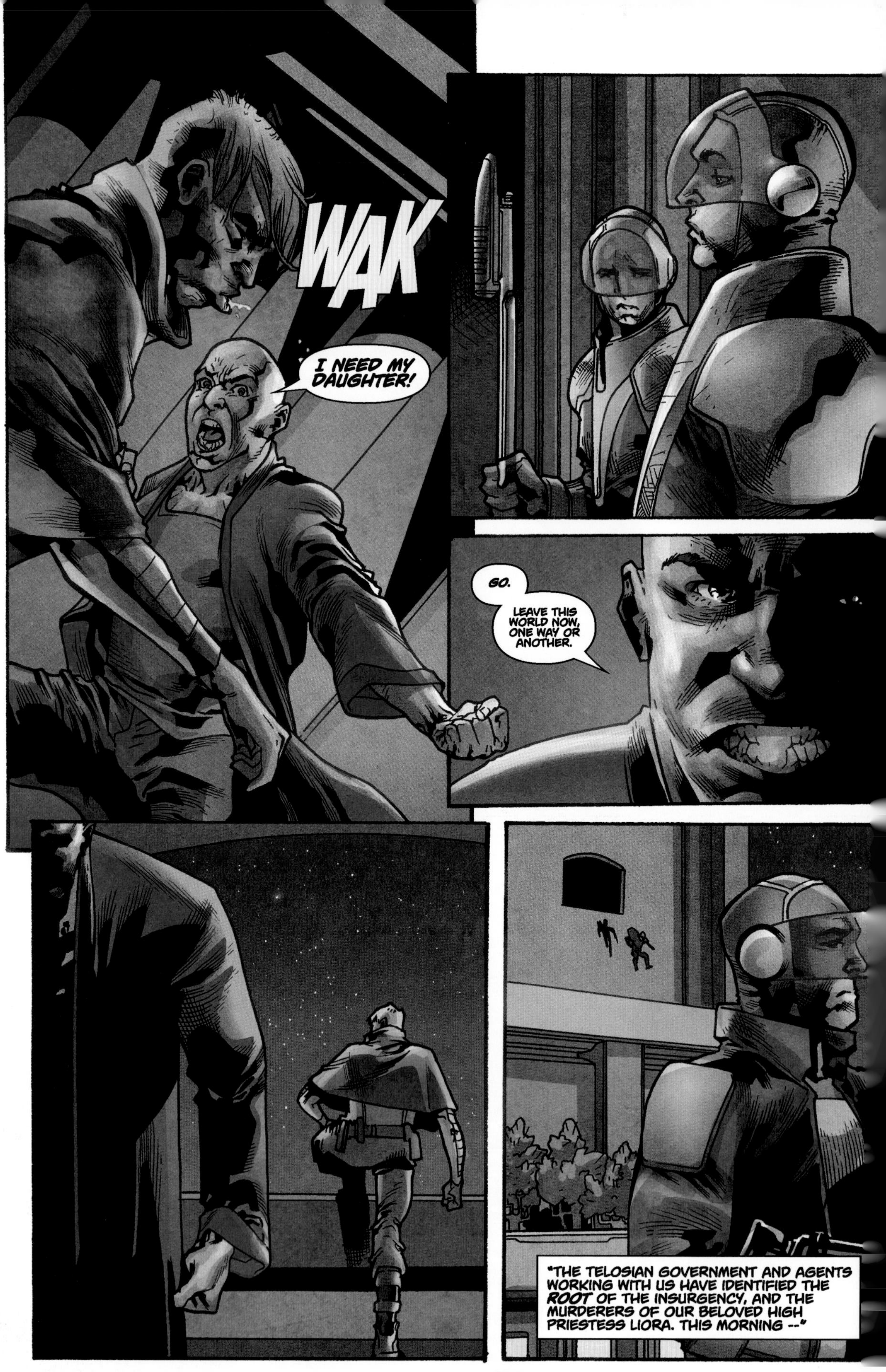
WAK
I NEED MY DAUGHTER!
GO.
LEAVE THIS WORLD NOW, ONE WAY OR ANOTHER.
"THE TELOSIAN GOVERNMENT AND AGENTS WORKING WITH US HAVE IDENTIFIED THE *ROOT* OF THE INSURGENCY, AND THE MURDERERS OF OUR BELOVED HIGH PRIESTESS LIORA. THIS MORNING --"

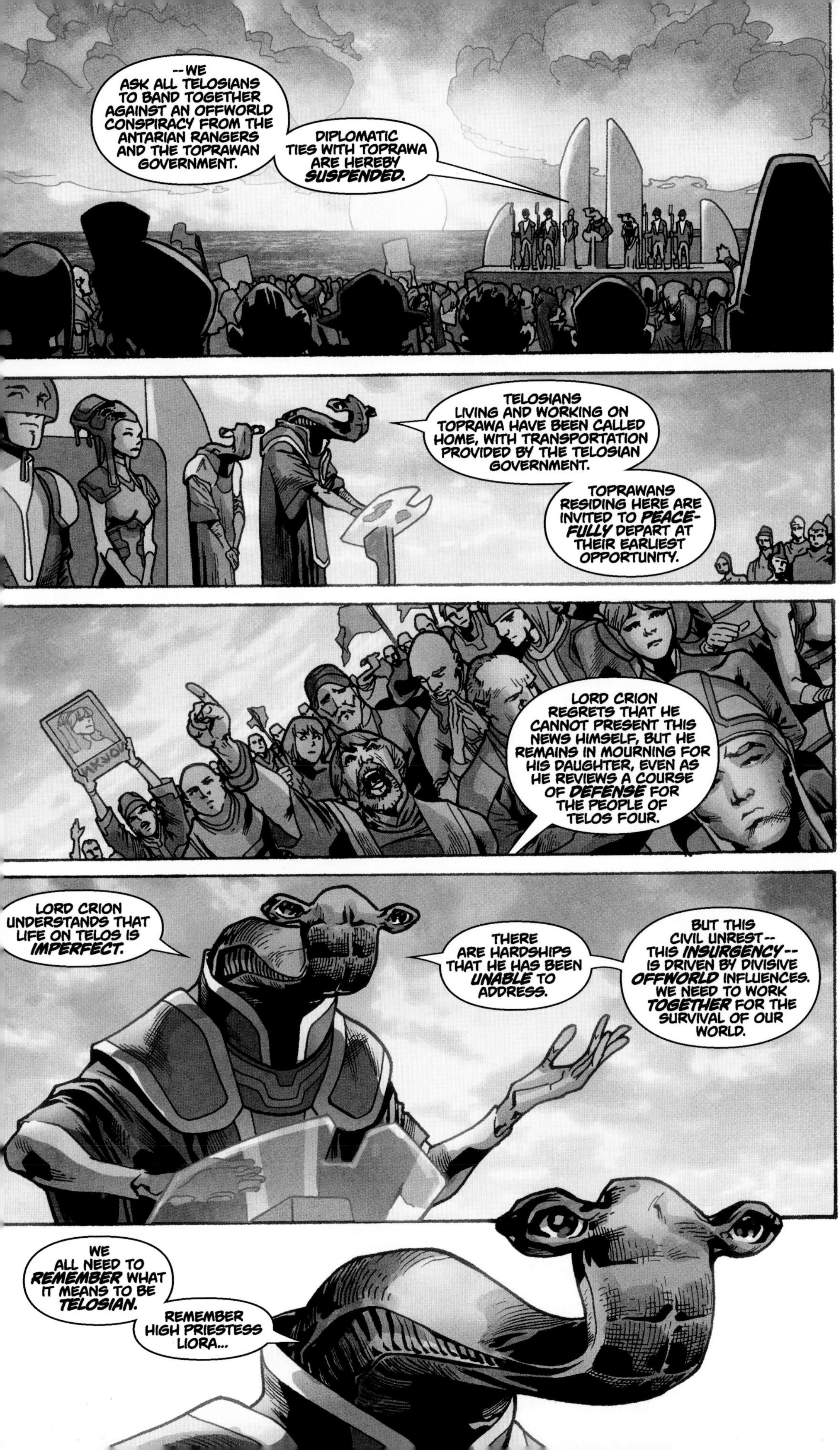
--WE ASK ALL TELOSIANS TO BAND TOGETHER AGAINST AN OFFWORLD CONSPIRACY FROM THE ANTARIAN RANGERS AND THE TOPRAWAN GOVERNMENT.
DIPLOMATIC TIES WITH TOPRAWA ARE HEREBY SUSPENDED.
TELOSIANS LIVING AND WORKING ON TOPRAWA HAVE BEEN CALLED HOME, WITH TRANSPORTATION PROVIDED BY THE TELOSIAN GOVERNMENT.
TOPRAWANS RESIDING HERE ARE INVITED TO PEACE-FULLY DEPART AT THEIR EARLIEST OPPORTUNITY.
LORD CRION REGRETS THAT HE CANNOT PRESENT THIS NEWS HIMSELF, BUT HE REMAINS IN MOURNING FOR HIS DAUGHTER, EVEN AS HE REVIEWS A COURSE OF DEFENSE FOR THE PEOPLE OF TELOS FOUR.
LORD CRION UNDERSTANDS THAT LIFE ON TELOS IS IMPERFECT.
THERE ARE HARDSHIPS THAT HE HAS BEEN UNABLE TO ADDRESS.
BUT THIS CIVIL UNREST-- THIS INSURGENCY-- IS DRIVEN BY DIVISIVE OFFWORLD INFLUENCES. WE NEED TO WORK TOGETHER FOR THE SURVIVAL OF OUR WORLD.
WE ALL NEED TO REMEMBER WHAT IT MEANS TO BE TELOSIAN.
REMEMBER HIGH PRIESTESS LIORA...

"...AND REMEMBER LORD CRION'S FALLEN DAUGHTER."

YOU'RE NOT WITH YOUR FATHER.

HE'S SURROUNDED BY HIS MOST LOYAL MILITARY LEADERS. HE'S SAFE.

BUT I SUPPOSE HE THOUGHT THAT YESTERDAY.

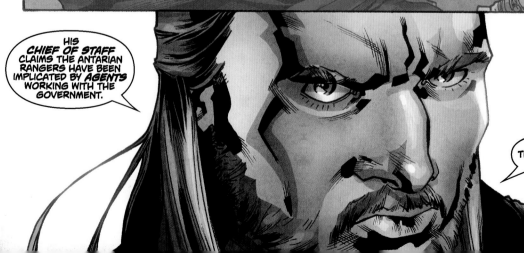

HIS *CHIEF OF STAFF* CLAIMS THE ANTARIAN RANGERS HAVE BEEN IMPLICATED BY *AGENTS* WORKING WITH THE GOVERNMENT.

ARE *WE* THOSE AGEN' XANATOS?

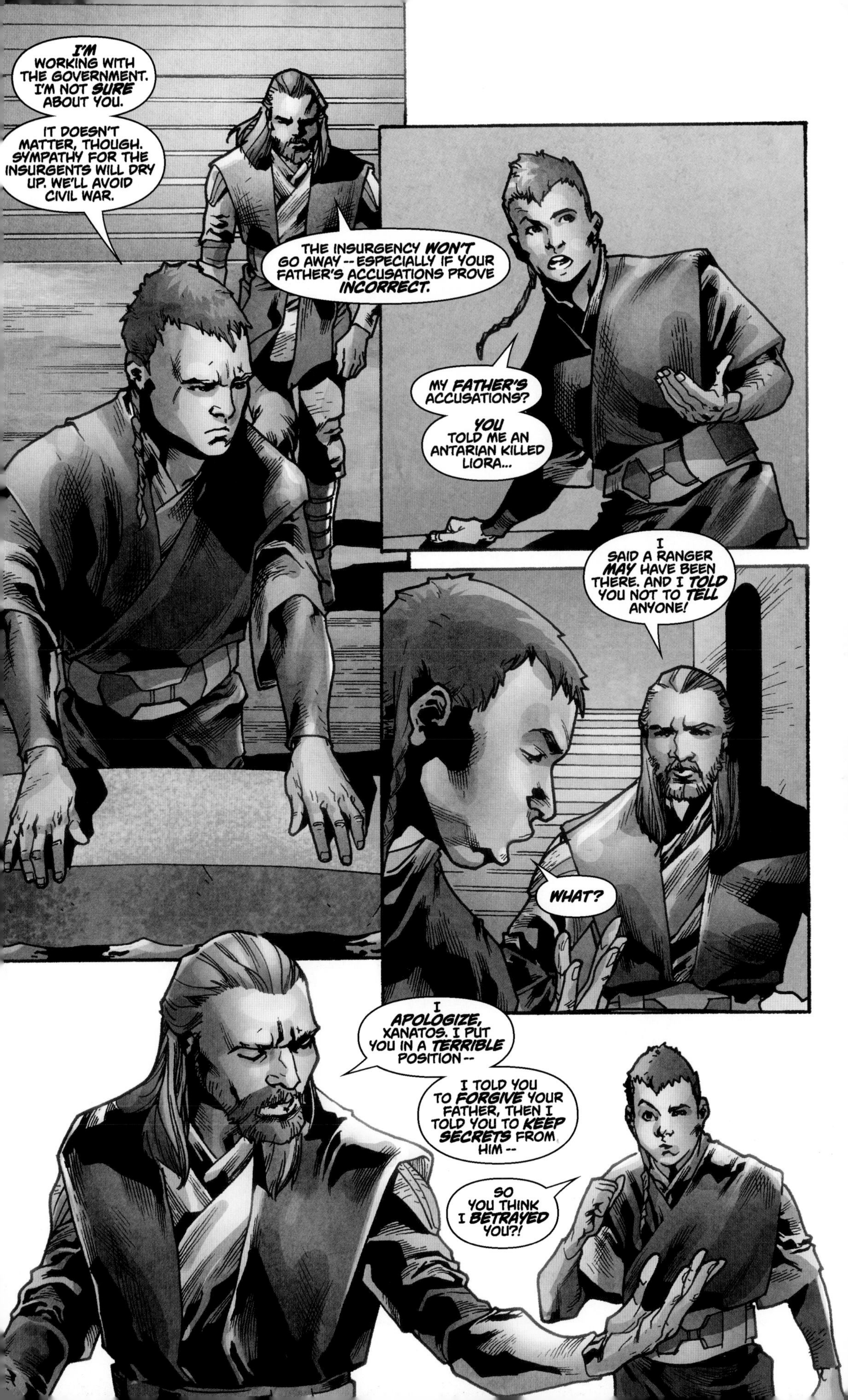
I'M WORKING WITH THE GOVERNMENT. I'M NOT SURE ABOUT YOU.
IT DOESN'T MATTER, THOUGH. SYMPATHY FOR THE INSURGENTS WILL DRY UP. WE'LL AVOID CIVIL WAR.
THE INSURGENCY WON'T GO AWAY -- ESPECIALLY IF YOUR FATHER'S ACCUSATIONS PROVE INCORRECT.
MY FATHER'S ACCUSATIONS?
YOU TOLD ME AN ANTARIAN KILLED LIORA...
I SAID A RANGER MAY HAVE BEEN THERE. AND I TOLD YOU NOT TO TELL ANYONE!
WHAT?
I APOLOGIZE, XANATOS. I PUT YOU IN A TERRIBLE POSITION --
I TOLD YOU TO FORGIVE YOUR FATHER, THEN I TOLD YOU TO KEEP SECRETS FROM HIM --
SO YOU THINK I BETRAYED YOU?!

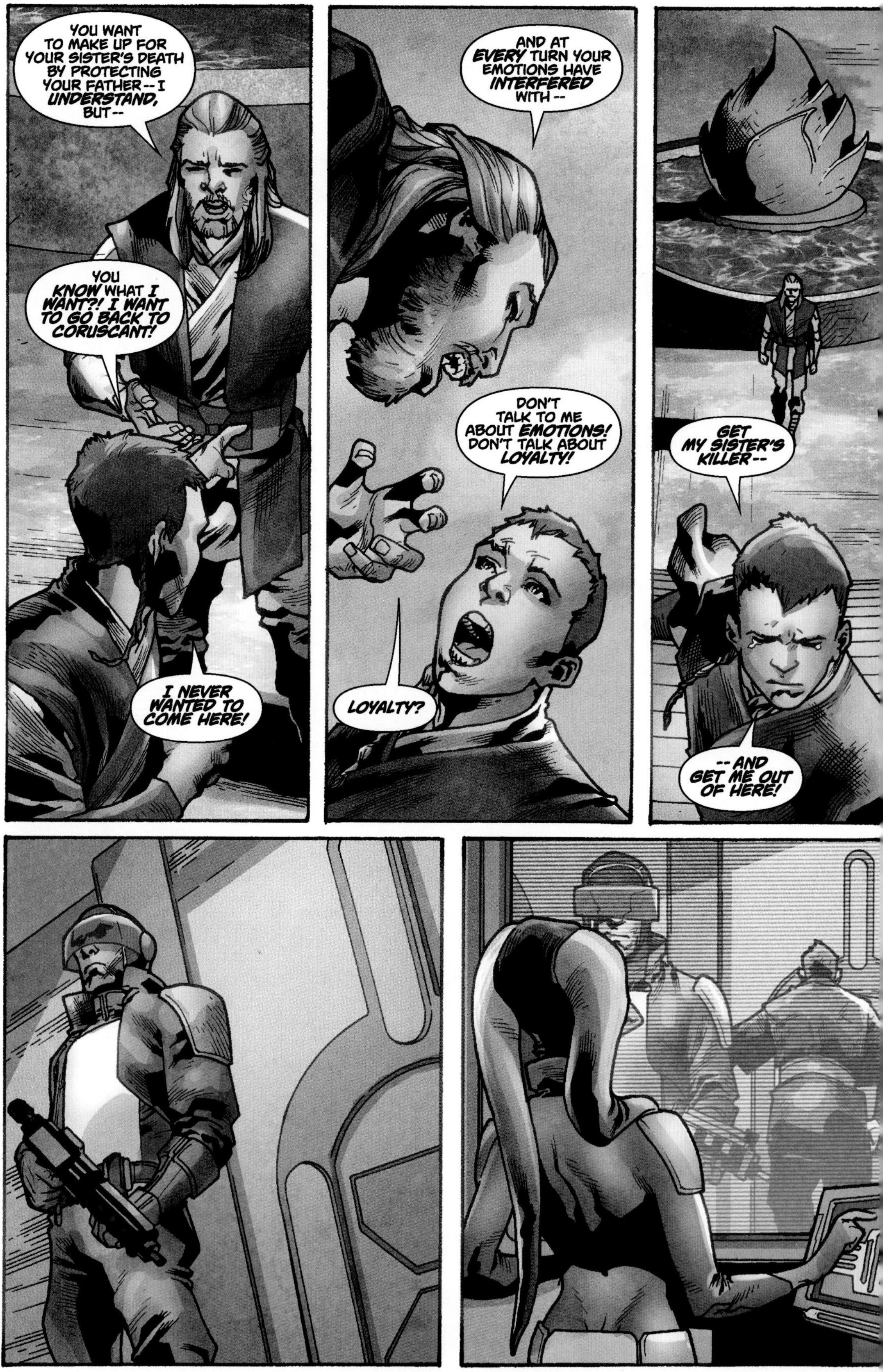
YOU WANT TO MAKE UP FOR YOUR SISTER'S DEATH BY PROTECTING YOUR FATHER -- I UNDERSTAND, BUT --
YOU KNOW WHAT I WANT?! I WANT TO GO BACK TO CORUSCANT!
I NEVER WANTED TO COME HERE!
AND AT EVERY TURN YOUR EMOTIONS HAVE INTERFERED WITH --
DON'T TALK TO ME ABOUT EMOTIONS! DON'T TALK ABOUT LOYALTY!
LOYALTY?
GET MY SISTER'S KILLER --
-- AND GET ME OUT OF HERE!

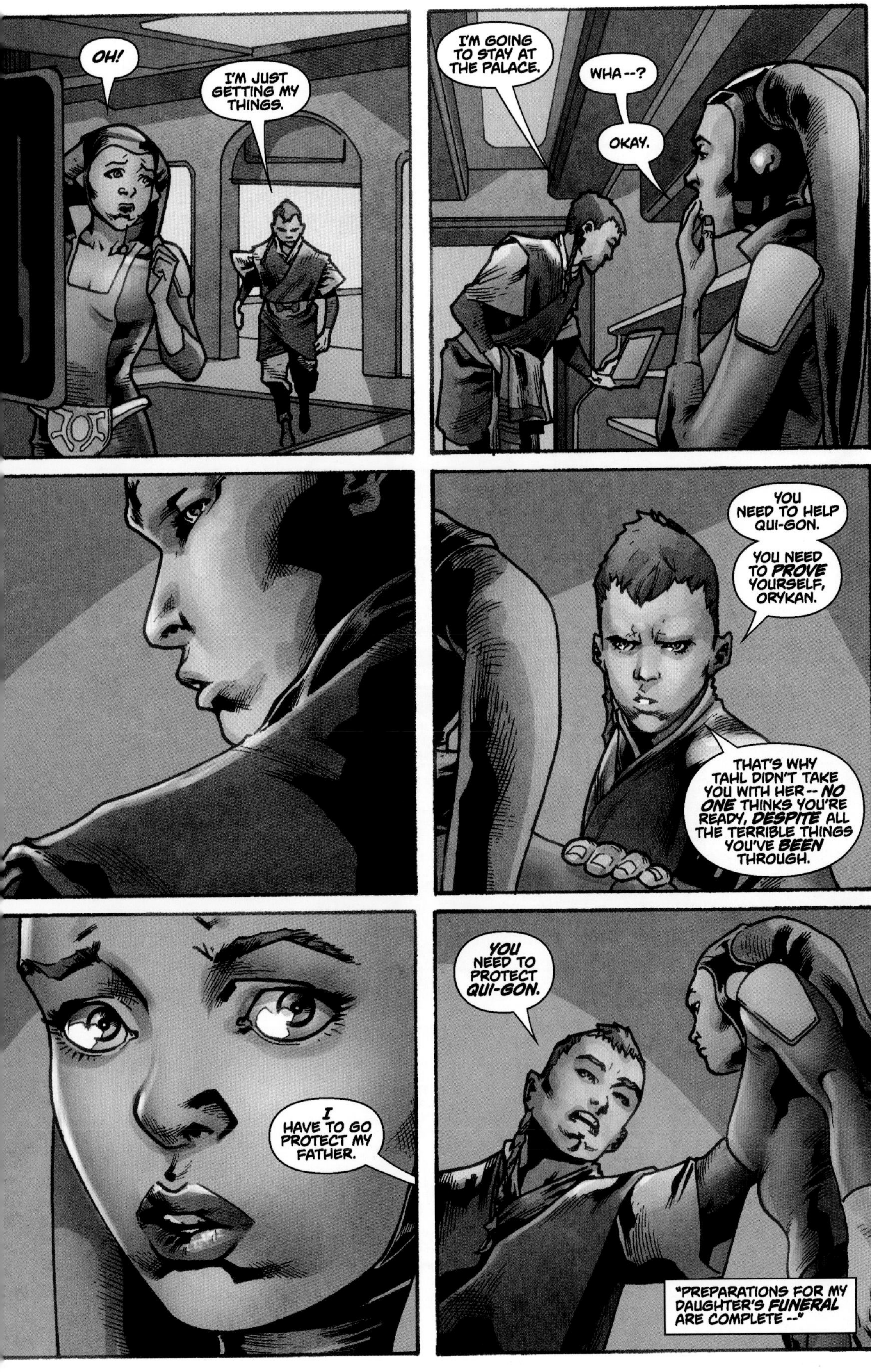

OH!
I'M JUST GETTING MY THINGS.
I'M GOING TO STAY AT THE PALACE.
WHA--?
OKAY.
YOU NEED TO HELP QUI-GON.
YOU NEED TO PROVE YOURSELF, ORYKAN.
THAT'S WHY TAHL DIDN'T TAKE YOU WITH HER--NO ONE THINKS YOU'RE READY, DESPITE ALL THE TERRIBLE THINGS YOU'VE BEEN THROUGH.
I HAVE TO GO PROTECT MY FATHER.
YOU NEED TO PROTECT QUI-GON.
"PREPARATIONS FOR MY DAUGHTER'S FUNERAL ARE COMPLETE--"

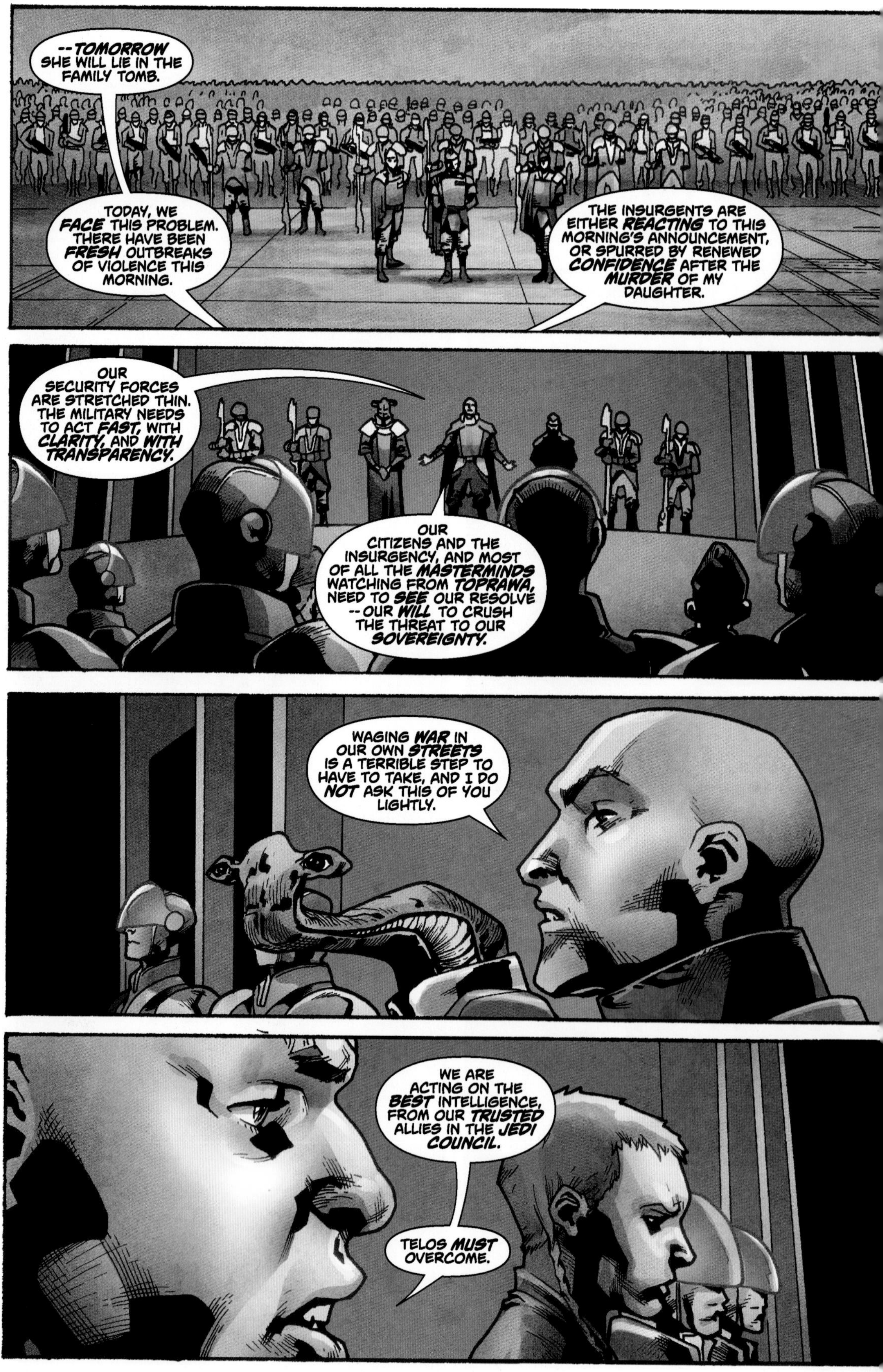
--TOMORROW SHE WILL LIE IN THE FAMILY TOMB.
TODAY, WE FACE THIS PROBLEM. THERE HAVE BEEN FRESH OUTBREAKS OF VIOLENCE THIS MORNING.
THE INSURGENTS ARE EITHER REACTING TO THIS MORNING'S ANNOUNCEMENT, OR SPURRED BY RENEWED CONFIDENCE AFTER THE MURDER OF MY DAUGHTER.
OUR SECURITY FORCES ARE STRETCHED THIN. THE MILITARY NEEDS TO ACT FAST, WITH CLARITY, AND WITH TRANSPARENCY.
OUR CITIZENS AND THE INSURGENCY, AND MOST OF ALL THE MASTERMINDS WATCHING FROM TOPRAWA, NEED TO SEE OUR RESOLVE --OUR WILL TO CRUSH THE THREAT TO OUR SOVEREIGNTY.
WAGING WAR IN OUR OWN STREETS IS A TERRIBLE STEP TO HAVE TO TAKE, AND I DO NOT ASK THIS OF YOU LIGHTLY.
WE ARE ACTING ON THE BEST INTELLIGENCE, FROM OUR TRUSTED ALLIES IN THE JEDI COUNCIL.
TELOS MUST OVERCOME.

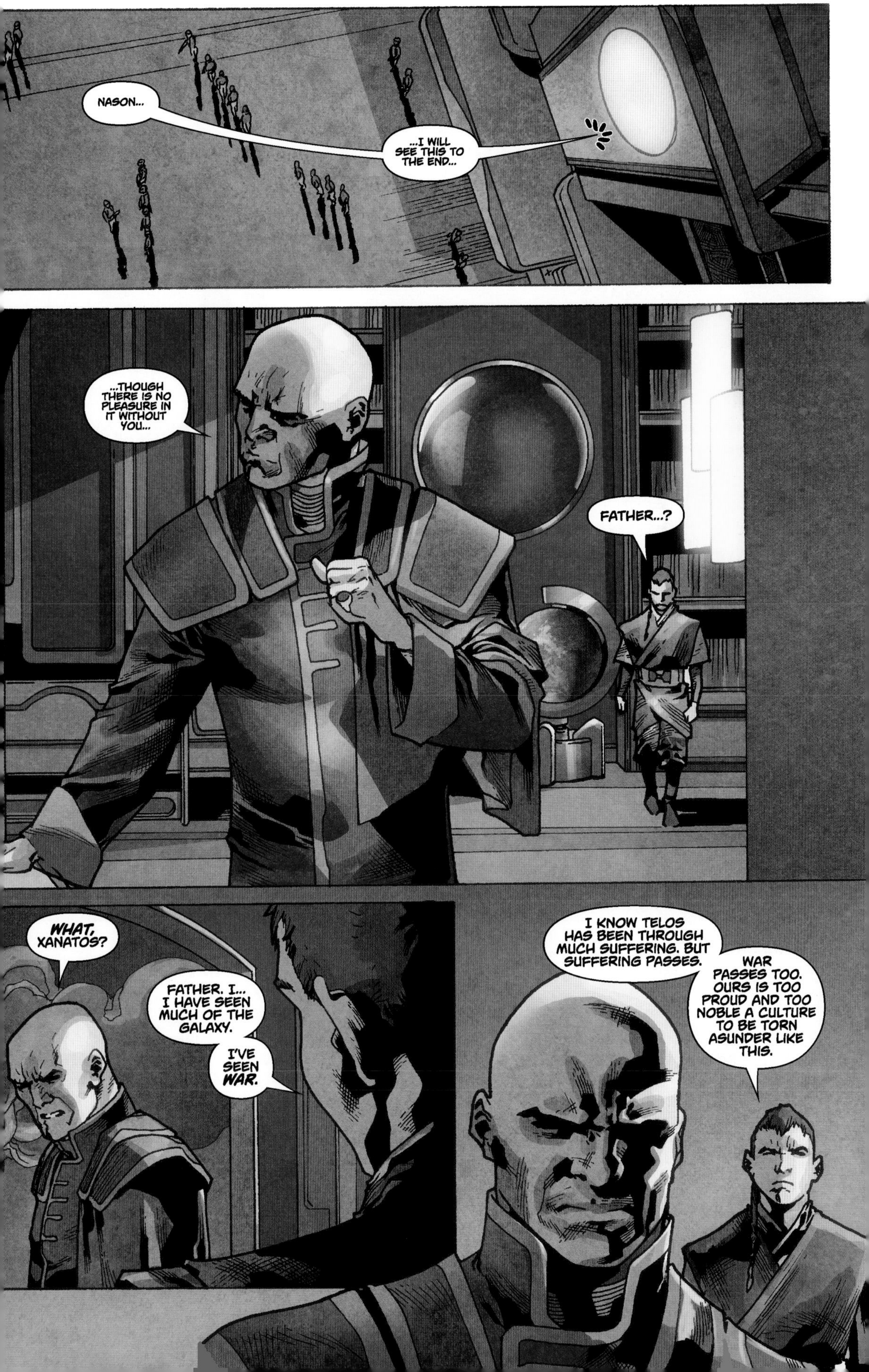
NASON...
...I WILL SEE THIS TO THE END...
...THOUGH THERE IS NO PLEASURE IN IT WITHOUT YOU...
FATHER...?
WHAT, XANATOS?
FATHER. I... I HAVE SEEN MUCH OF THE GALAXY.
I'VE SEEN WAR.
I KNOW TELOS HAS BEEN THROUGH MUCH SUFFERING. BUT SUFFERING PASSES.
WAR PASSES TOO. OURS IS TOO PROUD AND TOO NOBLE A CULTURE TO BE TORN ASUNDER LIKE THIS.

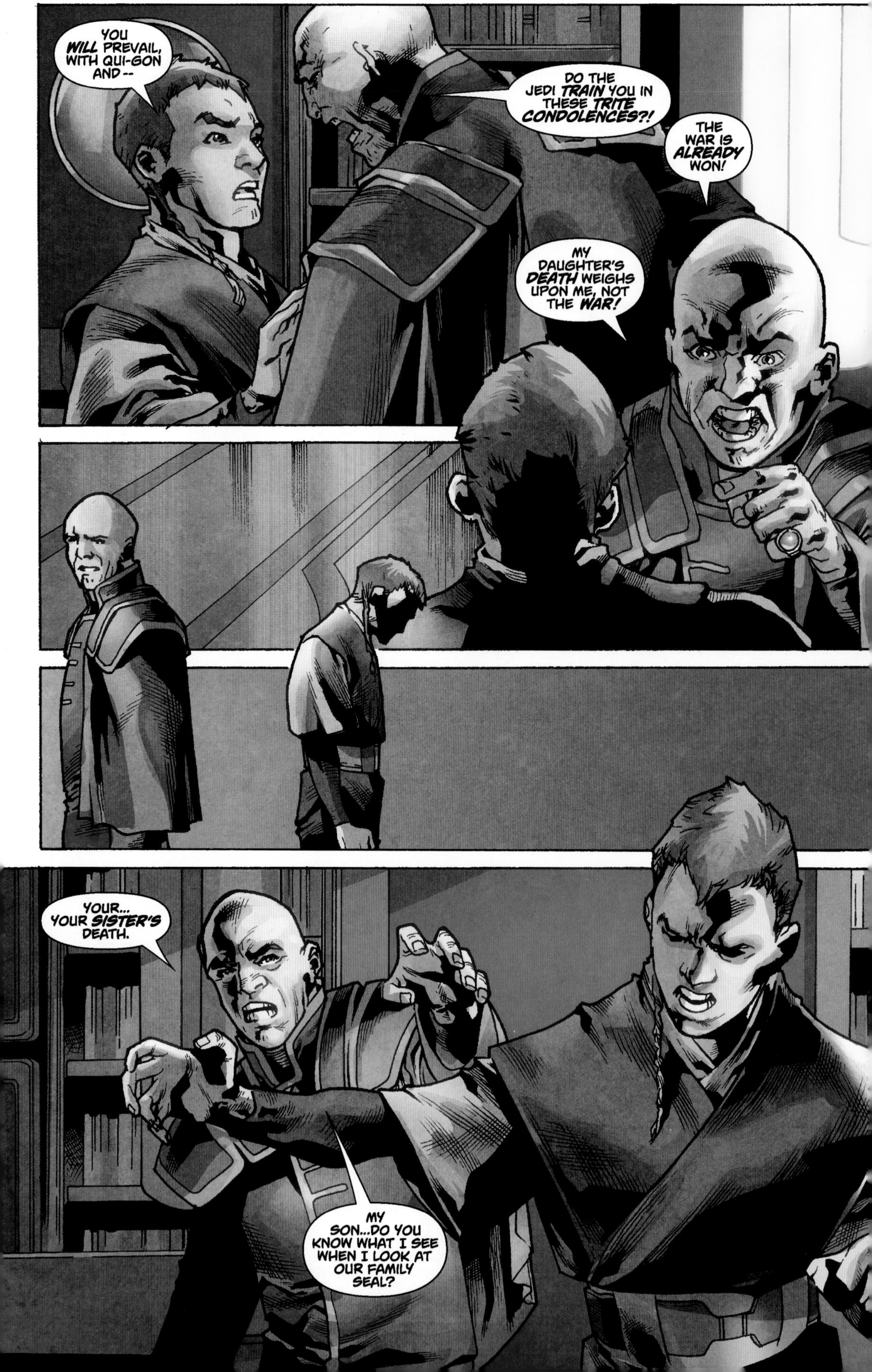
YOU WILL PREVAIL, WITH QUI-GON AND --
DO THE JEDI TRAIN YOU IN THESE TRITE CONDOLENCES?!
THE WAR IS ALREADY WON!
MY DAUGHTER'S DEATH WEIGHS UPON ME, NOT THE WAR!
YOUR... YOUR SISTER'S DEATH.
MY SON...DO YOU KNOW WHAT I SEE WHEN I LOOK AT OUR FAMILY SEAL?

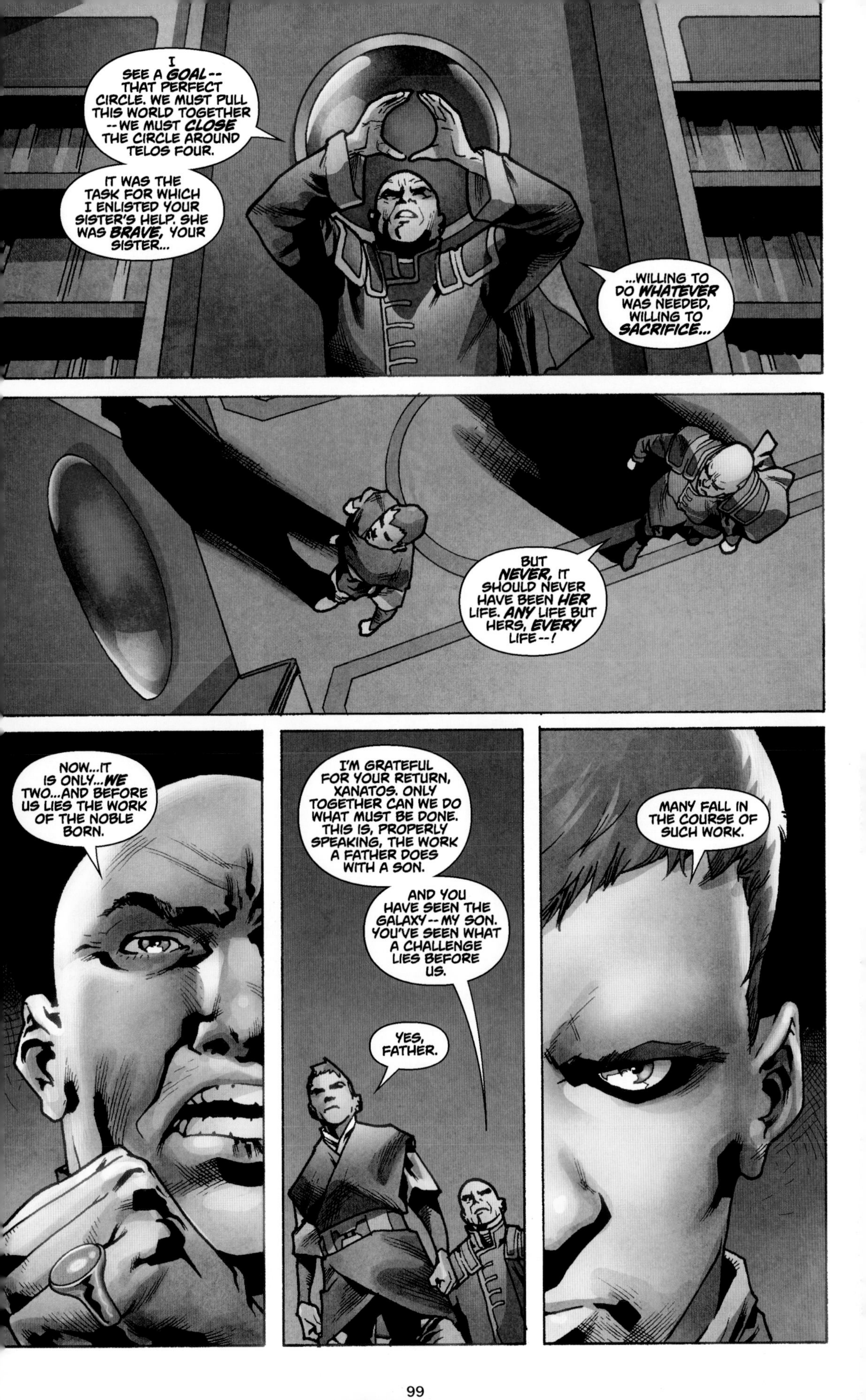
I SEE A GOAL-- THAT PERFECT CIRCLE. WE MUST PULL THIS WORLD TOGETHER --WE MUST CLOSE THE CIRCLE AROUND TELOS FOUR.
IT WAS THE TASK FOR WHICH I ENLISTED YOUR SISTER'S HELP. SHE WAS BRAVE, YOUR SISTER...
...WILLING TO DO WHATEVER WAS NEEDED, WILLING TO SACRIFICE...
BUT NEVER, IT SHOULD NEVER HAVE BEEN HER LIFE. ANY LIFE BUT HERS, EVERY LIFE--!
NOW...IT IS ONLY...WE TWO...AND BEFORE US LIES THE WORK OF THE NOBLE BORN.
I'M GRATEFUL FOR YOUR RETURN, XANATOS. ONLY TOGETHER CAN WE DO WHAT MUST BE DONE. THIS IS, PROPERLY SPEAKING, THE WORK A FATHER DOES WITH A SON.
AND YOU HAVE SEEN THE GALAXY--MY SON. YOU'VE SEEN WHAT A CHALLENGE LIES BEFORE US.
YES, FATHER.
MANY FALL IN THE COURSE OF SUCH WORK.

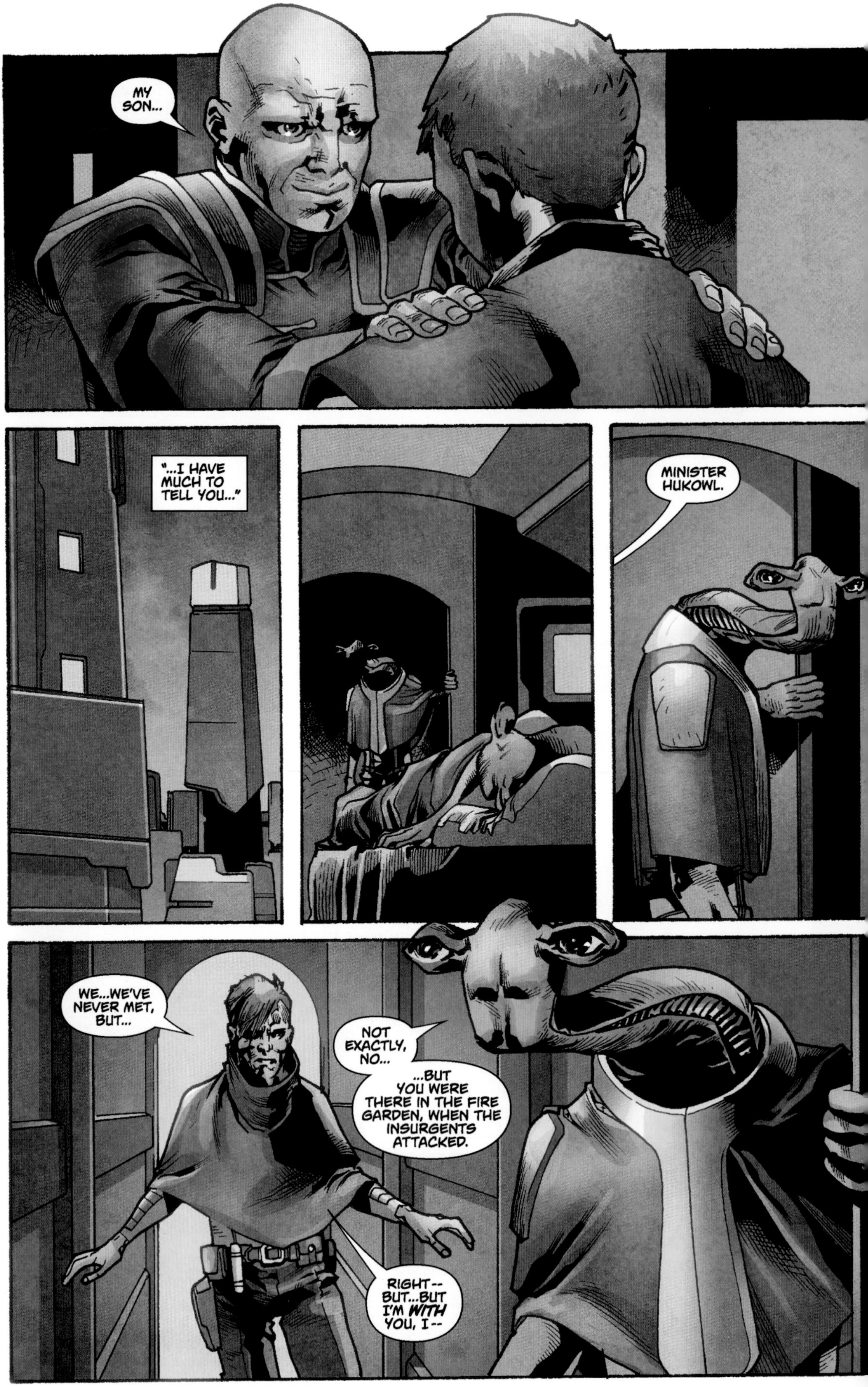
MY SON...
"...I HAVE MUCH TO TELL YOU..."
MINISTER HUKOWL.
WE...WE'VE NEVER MET, BUT...
NOT EXACTLY, NO...
...BUT YOU WERE THERE IN THE FIRE GARDEN, WHEN THE INSURGENTS ATTACKED.
RIGHT-- BUT...BUT I'M *WITH* YOU, I--

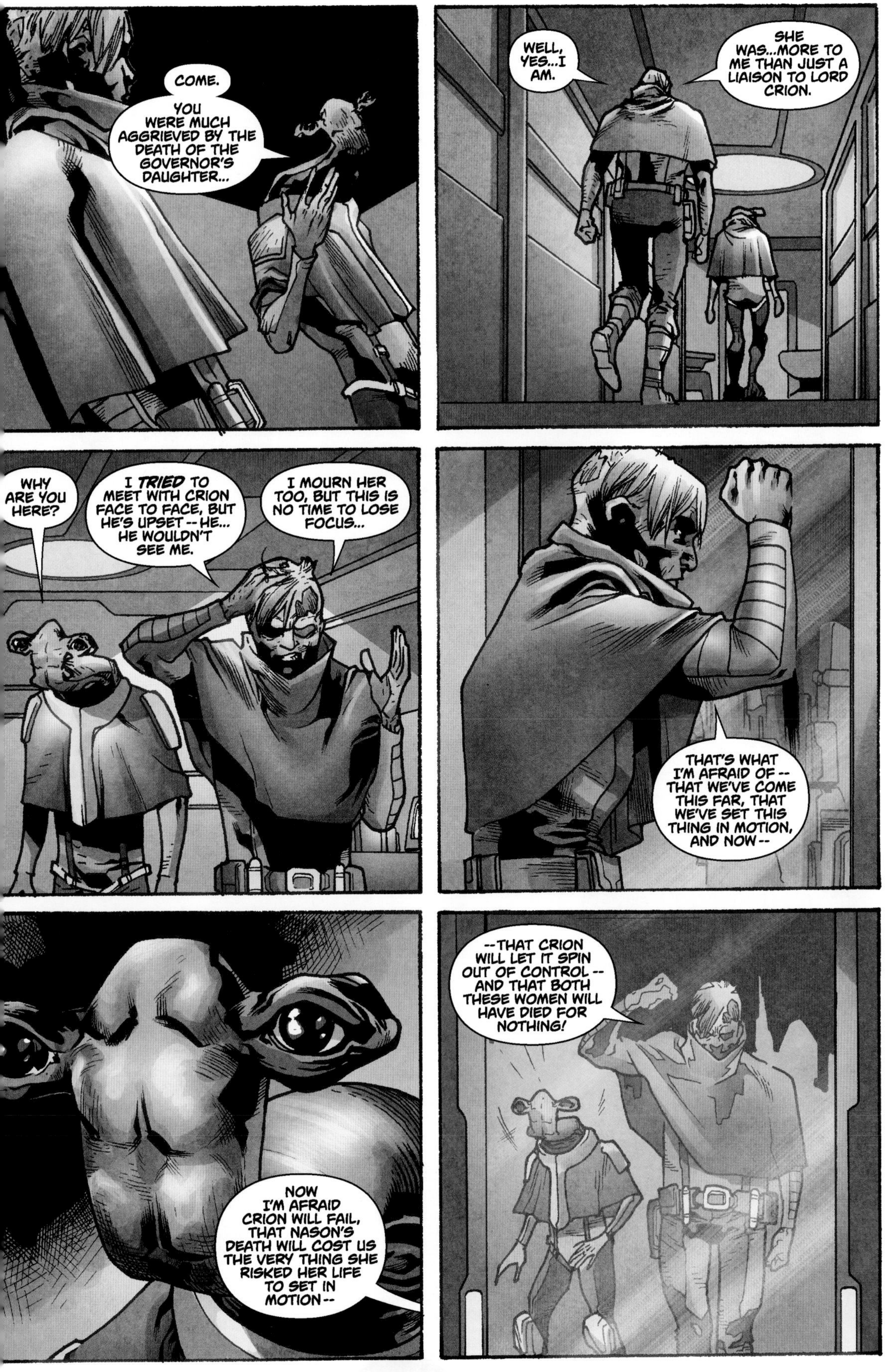
COME.
YOU WERE MUCH AGGRIEVED BY THE DEATH OF THE GOVERNOR'S DAUGHTER...
WELL, YES...I AM.
SHE WAS...MORE TO ME THAN JUST A LIAISON TO LORD CRION.
WHY ARE YOU HERE?
I *TRIED* TO MEET WITH CRION FACE TO FACE, BUT HE'S UPSET -- HE... HE WOULDN'T SEE ME.
I MOURN HER TOO, BUT THIS IS NO TIME TO LOSE FOCUS...
THAT'S WHAT I'M AFRAID OF -- THAT WE'VE COME THIS FAR, THAT WE'VE SET THIS THING IN MOTION, AND NOW --
NOW I'M AFRAID CRION WILL FAIL, THAT NASON'S DEATH WILL COST US THE VERY THING SHE RISKED HER LIFE TO SET IN MOTION --
--THAT CRION WILL LET IT SPIN OUT OF CONTROL -- AND THAT BOTH THESE WOMEN WILL HAVE DIED FOR NOTHING!

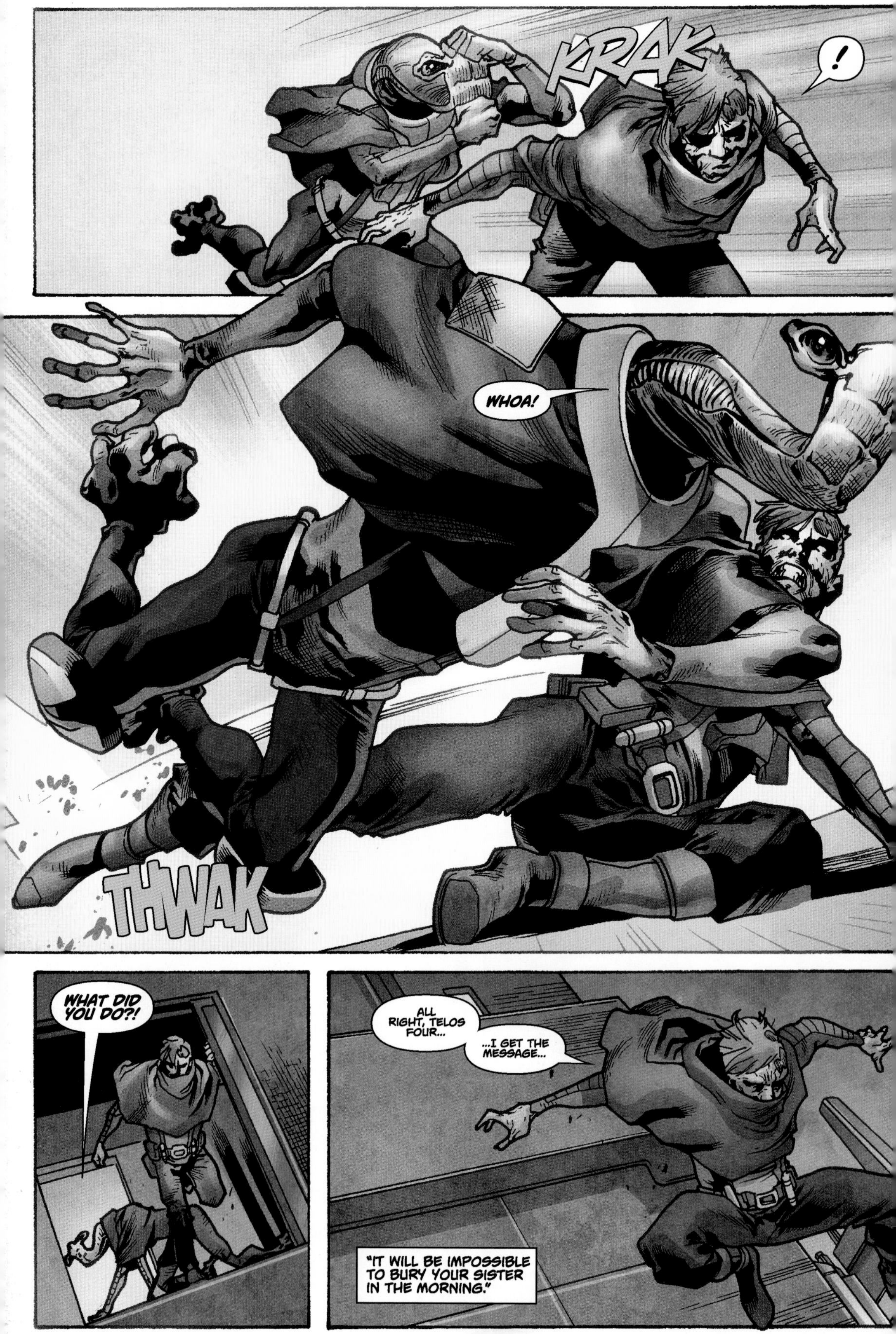
KRAK
!
WHOA!
THWAK
WHAT DID YOU DO?!
ALL RIGHT, TELOS FOUR...
...I GET THE MESSAGE...
"IT WILL BE IMPOSSIBLE TO BURY YOUR SISTER IN THE MORNING."

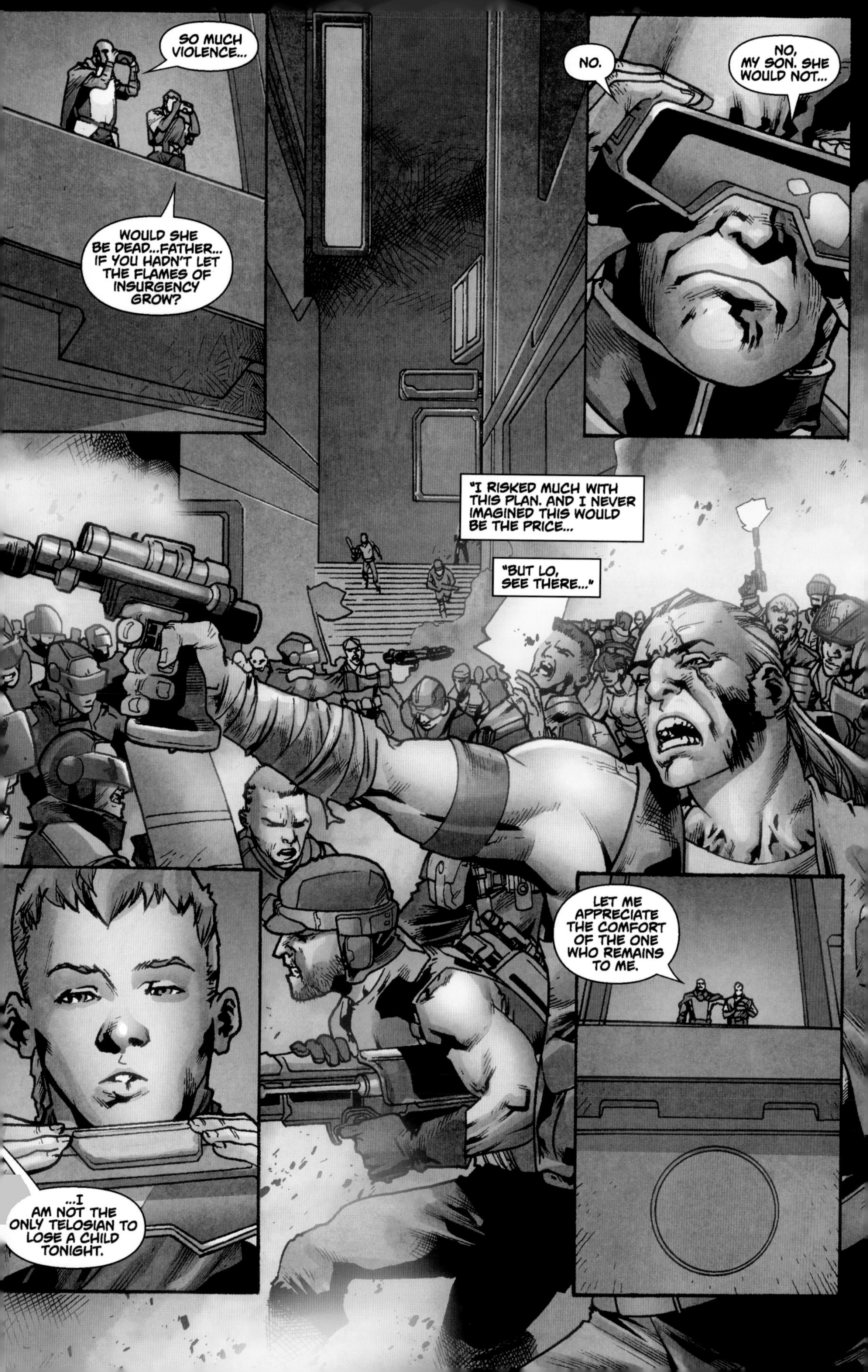
SO MUCH VIOLENCE...
WOULD SHE BE DEAD...FATHER... IF YOU HADN'T LET THE FLAMES OF INSURGENCY GROW?
NO.
NO, MY SON. SHE WOULD NOT...
"I RISKED MUCH WITH THIS PLAN. AND I NEVER IMAGINED THIS WOULD BE THE PRICE...
"BUT LO, SEE THERE..."
...I AM NOT THE ONLY TELOSIAN TO LOSE A CHILD TONIGHT.
LET ME APPRECIATE THE COMFORT OF THE ONE WHO REMAINS TO ME.

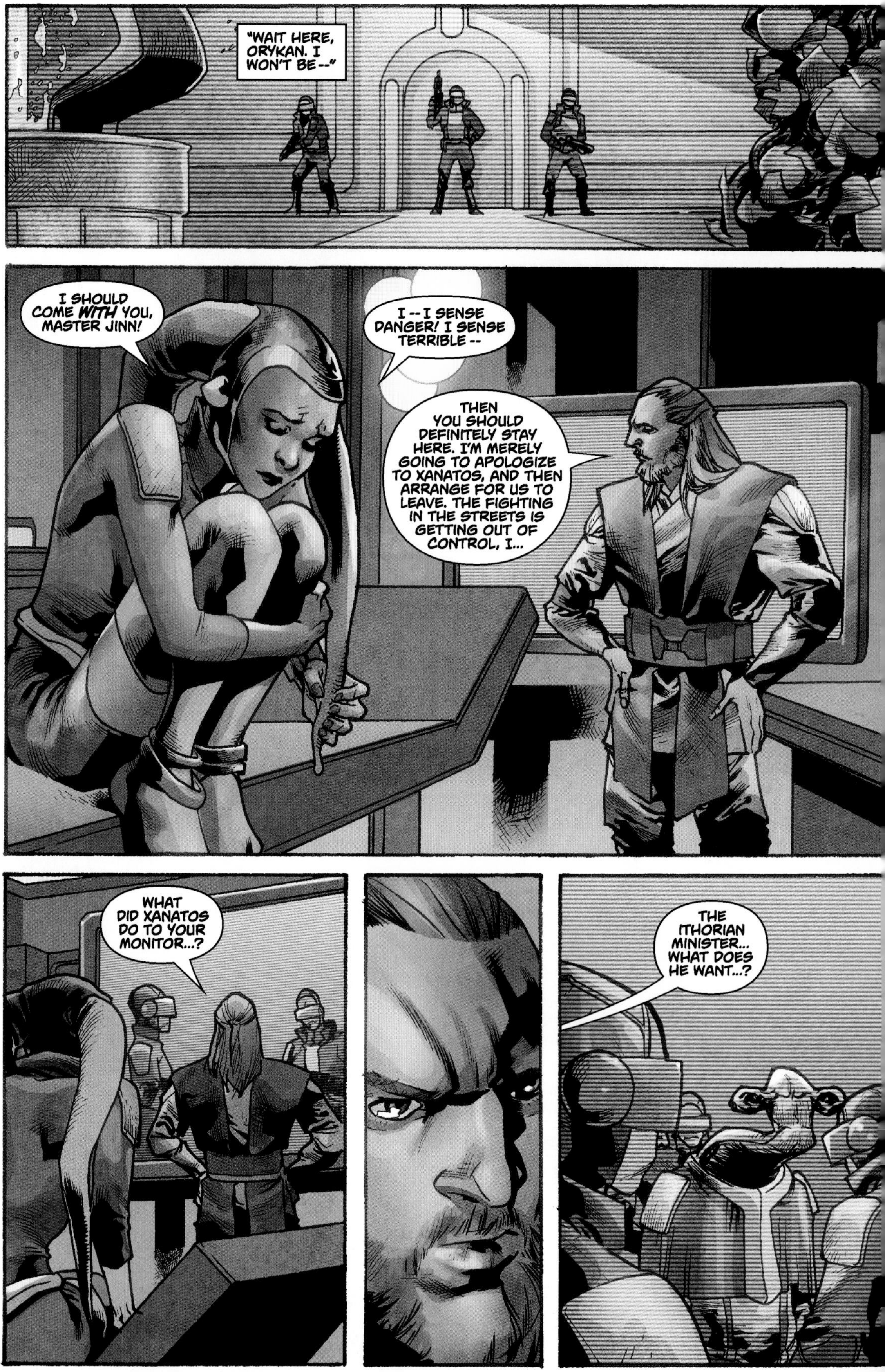
"WAIT HERE, ORYKAN. I WON'T BE--"
I SHOULD COME WITH YOU, MASTER JINN!
I -- I SENSE DANGER! I SENSE TERRIBLE --
THEN YOU SHOULD DEFINITELY STAY HERE. I'M MERELY GOING TO APOLOGIZE TO XANATOS, AND THEN ARRANGE FOR US TO LEAVE. THE FIGHTING IN THE STREETS IS GETTING OUT OF CONTROL, I...
WHAT DID XANATOS DO TO YOUR MONITOR...?
THE ITHORIAN MINISTER... WHAT DOES HE WANT...?

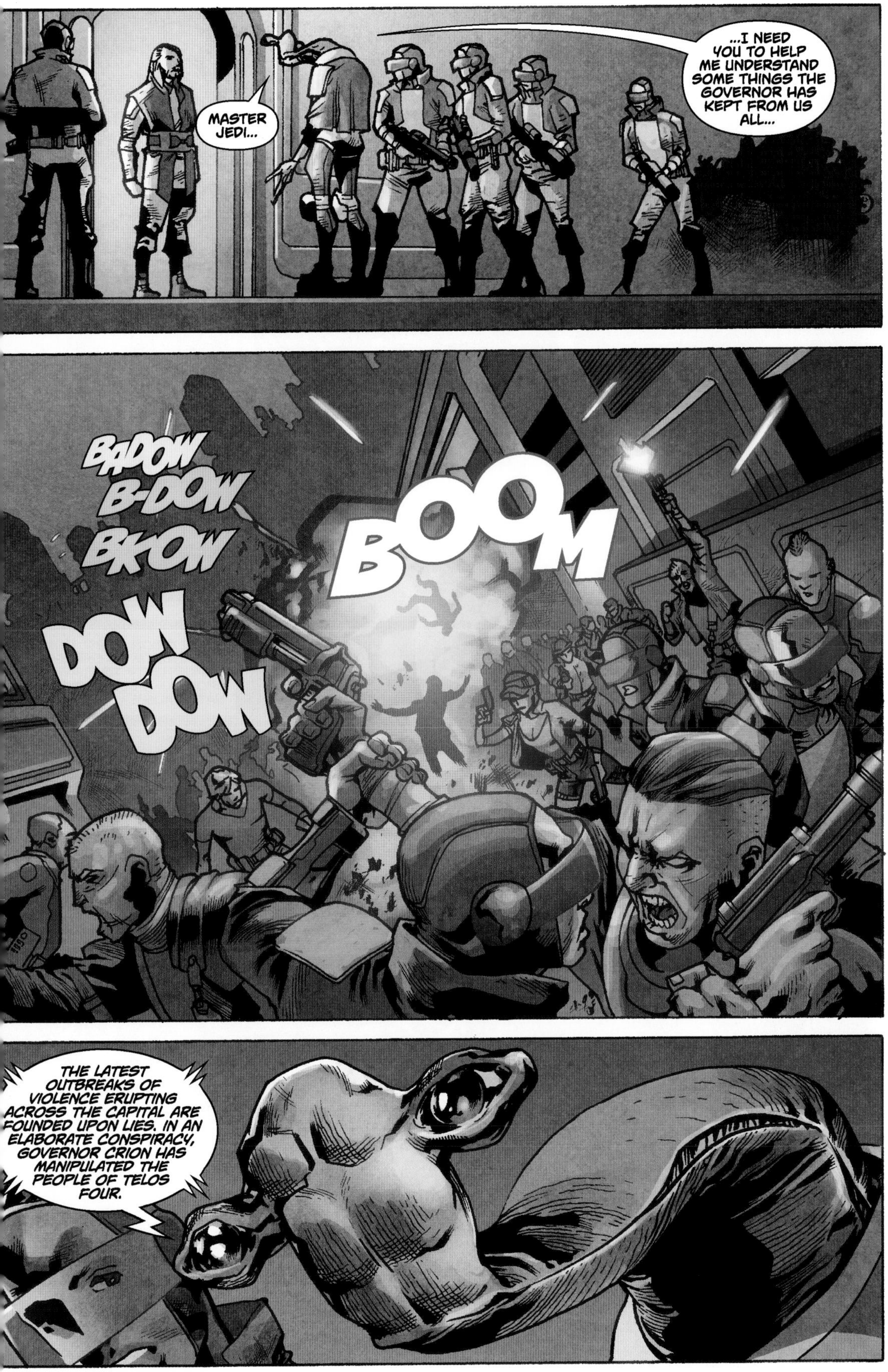
MASTER JEDI...
...I NEED YOU TO HELP ME UNDERSTAND SOME THINGS THE GOVERNOR HAS KEPT FROM US ALL...
BADOW
B-DOW
BK-OW
DOW DOW
BOOM
THE LATEST OUTBREAKS OF VIOLENCE ERUPTING ACROSS THE CAPITAL ARE FOUNDED UPON LIES. IN AN ELABORATE CONSPIRACY, GOVERNOR CRION HAS MANIPULATED THE PEOPLE OF TELOS FOUR.

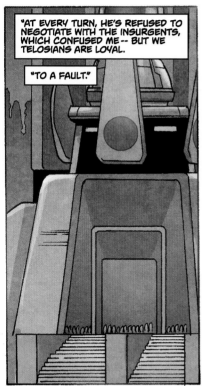

"AT EVERY TURN, HE'S REFUSED TO NEGOTIATE WITH THE INSURGENTS, WHICH CONFUSED ME-- BUT WE TELOSIANS ARE LOYAL.

"TO A FAULT."

I TRUSTED MY LORD.

BUT NOW I UNDERSTAND.

"LORD CRION *USED* THE INSURGENTS. HE SAW AN OPPORTUNITY TO PLAY UPON OUR FEELINGS OF NATIONALISM.

"HE FABRICATED A LINK BETWEEN THE OFFWORLD FORCES OF THE TOPRAWA GOVERNMENT AND THE *NATIVE* REBELLION ON TELOS FOUR. HIS *GOAL* WAS THE ESCALATION OF VIOLENCE WE'VE SEEN TODAY.

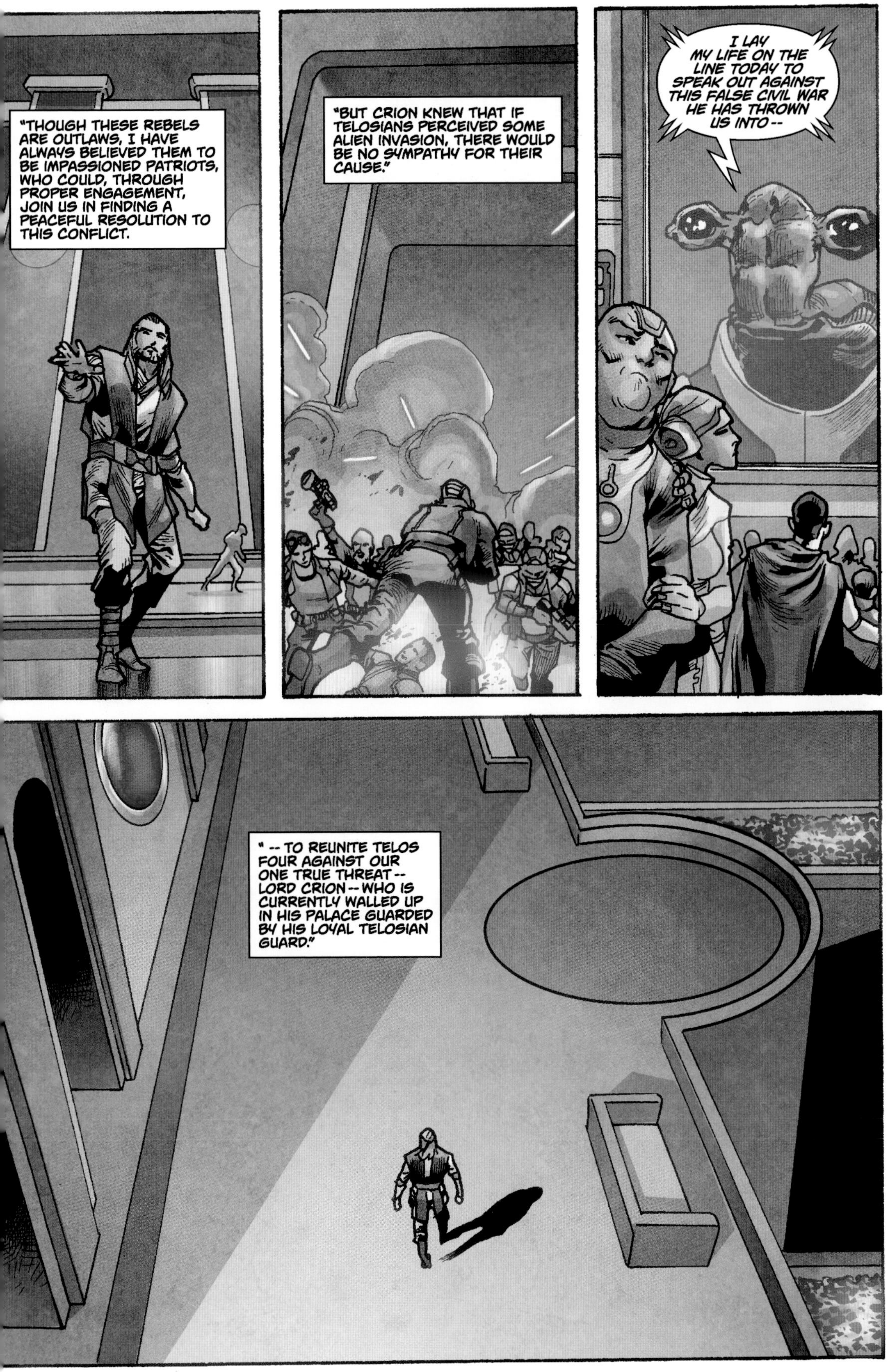
"THOUGH THESE REBELS ARE OUTLAWS, I HAVE ALWAYS BELIEVED THEM TO BE IMPASSIONED PATRIOTS, WHO COULD, THROUGH PROPER ENGAGEMENT, JOIN US IN FINDING A PEACEFUL RESOLUTION TO THIS CONFLICT.
"BUT CRION KNEW THAT IF TELOSIANS PERCEIVED SOME ALIEN INVASION, THERE WOULD BE NO SYMPATHY FOR THEIR CAUSE."
I LAY MY LIFE ON THE LINE TODAY TO SPEAK OUT AGAINST THIS FALSE CIVIL WAR HE HAS THROWN US INTO --
" -- TO REUNITE TELOS FOUR AGAINST OUR ONE TRUE THREAT -- LORD CRION -- WHO IS CURRENTLY WALLED UP IN HIS PALACE GUARDED BY HIS LOYAL TELOSIAN GUARD."

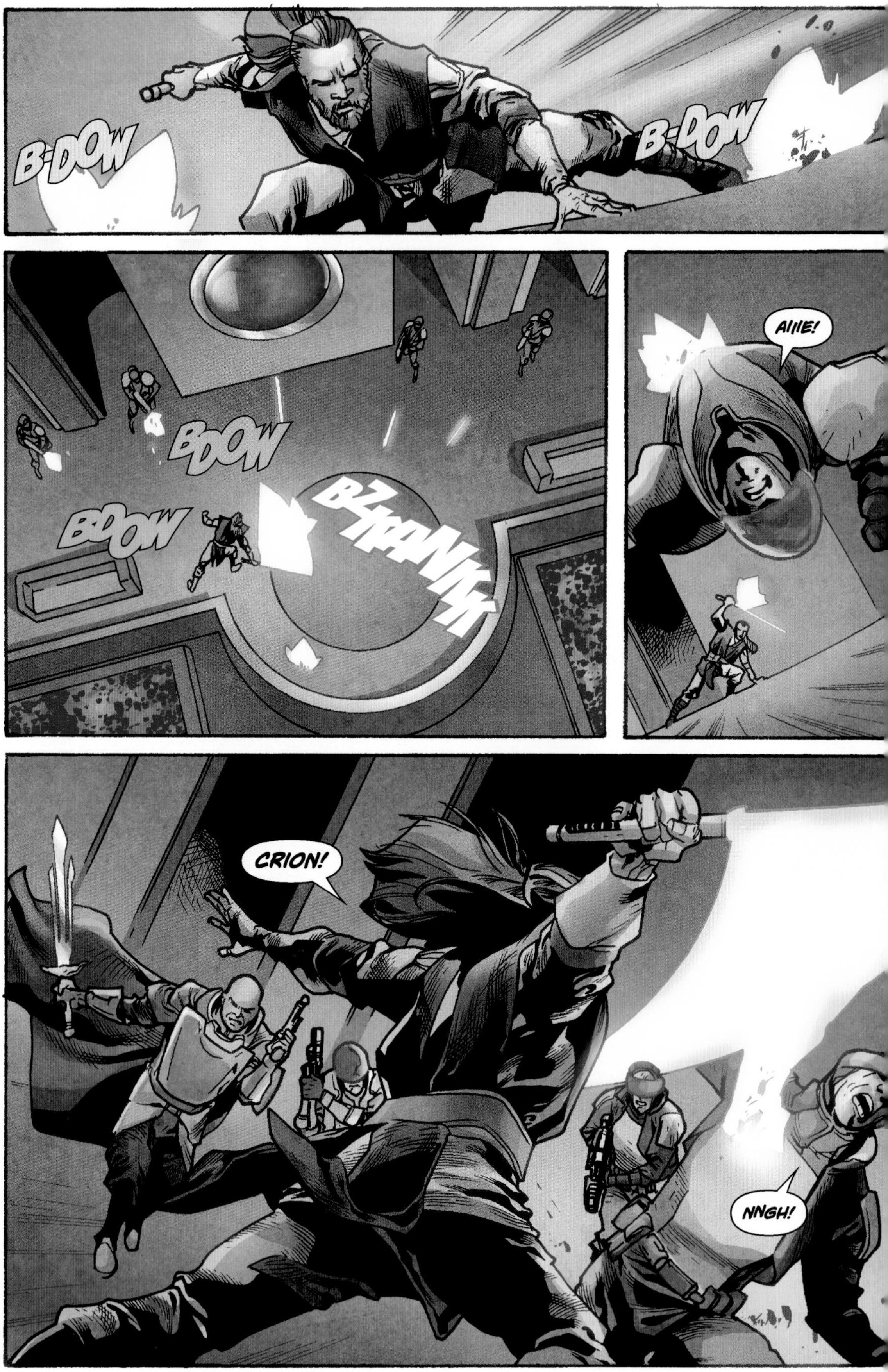
B-DOW
B-DOW
BDOW
BDOW
BZZANKK
AIIIE!
CRION!
NNGH!

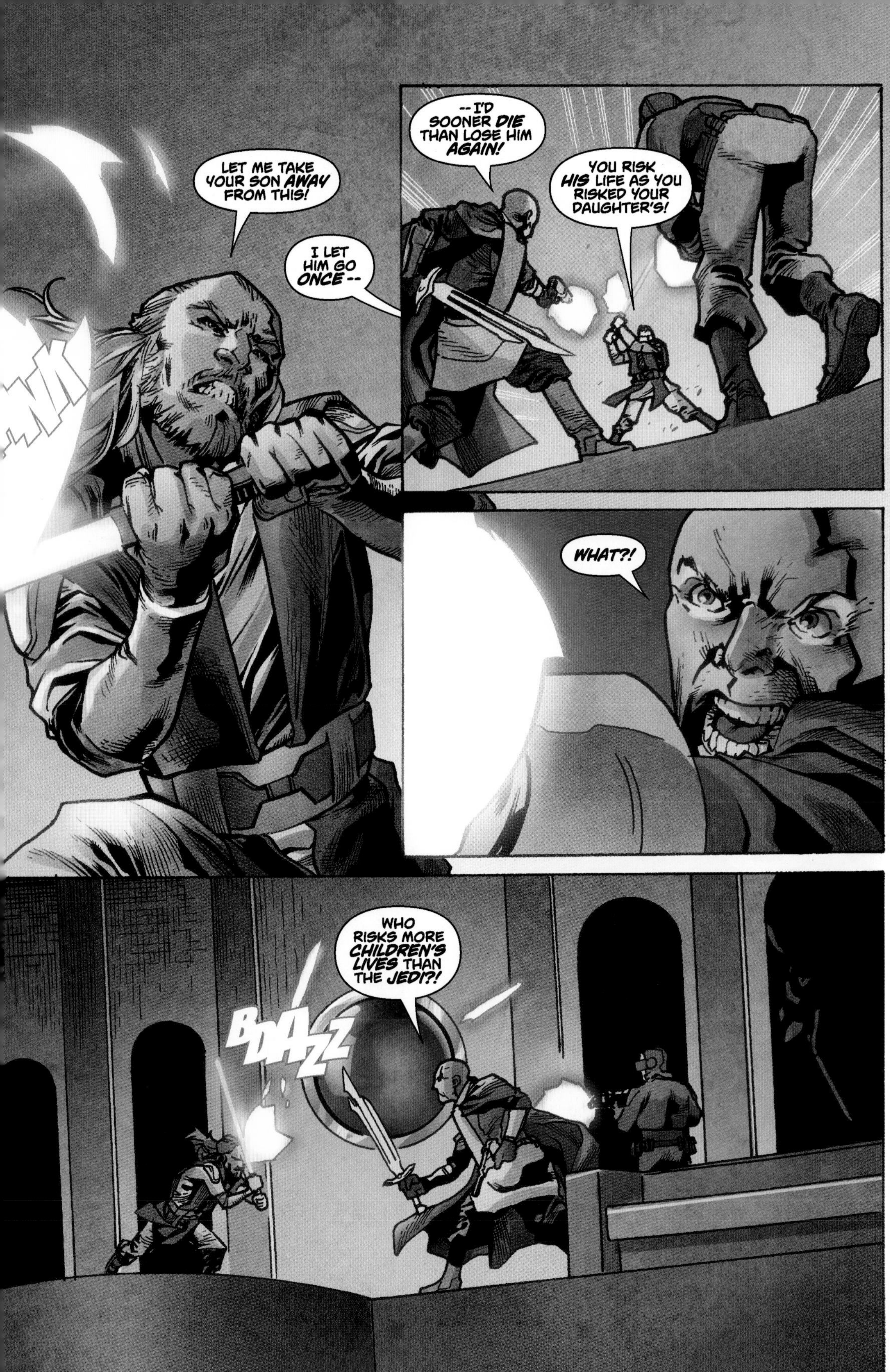
LET ME TAKE YOUR SON AWAY FROM THIS!
I LET HIM GO ONCE --
-- I'D SOONER DIE THAN LOSE HIM AGAIN!
YOU RISK HIS LIFE AS YOU RISKED YOUR DAUGHTER'S!
WHAT?!
WHO RISKS MORE CHILDREN'S LIVES THAN THE JEDI?!
BDAZZ

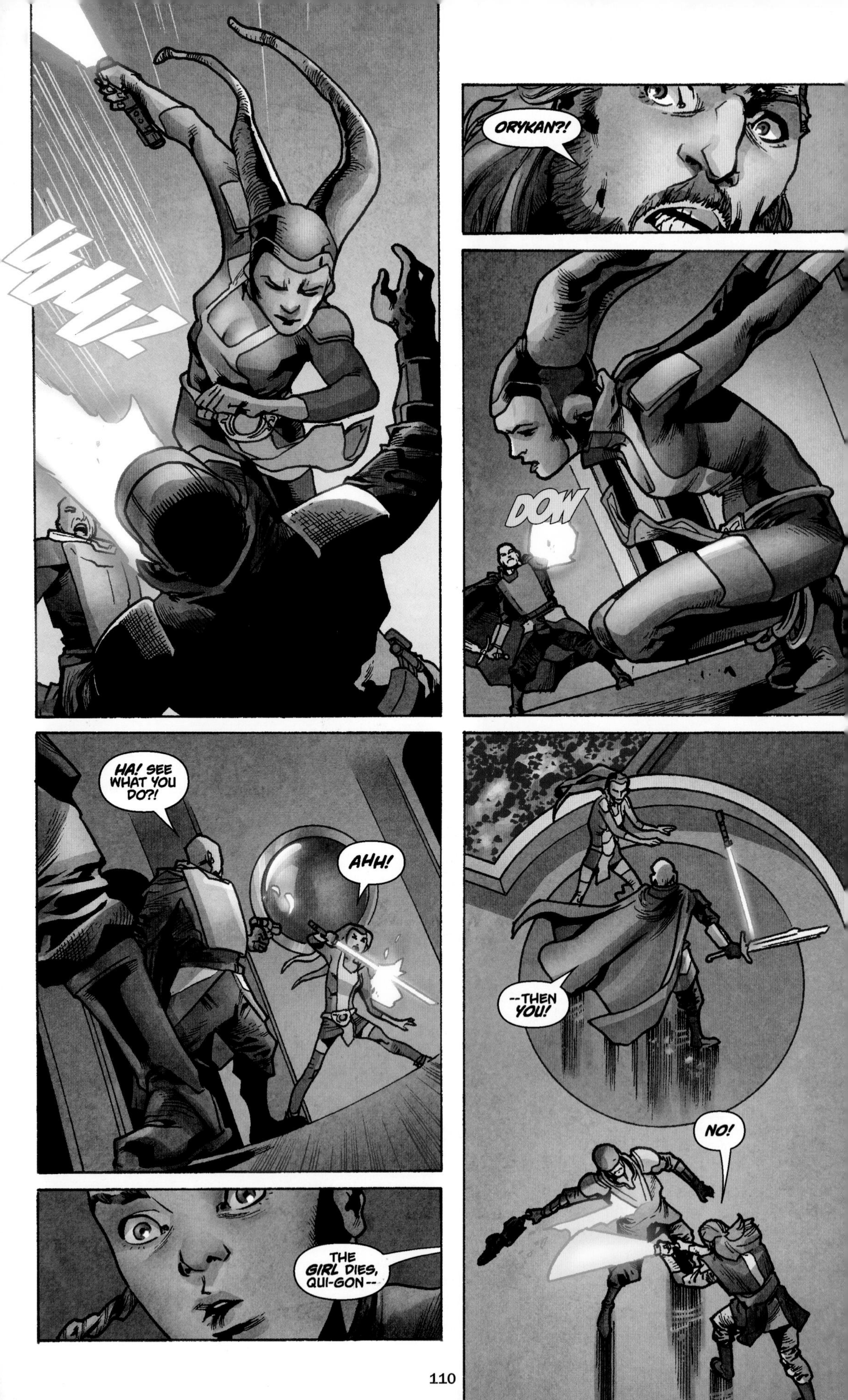
VVVVZ
ORYKAN?!
DOW
HA! SEE WHAT YOU DO?!
AHH!
THE GIRL DIES, QUI-GON--
--THEN YOU!
NO!

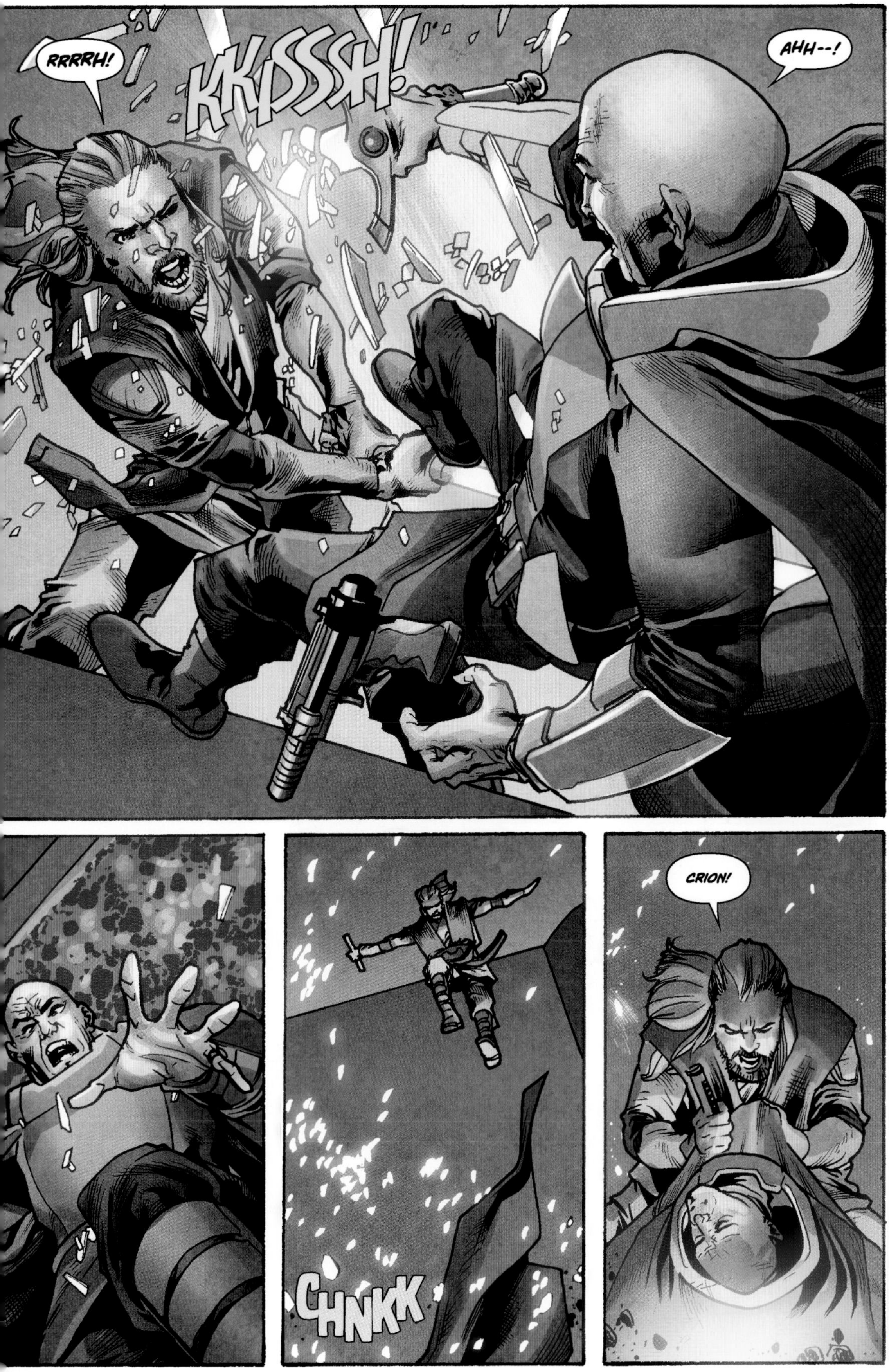
RRRRH!
KKISSSH!
AHH--!
CHNKK
CRION!

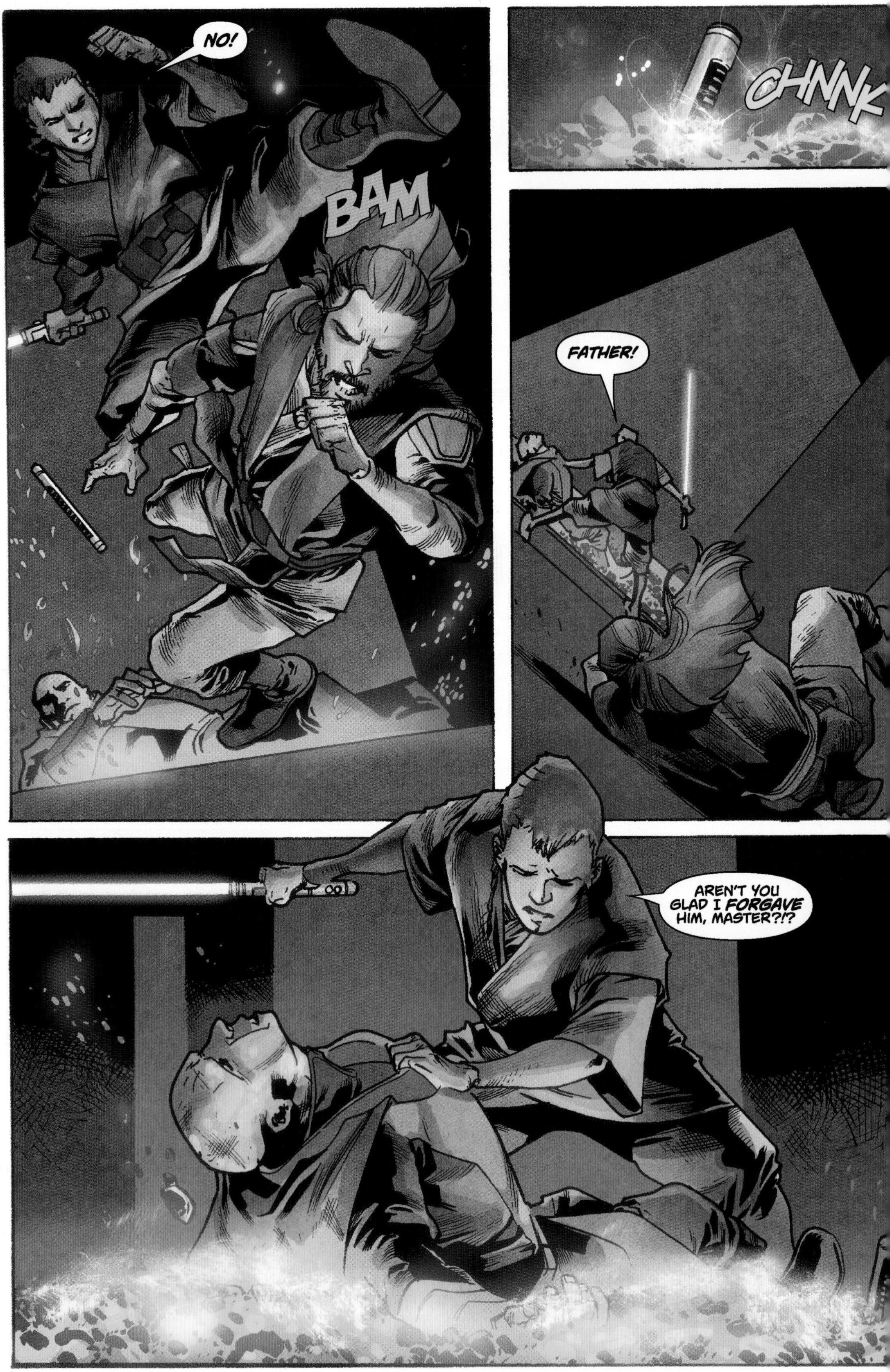
NO!
BAM
CHNNK
FATHER!
AREN'T YOU GLAD I FORGAVE HIM, MASTER?!?

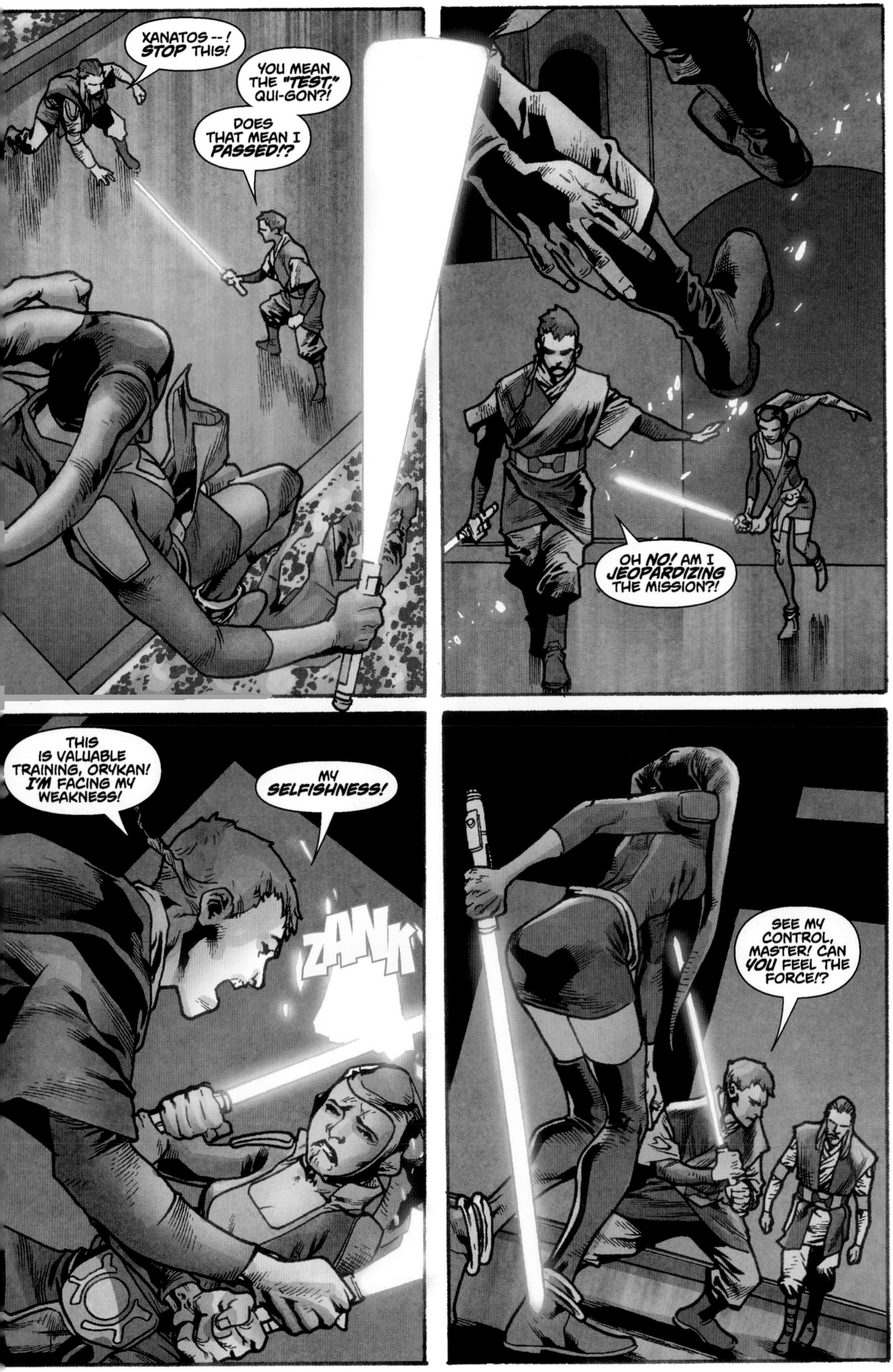
XANATOS --! STOP THIS!
YOU MEAN THE "TEST," QUI-GON?!
DOES THAT MEAN I PASSED!?
OH NO! AM I JEOPARDIZING THE MISSION?!
THIS IS VALUABLE TRAINING, ORYKAN! I'M FACING MY WEAKNESS!
MY SELFISHNESS!
ZANK
SEE MY CONTROL, MASTER! CAN YOU FEEL THE FORCE!?

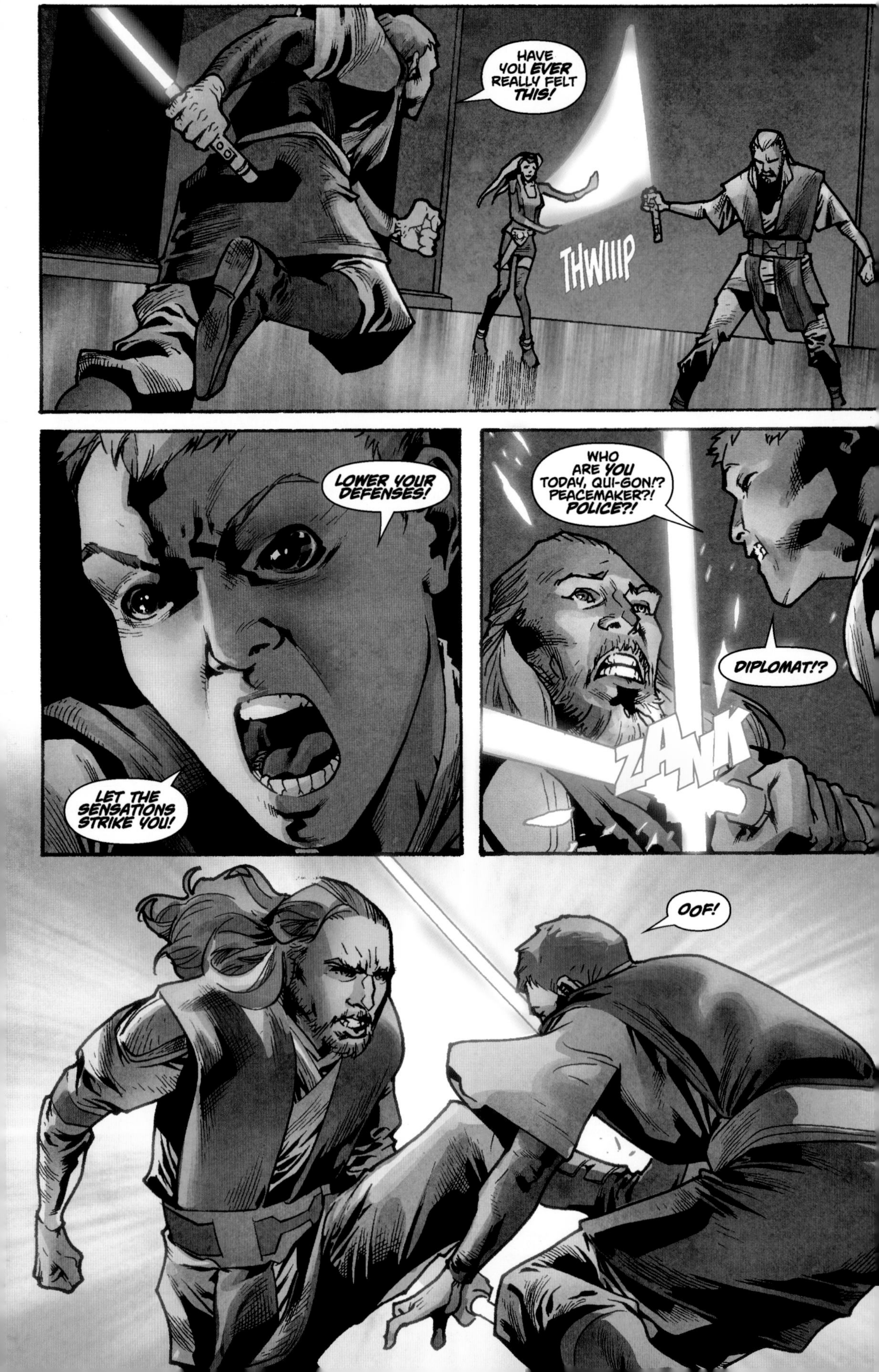
HAVE YOU EVER REALLY FELT THIS!
THWIIIP
LOWER YOUR DEFENSES!
LET THE SENSATIONS STRIKE YOU!
WHO ARE YOU TODAY, QUI-GON!? PEACEMAKER?! POLICE?!
DIPLOMAT!?
ZANK
OOF!

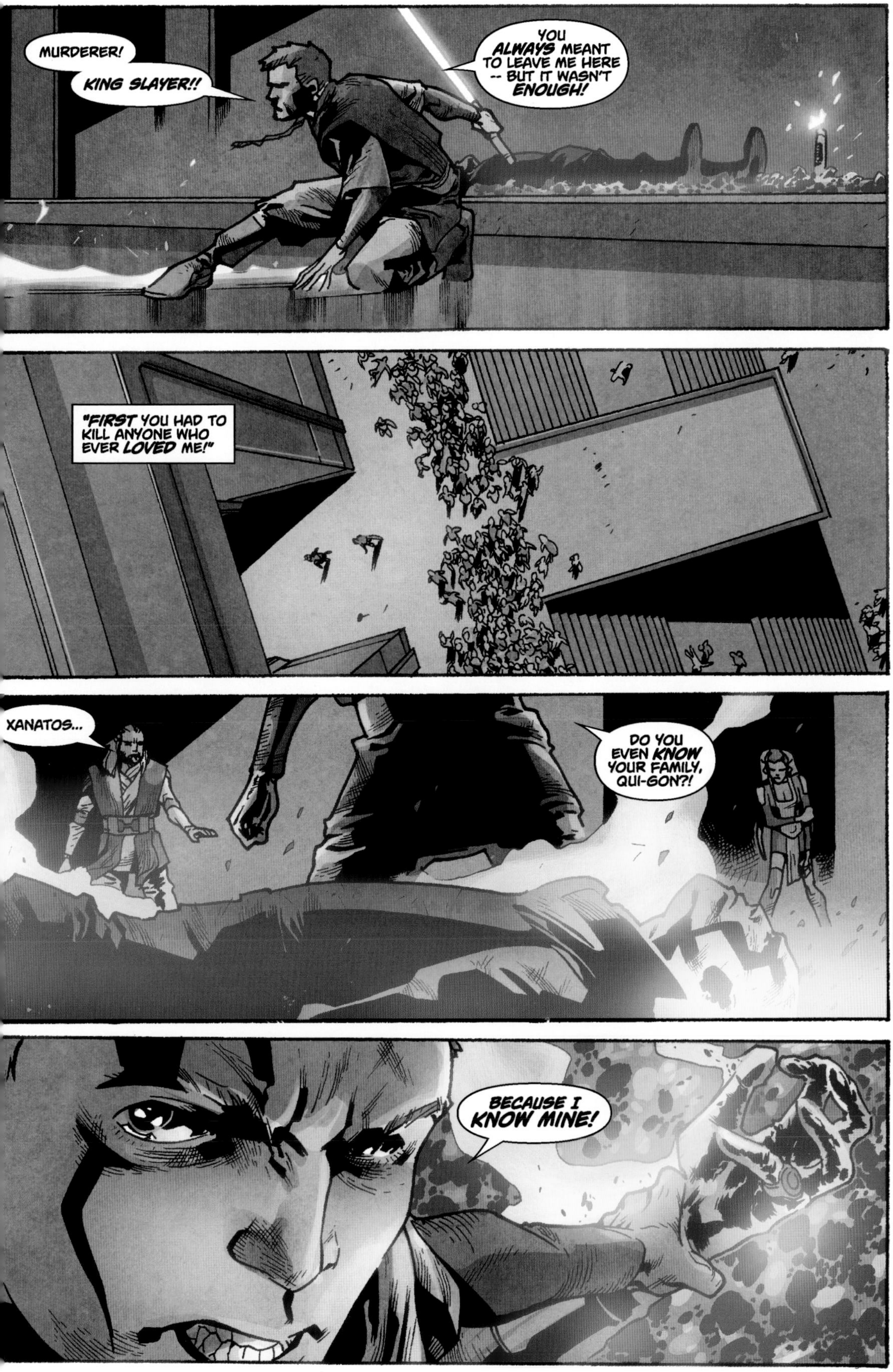
MURDERER!
KING SLAYER!!
YOU ALWAYS MEANT TO LEAVE ME HERE -- BUT IT WASN'T ENOUGH!
"FIRST YOU HAD TO KILL ANYONE WHO EVER LOVED ME!"
XANATOS...
DO YOU EVEN KNOW YOUR FAMILY, QUI-GON?!
BECAUSE I KNOW MINE!

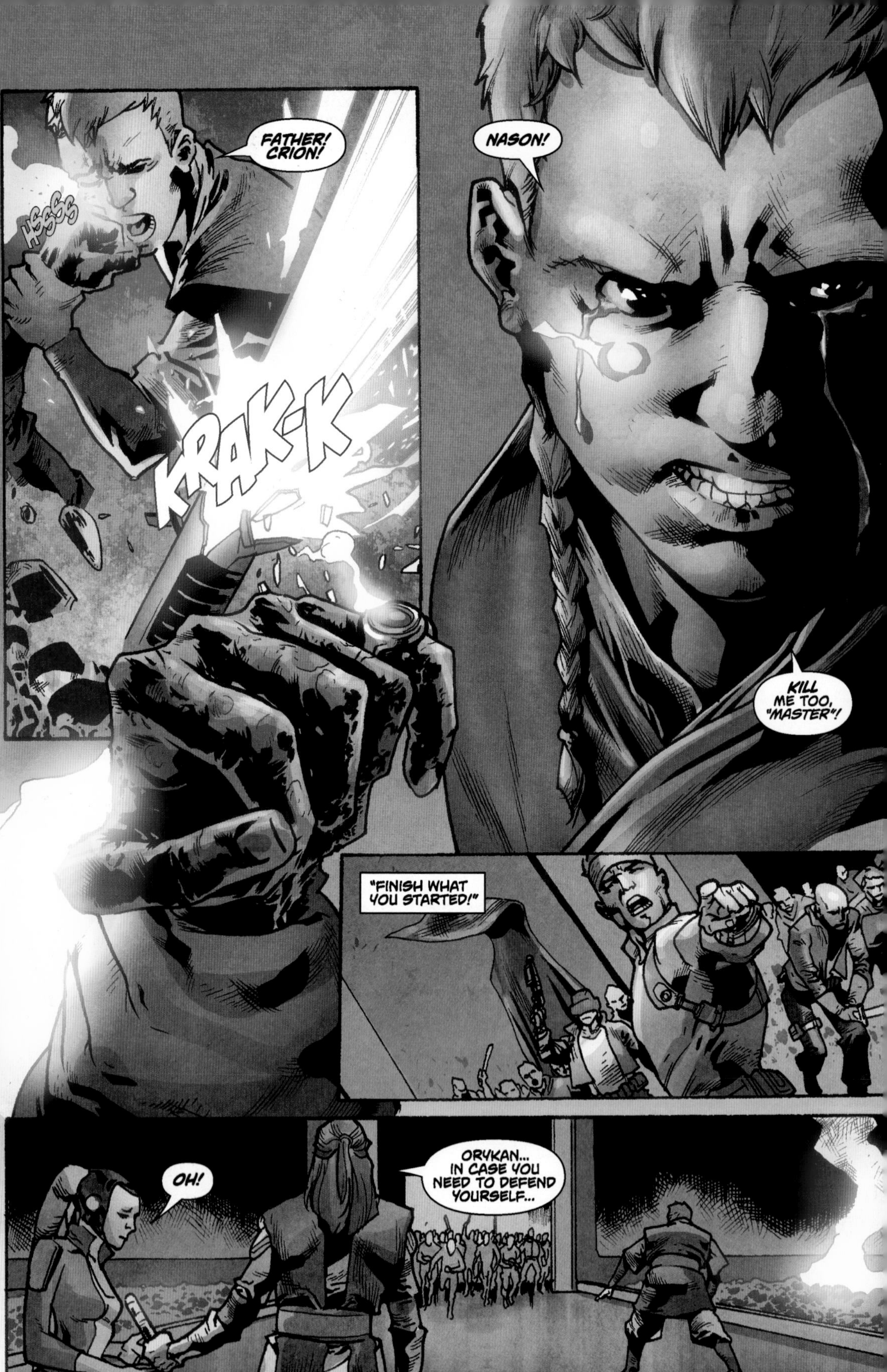
FATHER! CRION!
HSSSS
KRAK-K
NASON!
KILL ME TOO, "MASTER"!
"FINISH WHAT YOU STARTED!"
OH!
ORYKAN... IN CASE YOU NEED TO DEFEND YOURSELF...

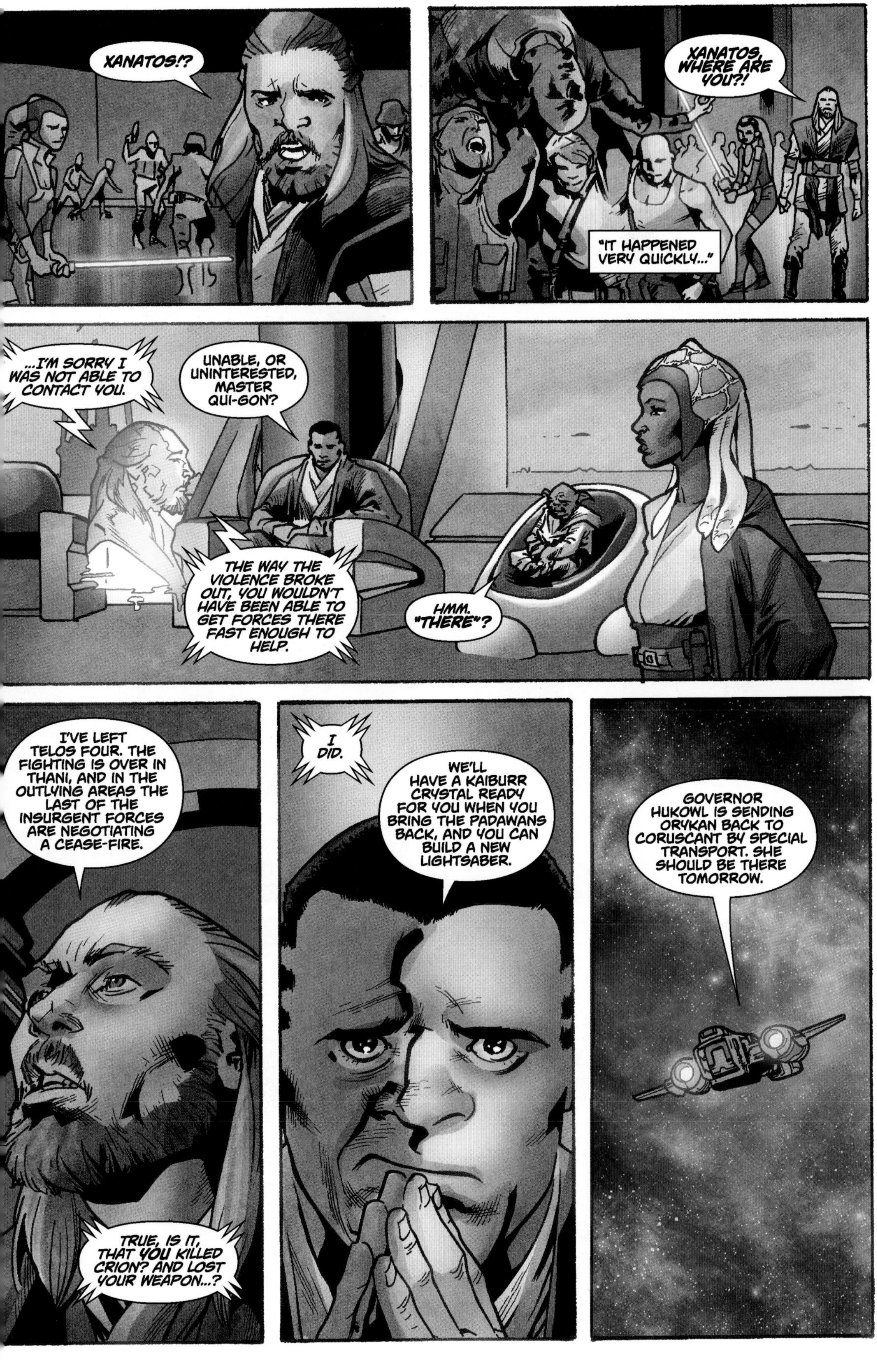
XANATOS!?
XANATOS, WHERE ARE YOU?!
"IT HAPPENED VERY QUICKLY..."
...I'M SORRY I WAS NOT ABLE TO CONTACT YOU.
UNABLE, OR UNINTERESTED, MASTER QUI-GON?
THE WAY THE VIOLENCE BROKE OUT, YOU WOULDN'T HAVE BEEN ABLE TO GET FORCES THERE FAST ENOUGH TO HELP.
HMM. "THERE"?
I'VE LEFT TELOS FOUR. THE FIGHTING IS OVER IN THANI, AND IN THE OUTLYING AREAS THE LAST OF THE INSURGENT FORCES ARE NEGOTIATING A CEASE-FIRE.
TRUE, IS IT, THAT YOU KILLED CRION? AND LOST YOUR WEAPON...?
I DID.
WE'LL HAVE A KAIBURR CRYSTAL READY FOR YOU WHEN YOU BRING THE PADAWANS BACK, AND YOU CAN BUILD A NEW LIGHTSABER.
GOVERNOR HUKOWL IS SENDING ORYKAN BACK TO CORUSCANT BY SPECIAL TRANSPORT. SHE SHOULD BE THERE TOMORROW.

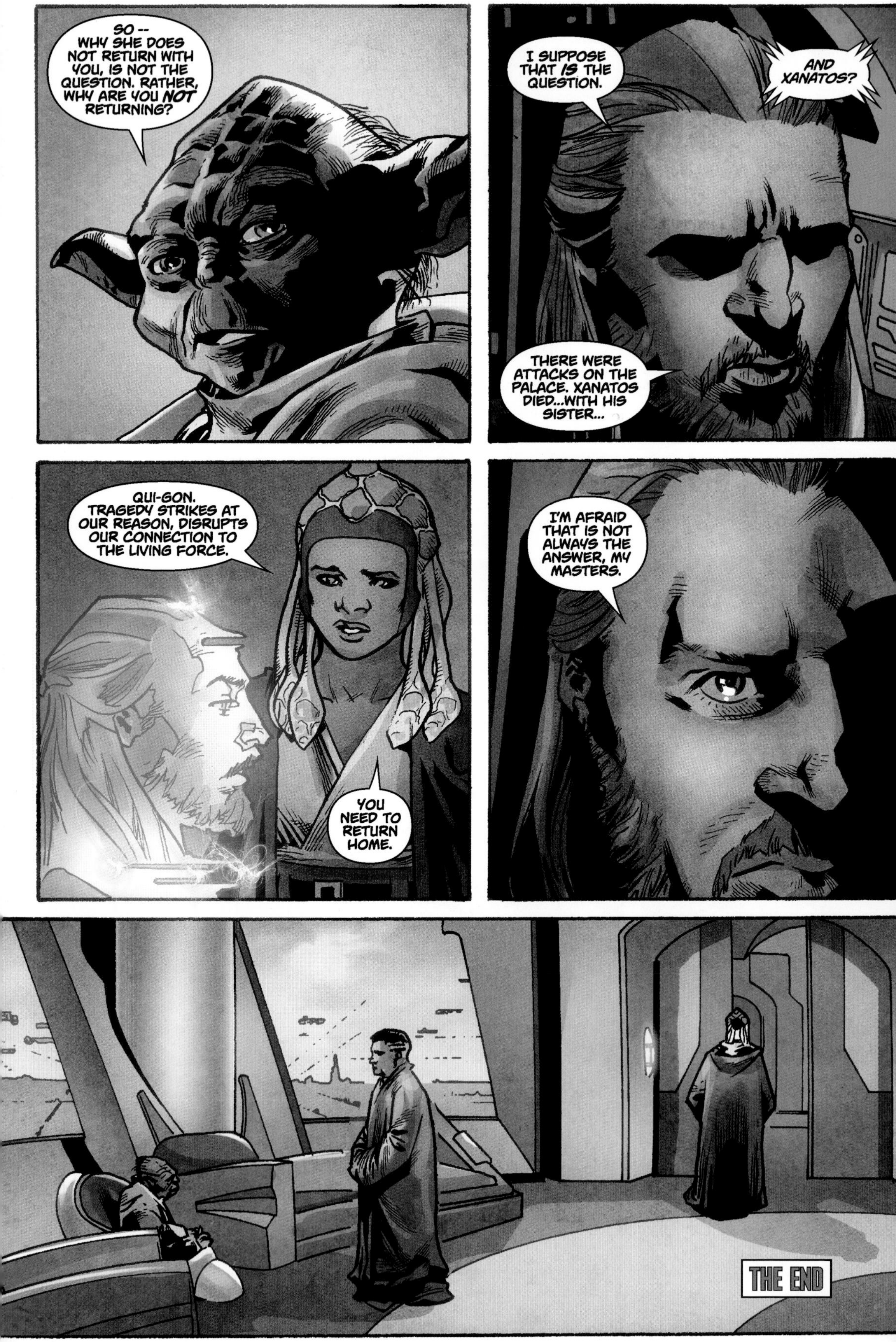
SO -- WHY SHE DOES NOT RETURN WITH YOU, IS NOT THE QUESTION. RATHER, WHY ARE YOU *NOT* RETURNING?
I SUPPOSE THAT *IS* THE QUESTION.
AND XANATOS?
THERE WERE ATTACKS ON THE PALACE. XANATOS DIED...WITH HIS SISTER...
QUI-GON. TRAGEDY STRIKES AT OUR REASON, DISRUPTS OUR CONNECTION TO THE LIVING FORCE.
YOU NEED TO RETURN HOME.
I'M AFRAID THAT IS NOT ALWAYS THE ANSWER, MY MASTERS.
THE END

TAR WARS GRAPHIC NOVEL TIMELINE (IN YEARS)

Omnibus: Tales of the Jedi—5,000–3,986 BSW4

Knights of the Old Republic—3,964–3,963 BSW4

The Old Republic—3653, 3678 BSW4

Knight Errant—1,032 BSW4

Jedi vs. Sith—1,000 BSW4

Omnibus: Rise of the Sith—33 BSW4

Episode I: The Phantom Menace—32 BSW4

Omnibus: Emissaries and Assassins—32 BSW4

Omnibus: Quinlan Vos—Jedi in Darkness—31–30 BSW4

Omnibus: Menace Revealed—31–22 BSW4

Honor and Duty—22 BSW4

Blood Ties—22 BSW4

Episode II: Attack of the Clones—22 BSW4

Clone Wars—22–19 BSW4

Clone Wars Adventures—22–19 BSW4

General Grievous—22–19 BSW4

Episode III: Revenge of the Sith—19 BSW4

Dark Times—19 BSW4

Omnibus: Droids—5.5 BSW4

Omnibus: Boba Fett—3 BSW4–10 ASW4

Underworld—1 BSW4

Episode IV: A New Hope—SW4

Classic Star Wars—0–3 ASW4

Omnibus: A Long Time Ago . . . —0–4 ASW4

Empire—0 ASW4

Rebellion—0 ASW4

Omnibus: Early Victories—0–3 ASW4

Jabba the Hutt: The Art of the Deal—1 ASW4

Episode V: The Empire Strikes Back—3 ASW4

Omnibus: Shadows of the Empire—3.5–4.5 ASW4

Episode VI: Return of the Jedi—4 ASW4

Omnibus: X-Wing Rogue Squadron—4–5 ASW4

Heir to the Empire—9 ASW4

Dark Force Rising—9 ASW4

The Last Command—9 ASW4

Dark Empire—10 ASW4

Crimson Empire—11 ASW4

Jedi Academy: Leviathan—12 ASW4

Union—19 ASW4

Chewbacca—25 ASW4

Invasion—25 ASW4

Legacy—130–137 ASW4

Old Republic Era
25,000 – 1000 years before
Star Wars: A New Hope

Rise of the Empire Era
1000 – 0 years before
Star Wars: A New Hope

Rebellion Era
0 – 5 years after
Star Wars: A New Hope

New Republic Era
5 – 25 years after
Star Wars: A New Hope

New Jedi Order Era
25+ years after
Star Wars: A New Hope

Legacy Era
130+ years after
Star Wars: A New Hope

Vector
Crosses four eras in the timeline

Volume 1 contains:
Knights of the Old Republic Volume 5
Dark Times Volume 3
Volume 2 contains:
Rebellion Volume 4
Legacy Volume 6

BSW4 = before *Episode IV: A New Hope*. ASW4 = after *Episode IV: A New Hope*.

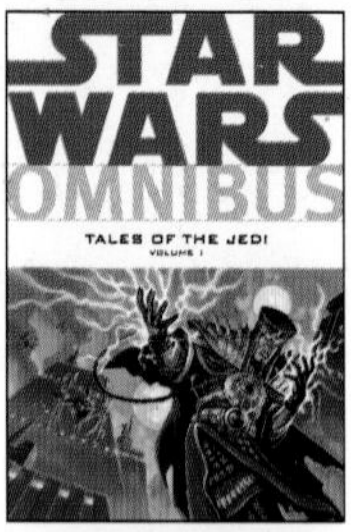
STAR WARS
OMNIBUS
TALES OF THE JEDI
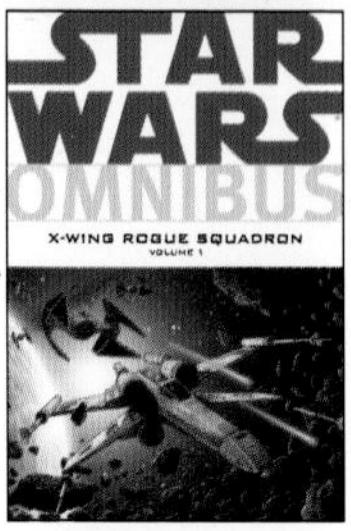
STAR WARS
OMNIBUS
X-WING ROGUE SQUADRON
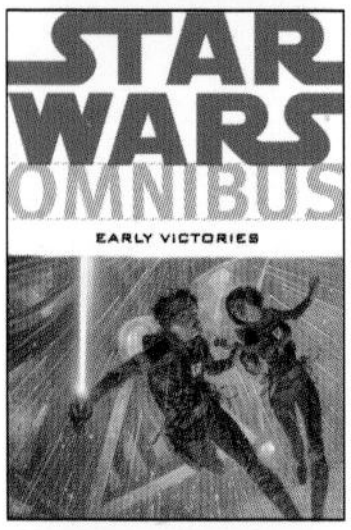
STAR WARS
OMNIBUS
EARLY VICTORIES
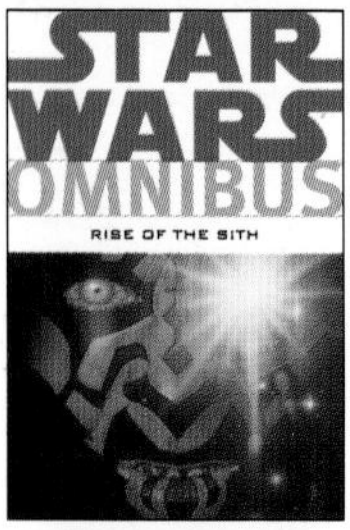
STAR WARS
OMNIBUS
RISE OF THE SITH
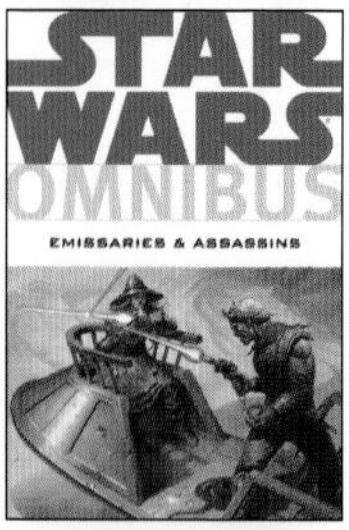
STAR WARS
OMNIBUS
EMISSARIES & ASSASSINS
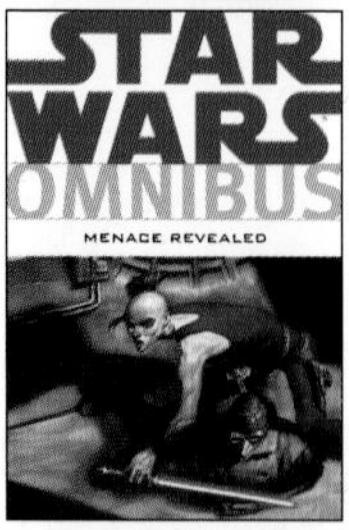
STAR WARS
OMNIBUS
MENACE REVEALED
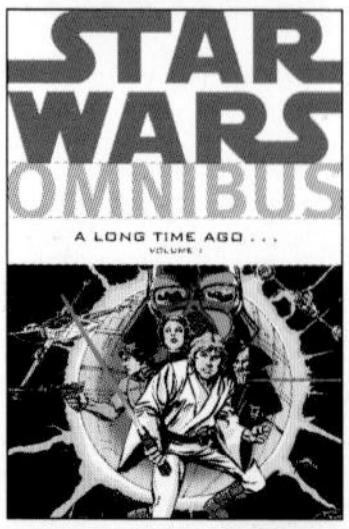
STAR WARS
OMNIBUS
A LONG TIME AGO . . .

STAR WARS OMNIBUS COLLECTIONS

STAR WARS: TALES OF THE JEDI

Including the *Tales of the Jedi* stories "The Golden Age of the Sith," "The Freedon Nadd Uprising," and "Knights of the Old Republic," these huge omnibus editions are the ultimate introduction to the ancient history of the *Star Wars* universe!

Volume 1 ISBN 978-1-59307-830-0 | $24.99   **Volume 2 ISBN 978-1-59307-911-6 | $24.99**

STAR WARS: X-WING ROGUE SQUADRON

The greatest starfighters of the Rebel Alliance become the defenders of a new Republic in this massive collection of stories featuring Wedge Antilles, hero of the Battle of Endor, and his team of ace pilots known throughout the galaxy as Rogue Squadron.

Volume 1 ISBN 978-1-59307-572-9 | $24.99   **Volume 2 ISBN 978-1-59307-619-1 | $24.99**

Volume 3 ISBN 978-1-59307-776-1 | $24.99

STAR WARS: BOBA FETT

Boba Fett, the most feared, most respected, and most loved bounty hunter in the galaxy, now has all of his comics stories collected into one massive volume!

ISBN 978-1-59582-418-9 | $24.99

STAR WARS: EARLY VICTORIES

Following the destruction of the first Death Star, Luke Skywalker is the new, unexpected hero of the Rebellion. But the galaxy hasn't been saved yet–Luke and Princess Leia find there are many more battles to be fought against the Empire and Darth Vader!

ISBN 978-1-59582-172-0 | $24.99

STAR WARS: RISE OF THE SITH

Before the name of Skywalker–or Vader–achieved fame across the galaxy, the Jedi Knights had long preserved peace and justice . . . as well as preventing the return of the Sith. These thrilling tales illustrate the events leading up to *The Phantom Menace*.

ISBN 978-1-59582-228-4 | $24.99

STAR WARS: EMISSARIES AND ASSASSINS

Discover more stories featuring Anakin Skywalker, Amidala, Obi-Wan, and Qui-Gon set during the time of Episode I: *The Phantom Menace* in this mega collection!

ISBN 978-1-59582-229-1 | $24.99

STAR WARS: MENACE REVEALED

This is our largest omnibus of never-before-collected and out-of-print *Star Wars* stories. Included here are one-shot adventures, short story arcs, specialty issues, and early Dark Horse Extra comic strips! All of these tales take place after Episode I: *The Phantom Menace*, and lead up to Episode II: *Attack of the Clones*.

ISBN 978-1-59582-273-4 | $24.99

STAR WARS: SHADOWS OF THE EMPIRE

Featuring all your favorite characters from the *Star Wars* trilogy—Luke Skywalker, Princess Leia, and Han Solo—this volume includes stories written by acclaimed novelists Timothy Zahn and Steve Perry!

ISBN 978-1-59582-434-9 | $24.99

STAR WARS: A LONG TIME AGO. . . .

Star Wars: A Long Time Ago. . . . omnibus volumes feature classic *Star Wars* stories not seen in over twenty years! Originally printed by Marvel Comics, these stories have been recolored and are sure to please *Star Wars* fans both new and old.

Volume 1: ISBN 978-1-59582-486-8 | $24.99   **Volume 2: ISBN 978-1-59582-554-4 | $24.99**

Volume 3: ISBN 978-1-59582-639-8 | $24.99   **Volume 4: ISBN 978-1-59582-640-4 | $24.99**

AVAILABLE AT YOUR LOCAL COMICS SHOP OR BOOKSTORE!

To find a comics shop in your area, call 1-888-266-4226

For more information or to order direct: • On the web: DarkHorse.com

• E-mail: mailorder@darkhorse.com • Phone: 1-800-862-0052 Mon.–Fri. 9 AM to 5 PM Pacific Time